Nebraska Barn Quilt
Coloring Book
Dawson County Barn Quilt Trail
John H. Lettau

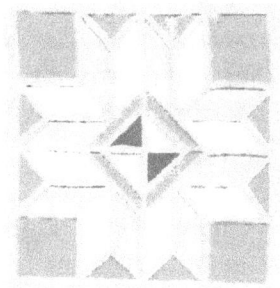 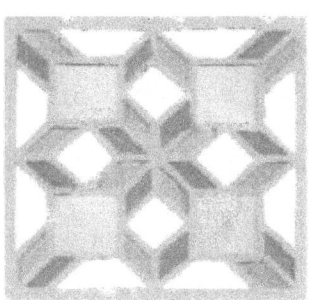 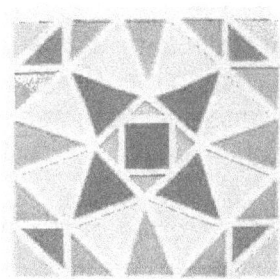 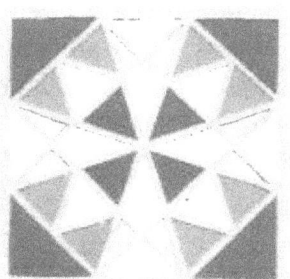

Barn Quilt Blocks on Cover

Double Card Trick   Piece by Piece
Our Version of Sunflower   The Compass: Finding Our Way

Featuring 50 Quilt Designs in Dawson County

History of Barn Quilts

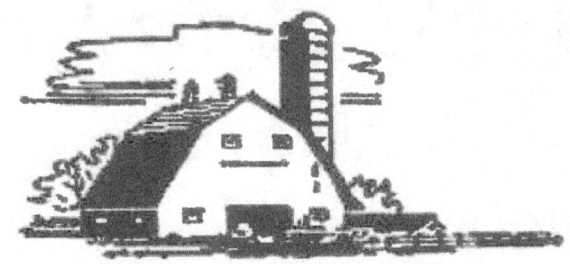

Today colorful barn quilts, also called quilt blocks, can be found along many highways, rural back roads and even in towns and cities through out America and Canada. The interest in this fast growing grass roots art movement started not many years ago in Ohio and continues to grow daily as communities, social clubs and clubs see what barn quilt blocks can do to promote tourism and the local history/heritage. Brilliant barn quilt patterns are displayed on barns, corn cribs, and other farm out-buildings through out farm country and even in towns and cities. This book is an opportunity for you to create many original color design patterns for the barn quilt blocks in this coloring book.

Barn Quilt Projects are usually supported and organized to educate, promote and celebrate the unique agricultural heritage of an area through the visual combination of barns and quilt patterns. Farms are vital to the economic well-being of many rural communities. Handmade barn quilt blocks provide warmth, beauty, and an outlet for individual artistic expression. Plus, promoting tourism is an important part of all local barn quilt projects.

How Barn Quilts are Constructed

A barn quilt is usually made by painting a barn quilt design on MDO signboard suitable for weathering outdoors in all forms of weather. Prior to painting the barn quilt pattern two or three coats of primer are applied to front, back and all edges of the signboard. Next, draw the barn quilt pattern. Frog Tape {painter tape} is then applied to outline all sections of the design. Two coats of each color are painted with each coat allowed to dry over night. After the quilt is finished it is allowed to cure for two weeks before being mounted on a barn or other building.

Barn quilt blocks located in the Dawson area of Nebraska are found in many different sizes...8 by 8, 4 by 4, and 2 by 2 so they can be placed on posts and displayed in yards and parks. The Dawson Barn Quilt Trail promotes the quilt art through the Cozad area as well as promoting the beauty and agricultural history of Dawson County and the state of Nebraska.

Each quilt design is usually painted by a team of volunteers and require a willing farmer or property owner to donate hanging area on their barn, building or other structure. Making the quilt squares allows volunteer groups from churches, schools, 4-H, other community service groups and even families the opportunity to create and paint their quilt block. The chosen square may represent a family pattern from a beloved family quilt.

Interesting Facts On Barn Quilts

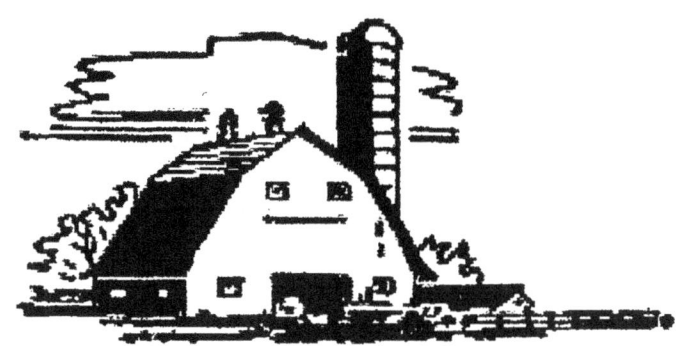

1. Common designs, such as Corn & Beans, are found in many states & rural areas.
2. The same quit pattern will be found with different color patterns.
3. It is not uncommon to find the same pattern with different names.
4. Some common patterns have small modification with a few extra lines.
5. Barn quilt patterns may honor individuals, families, and/or groups.
6. Many times color selections may have a special family meaning.
7. Quilts may be family designed and named.
8. Some city libraries and social clubs are organizing senior coloring programs.
9. Some select a common pattern and just change coloring pattern and/or name.
10. Some find popular patterns and change name and/or meaning.

Typical Barn Quilt Project Objectives

1. Reflects the agricultural heritage of the region.
2. Barns or buildings are highly visible from highway or road.
3. Bring pride to the area.
4. Notes well maintained barns and other farm buildings.
5. Promotes tourism for and in the area.

Objectives of Coloring Books

1. Provide a relaxing hobby for seniors and families.
2. Reduce tension in daily life.
3. Create a fun activity for all age groups.
4. Promote barn quilts around the country.

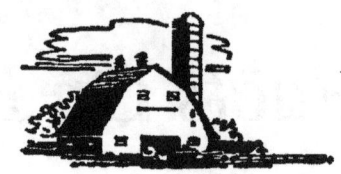

Dawson County Nebraska Barn Quilt Trail Listing

Agricultural Compass	Plum Creek Parkway	Lexington, Nebraska
Americana	Road 761	Cozad, Nebraska
American Flag	Avenue E & E 10th Street	Cozad, Nebraska
Army Star	West 9th Street	**Cozad, Nebraska**
Bank Colors	Meridian Avenue	Cozad, Nebraska
Bread Basket	West 12th Street	Cozad, Nebraska
Business in Progress	West 8th Street	Cozad, Nebraska
Churn Dash	West 13th Street	Cozad, Nebraska
Clipper Herald	West 5th Street	Cozad ,Nebraska
Cross & Stars	Avenue E & E 10th Street	Cozad, Nebraska
Crossroads	West 10th Street	Cozad, Nebraska
Crown of Thorns	Avenue E	Cozad, Nebraska
Deconstructed Sunflower	Road 419	Cozad, Nebraska
Double Aster	Lincoln Avenue	Cozad, Nebraska
Double Card Trick	Avenue J	Cozad, Nebraska
Eclipse	East 12th Street	Cozad, Nebraska
Elks	J Street	Cozad, Nebraska
Elks Lodge Flag Colors	J Street	Cozad, Nebraska
Friendship Star	Road 761	Cozad, Nebraska
Gensenbach's Creation	Road 419	Cozad, Nebraska
God Bless America	Meridian Avenue	Cozad, Nebraska
Haymaker Spirit	Meridian Avenue	Cozad, Nebraska
Heaven a Blazin'	East 12th Street	Cozad, Nebraska
Jane's Place	Road 421	Cozad, Nebraska
Lots of Fun	West 8th Street	Cozad, Nebraska
Love Flag	Road 761	Cozad, Nebraska
Love Learning	East 14th Street	Cozad, Nebraska
Maple Leaf & Sunshine	East 8th Street	Cozad, Nebraska
Meridian Museum Quilt	East 8th Street	Cozad, Nebraska
Missouri Star	Lincoln Avenue	Cozad, Nebraska
Nebraska 4-H star	Plum Creek Parkway	Cozad, Nebraska
Nebraska National Forest	West 17th Street	Cozad, Nebraska
Our Version of Sunflower	East 22nd Street	Cozad, Nebraska
Patriotic Star	Avenue C	Cozad, Nebraska
Piece by Piece	East 12th Street	Cozad, Nebraska
Pinwheel in Pinwheel	Avenue J	Cozad, Nebraska
Prairie Wildfire	Road 419	Eusits, Nebraska
Red, white & Blue Runs True	East 12th Street	Cozad, Nebraska
Scatter Joy	West 13th Street	Cozad, Nebraskad

Dawson County Nebraska Barn Quilt Trail Listing Continued

Security First Bank	Avenue F	Cozad, Nebraska
Sesqui Ear	North Taft	Lexington, Nebraska
Staton Shop	Adams Street	Cozad, Nebraska
Summer Bliss	21st Street	Gothenburg, Nebraska
Swedish Weathervane	Lake Avenue	Gothenburg, Nebraska
Thank You	North Shore Drive	Johnson Lake, Nebraska
The Compass Finding Our Way	Meridian Avenue	Cozad, Nebraska
Variable Square	West 14th Street	Cozad, Nebraska
Vetters Corn	Road 761	Cozad, Nebraska
Wabi Sabi	East 6th Street	Cozad, Nebraska
Weller	C Street	Cozad, Nebraska

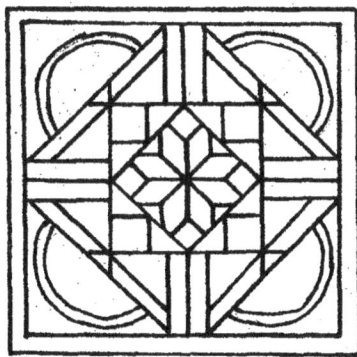 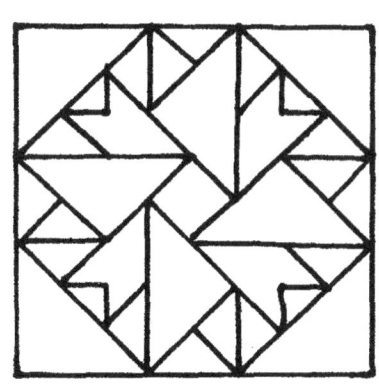 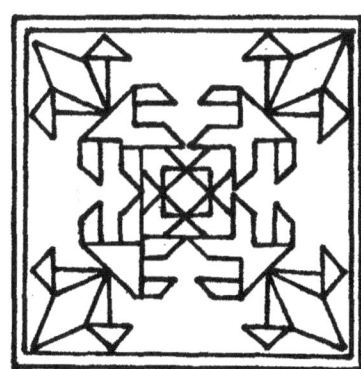

Agricultural Compass
Dawson County Nebraska Barn Quilt Trail

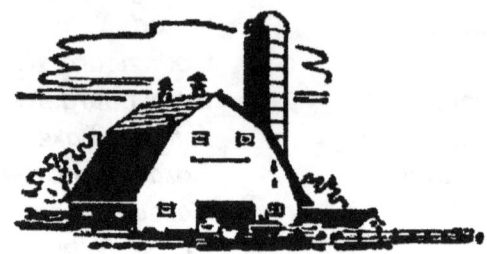

Barn Quilt Location
Plum Creek Parkway
Lexington, Nebraska

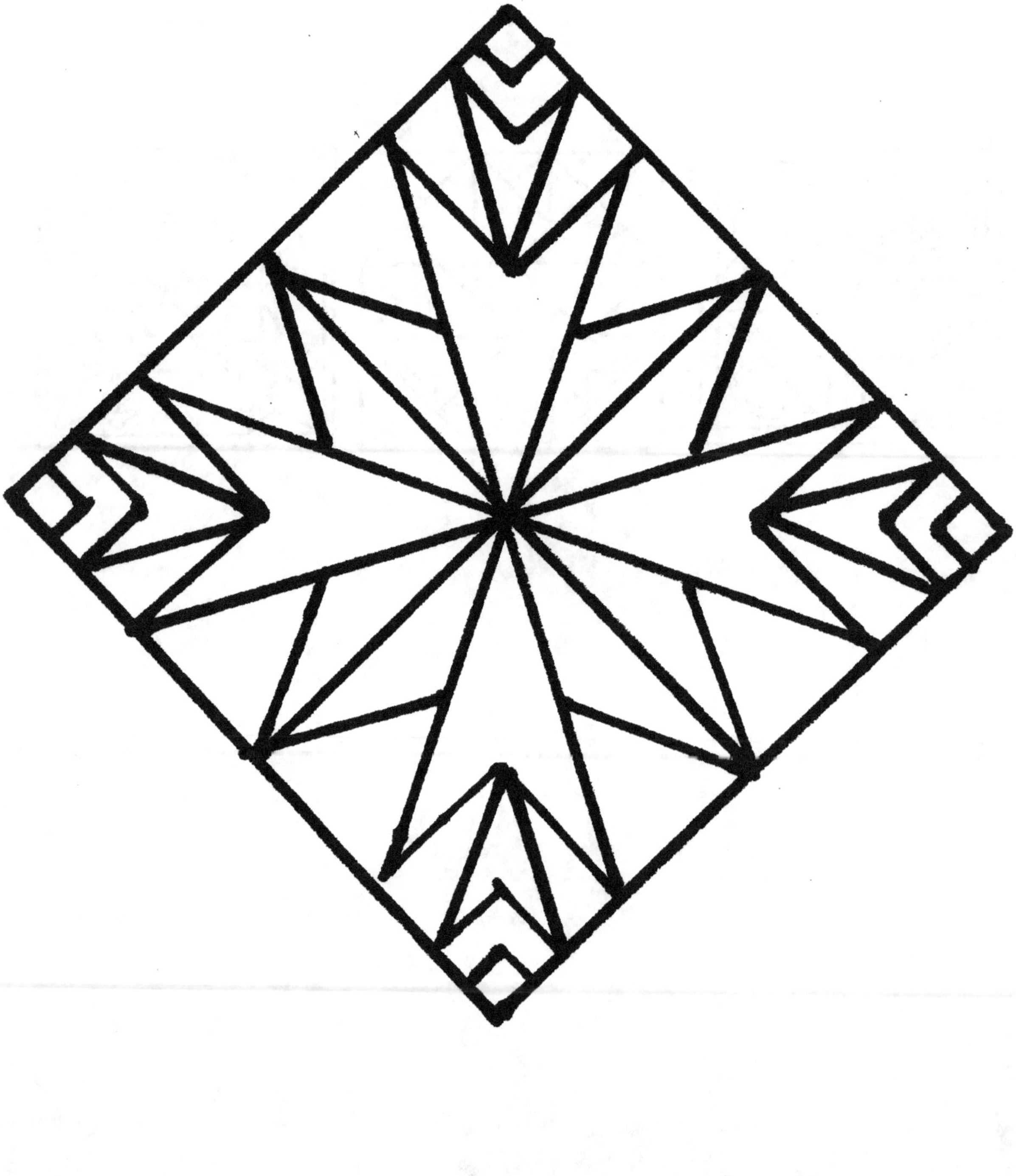

Dawson County Nebraska Barn Quilt Agricultural Compass

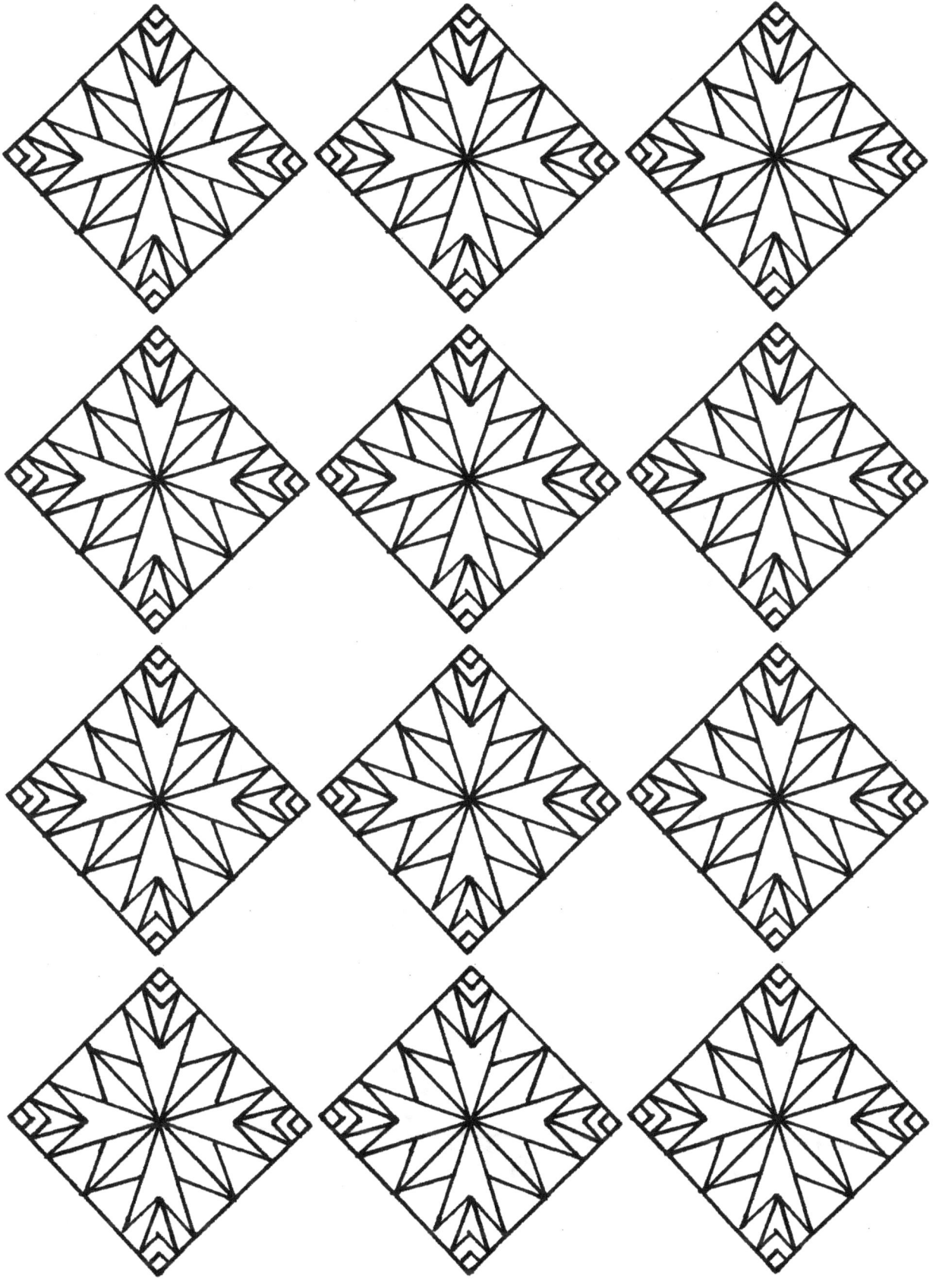

Americana
Dawson County Nebraska Barn Quilt Trail

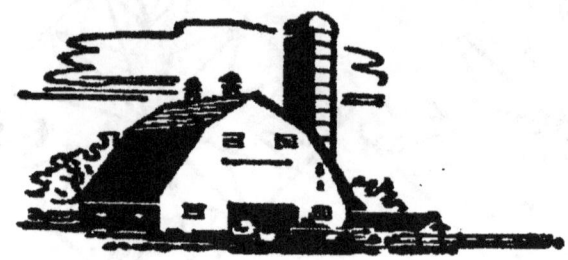

Quilt Block Location
Road 761
Cozad, Nebraska

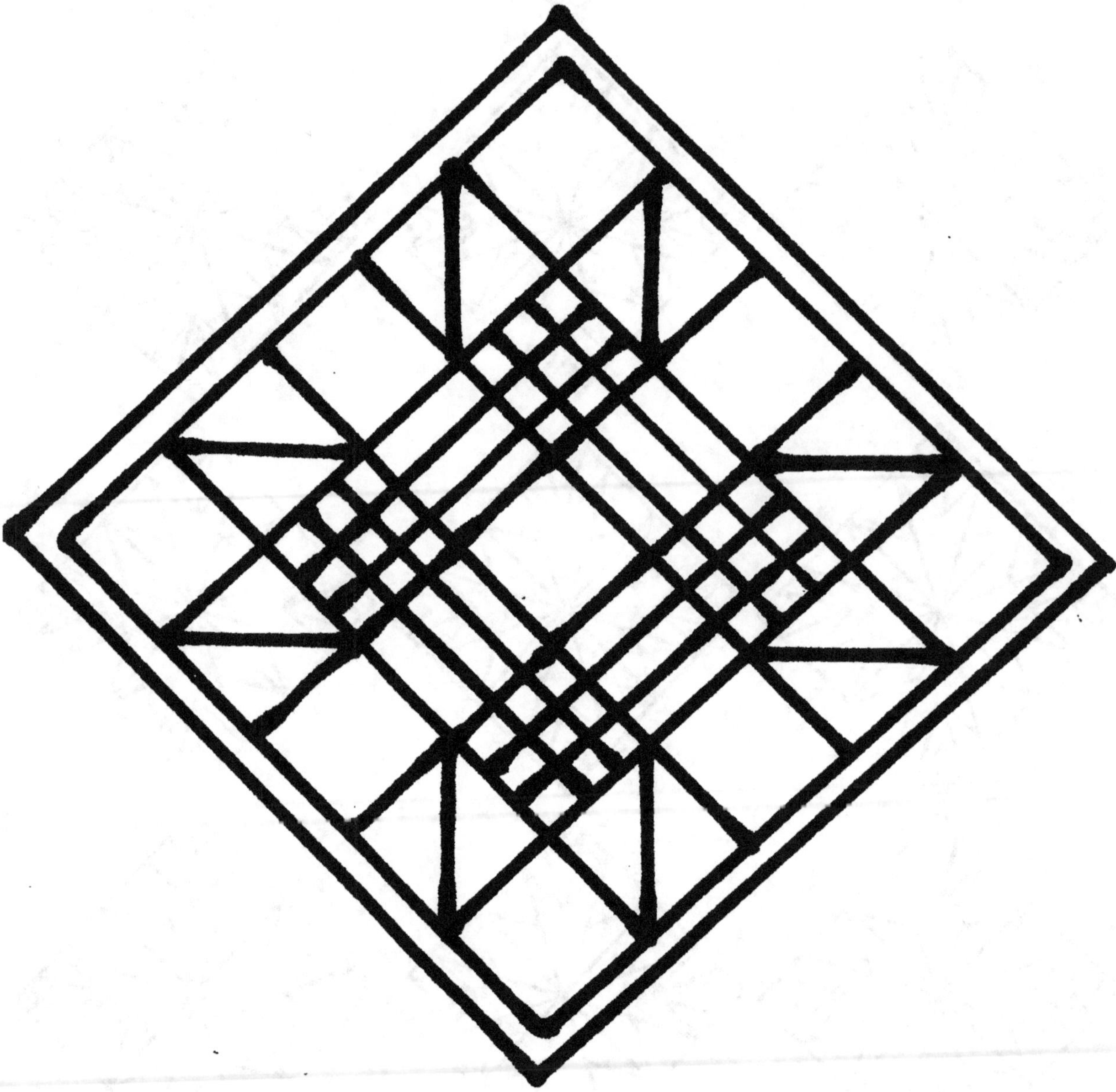

Dawson County Nebraska Barn Quilt Americana

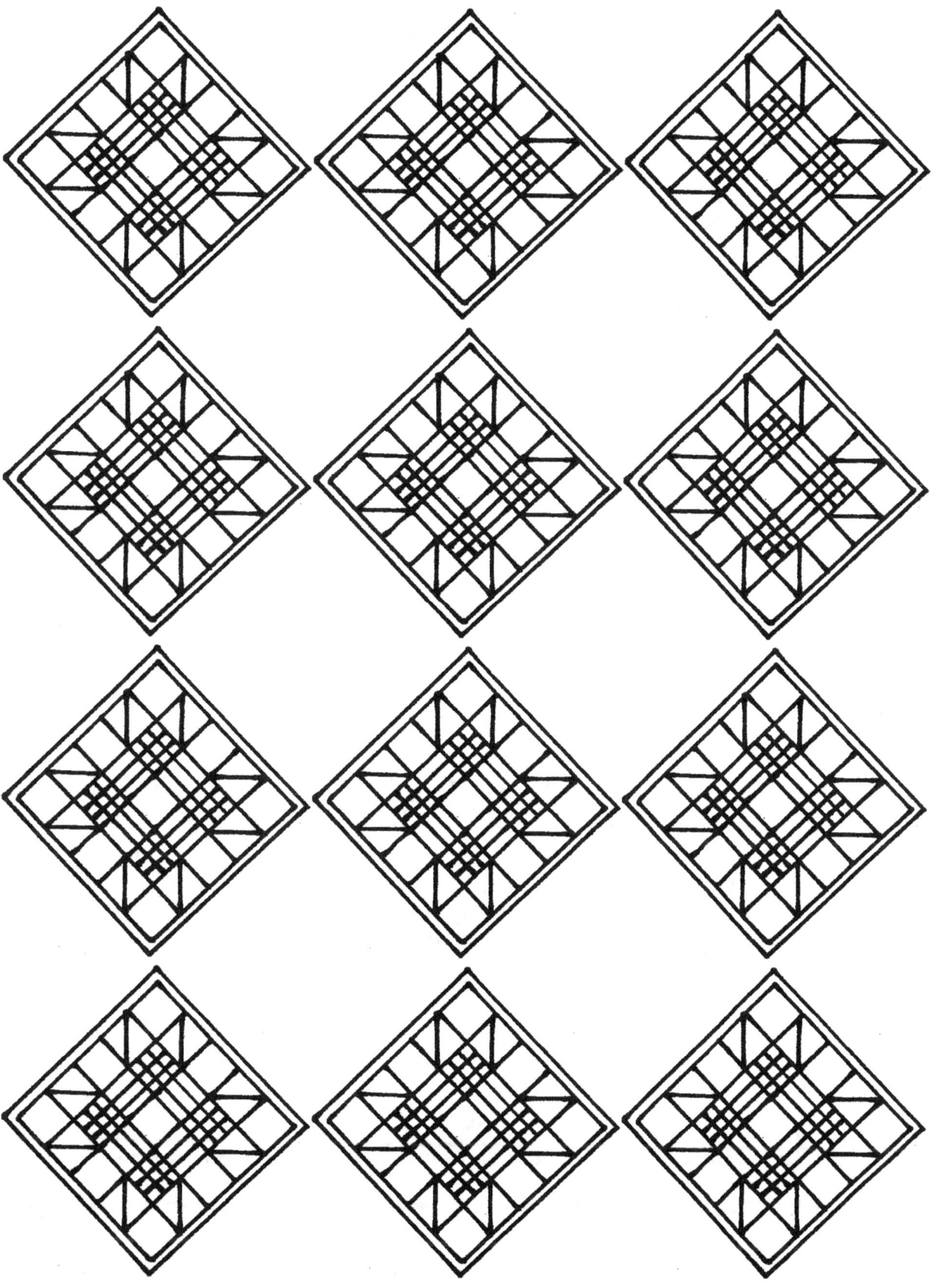

American Flag
Dawson County Nebraska Barn Quilt Trail

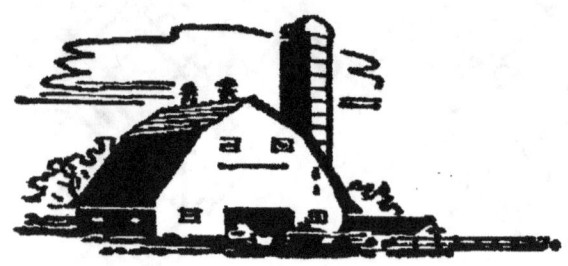

Quilt Block Location
Avenue E & E Street
Cozad, Nebraska

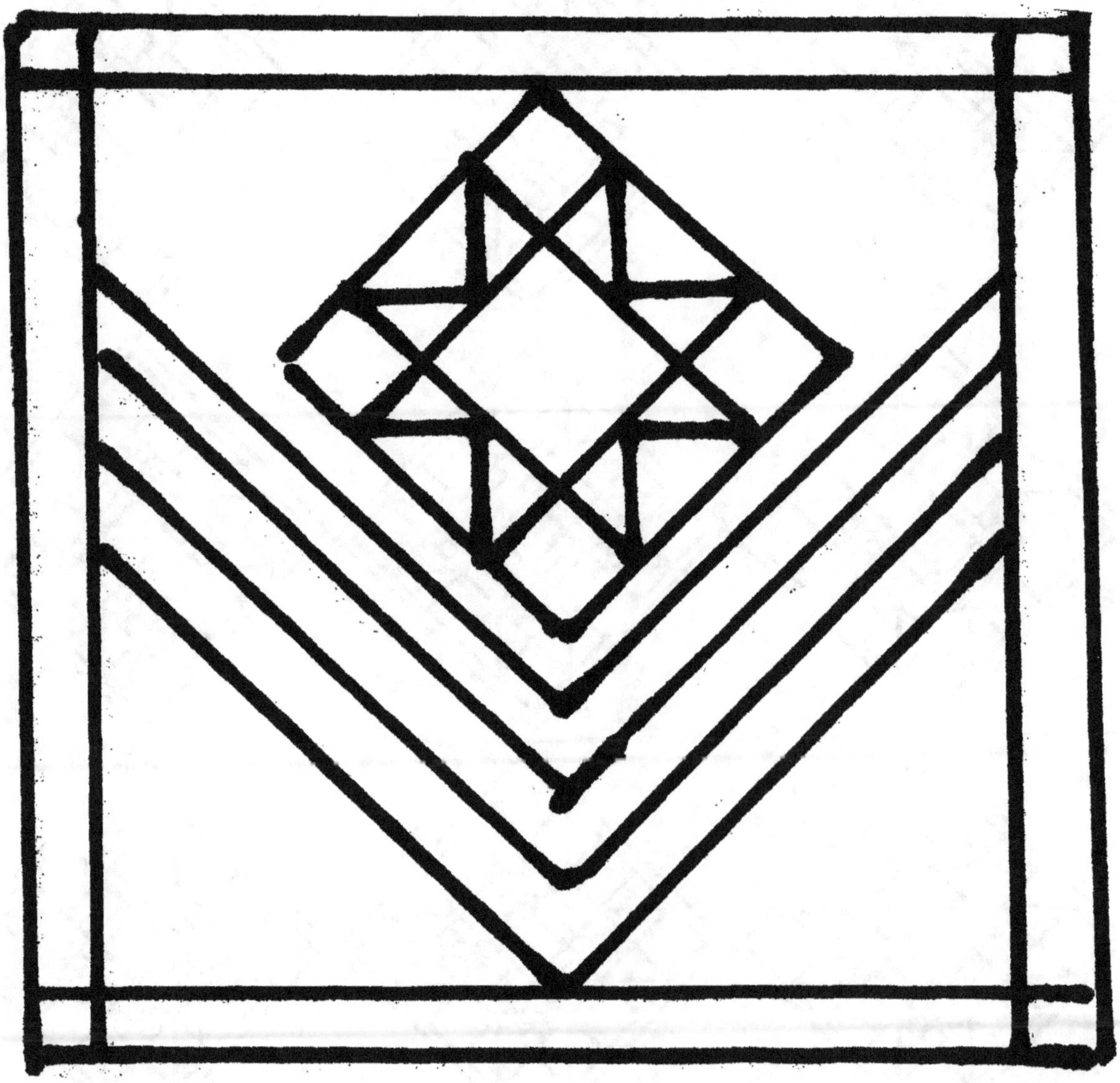

Dawson County Nebraska Barn Quilt American Flag

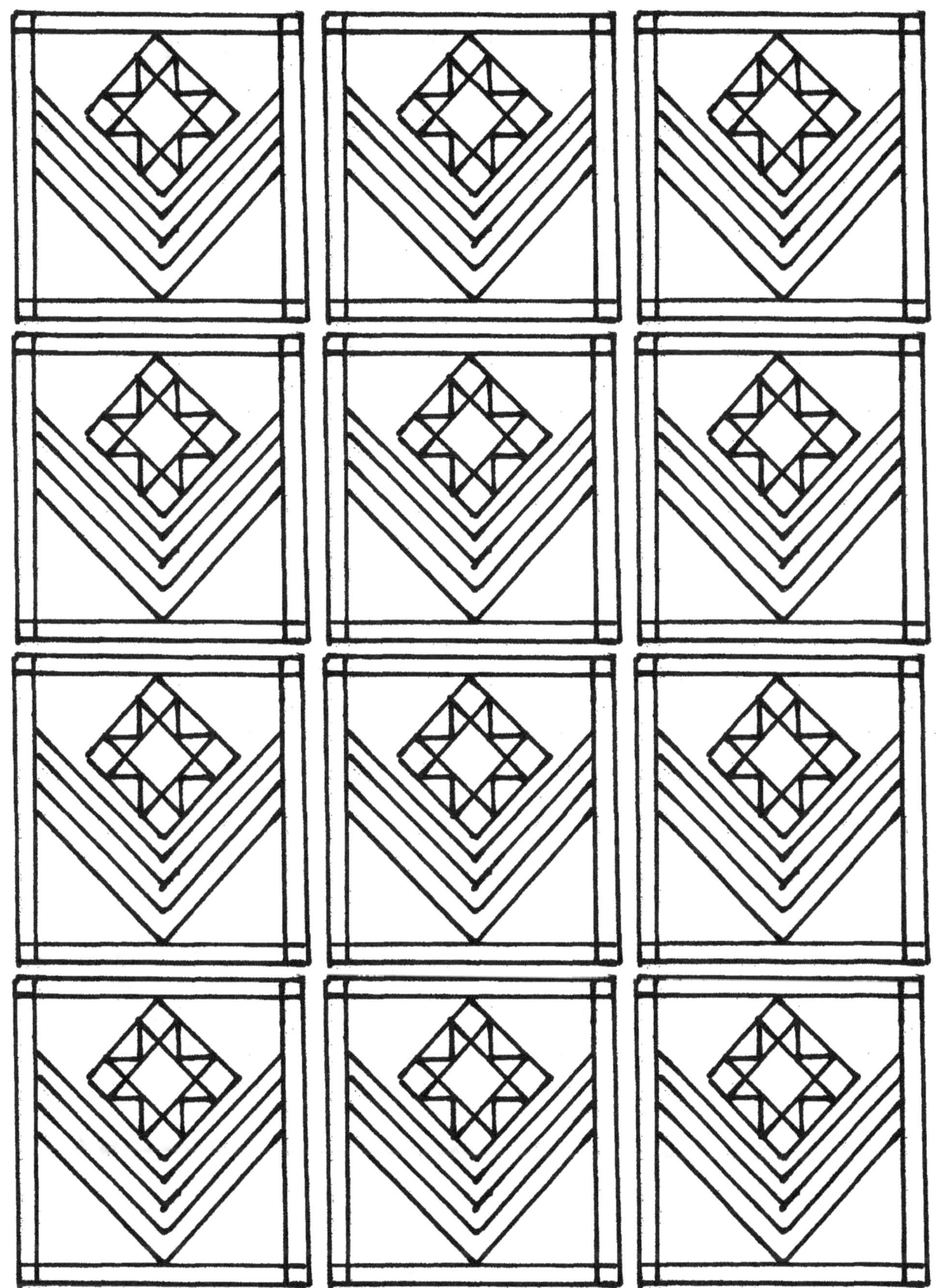

Army Star

Dawson County Nebraska Barn Quilt Trail

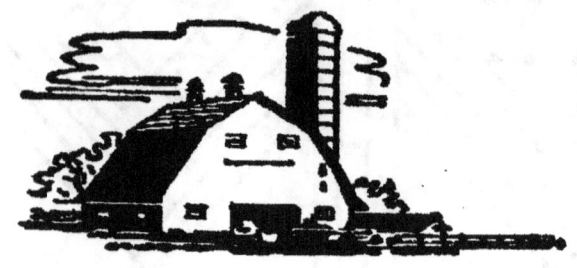

Quilt Block Location
West 9th Street
Cozad, Nebraska

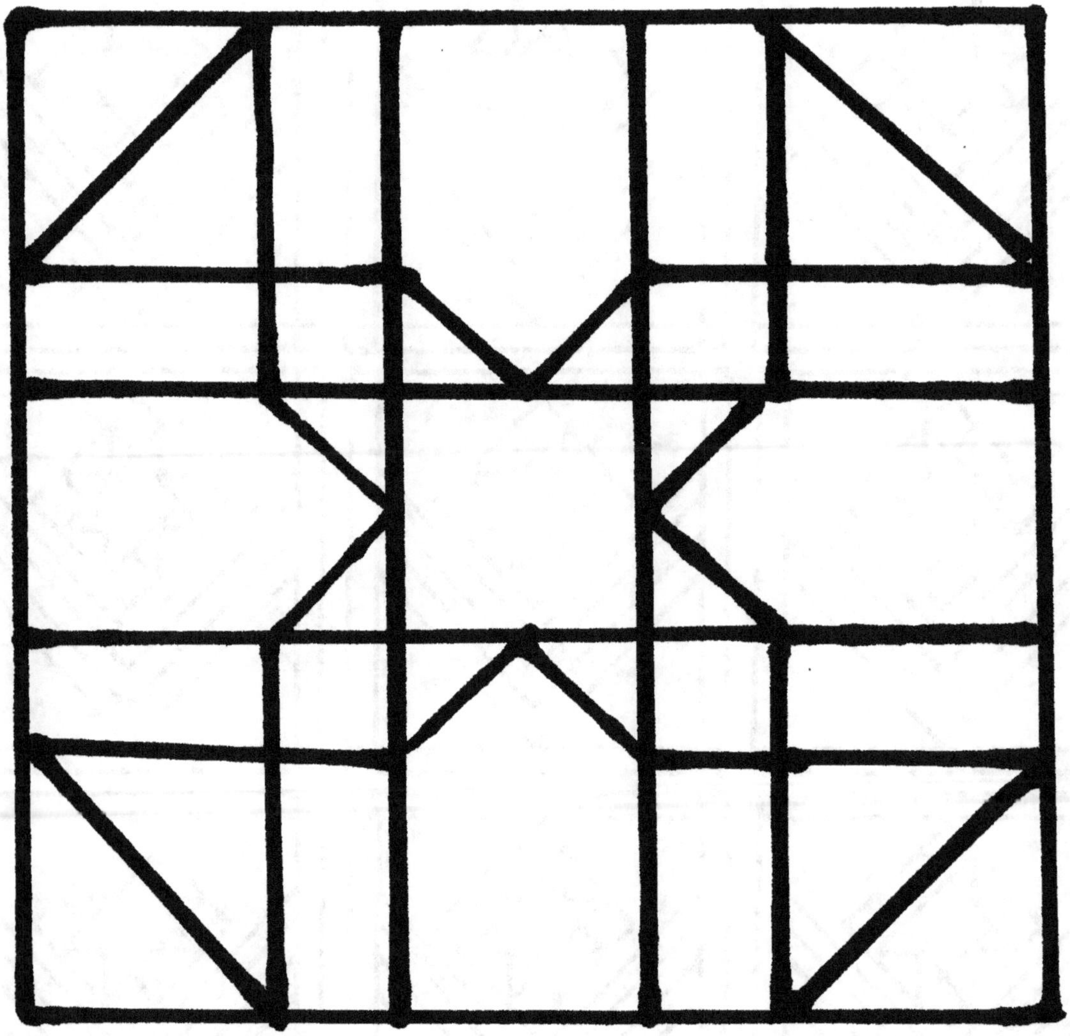

Dawson County Nebraska Barn Quilt Army Star

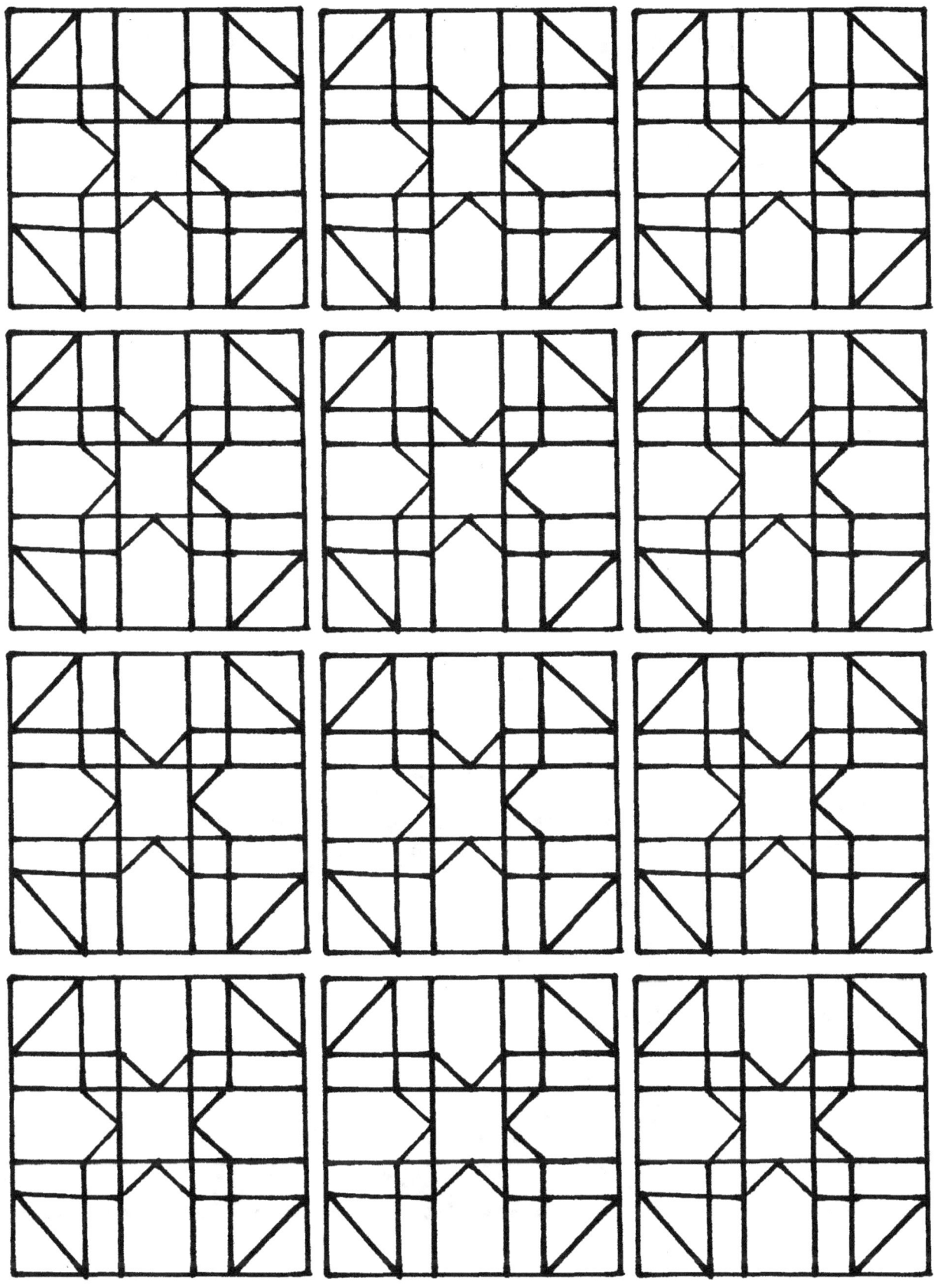

Bank Colors
Dawson County Nebraska Barn Quilt Trail

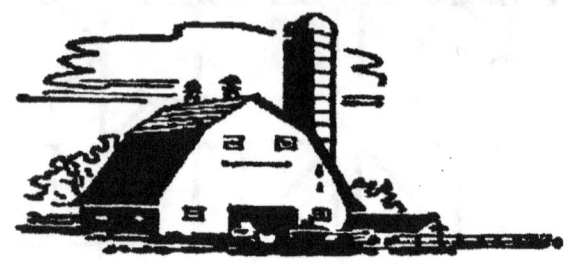

Quilt Block Location
Meridian Avenue
Cozad, Nebraska

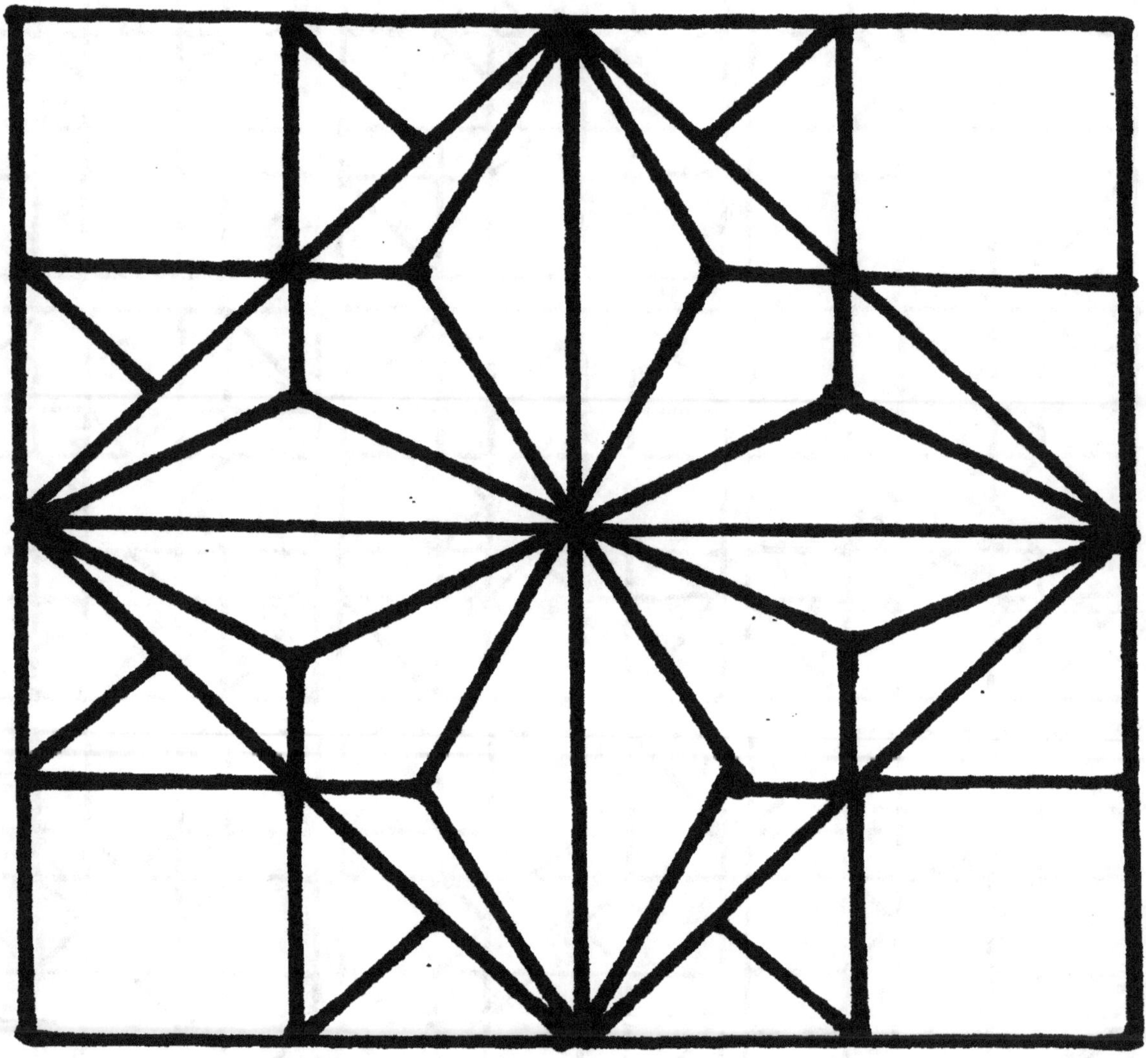

Dawson County Nebraska Barn Quit Bank Colors

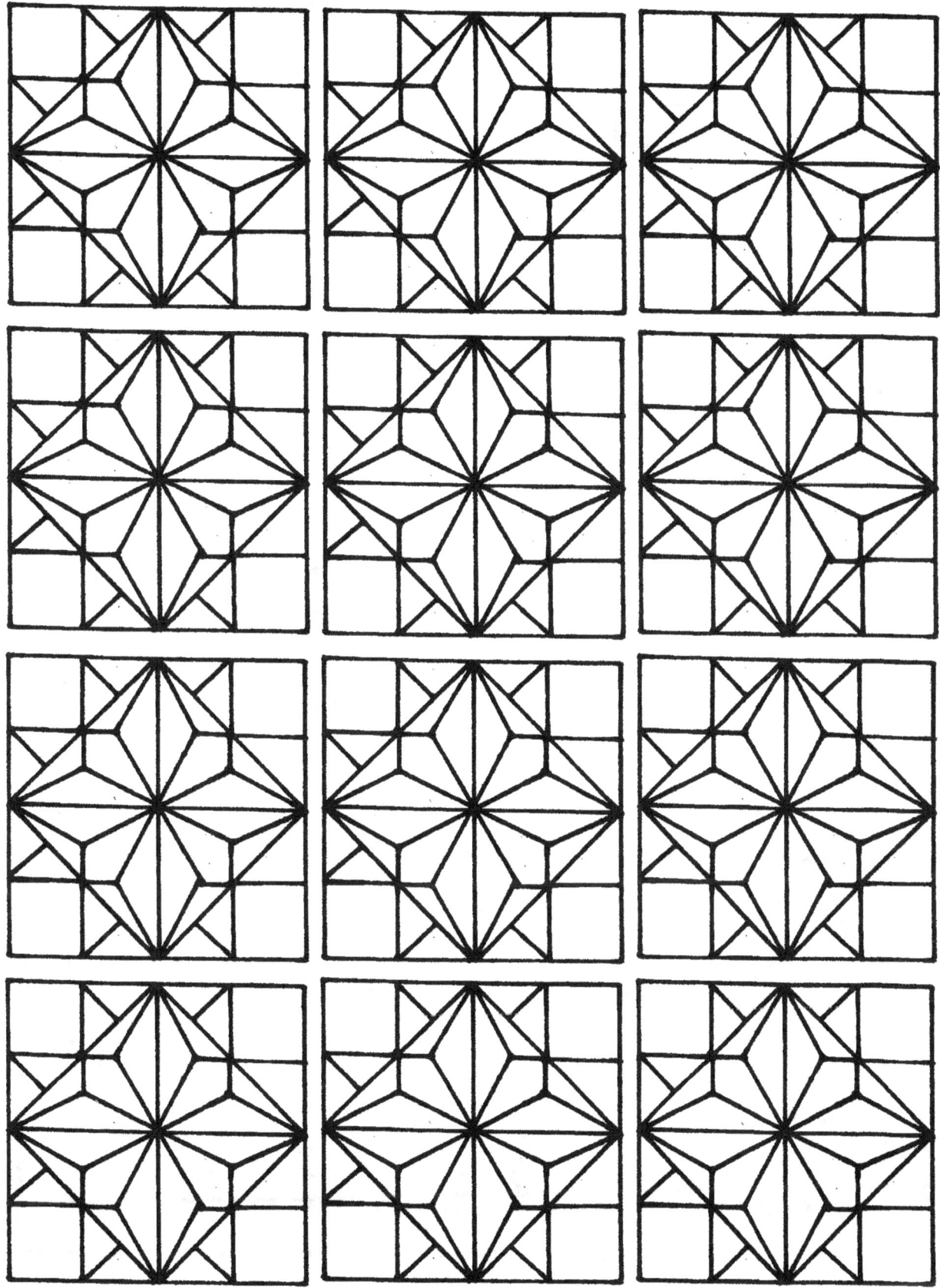

Bread Basket
Dawson County Nebraska Barn Quilt Trail

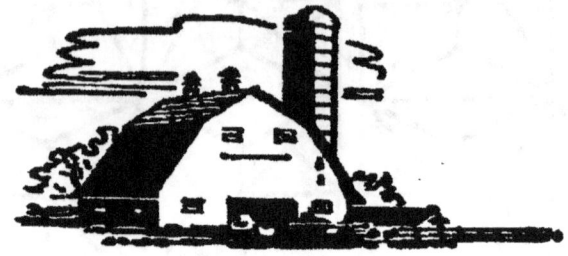

Quilt Block Location
West 12th Street
Cozad, Nebraska

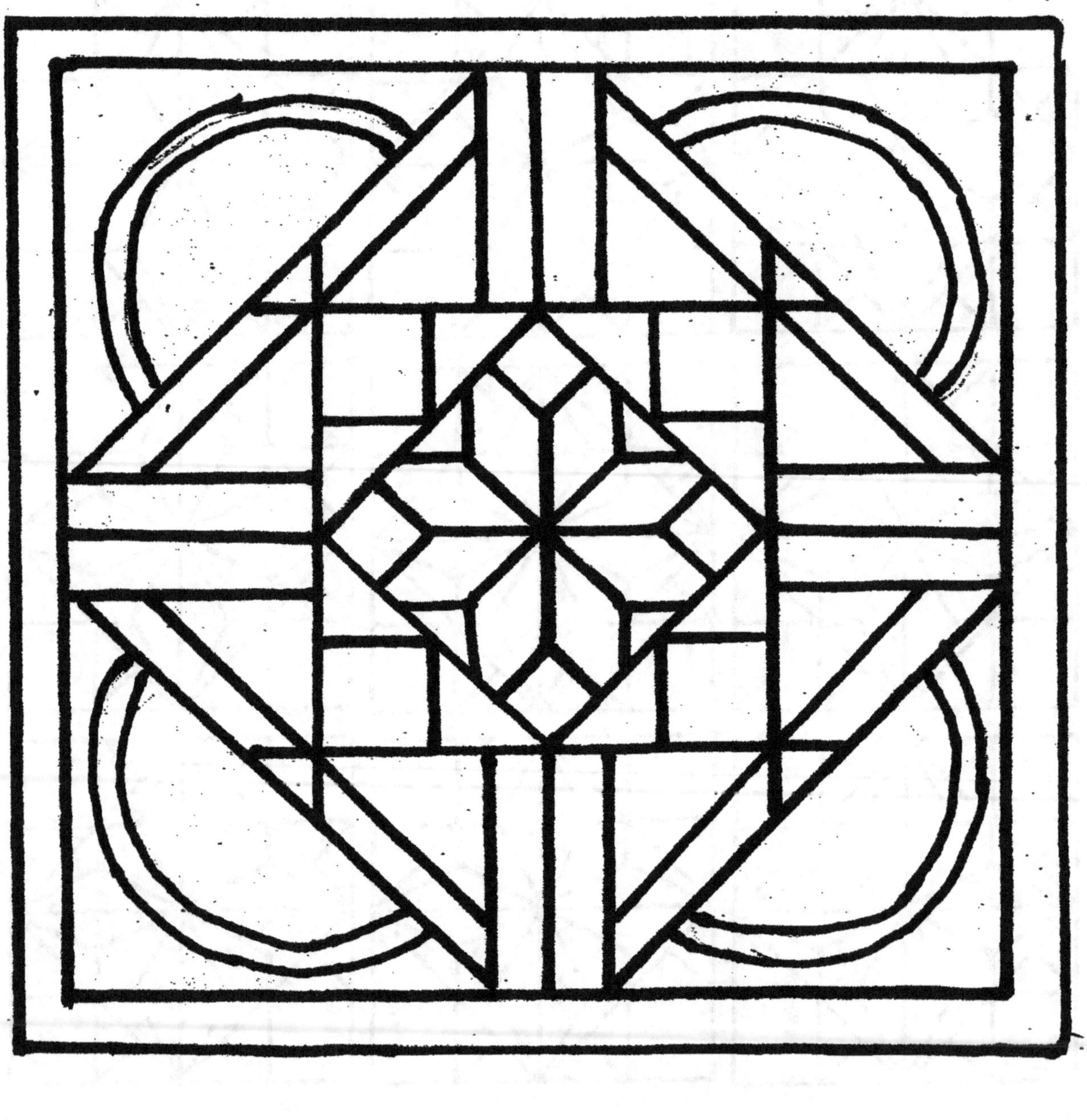

Dawson County Nebraska Barn Quilt Bread Basket

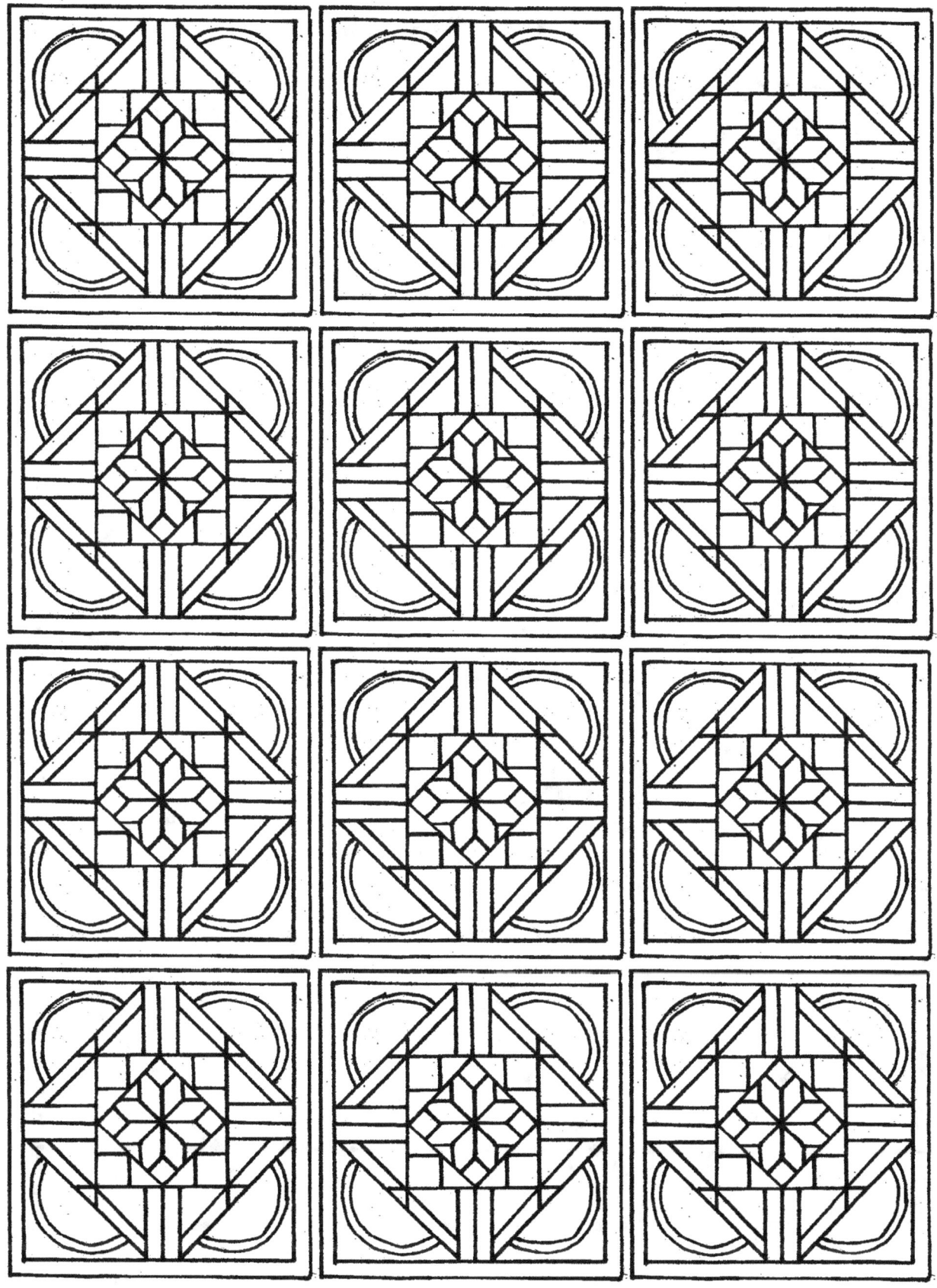

Business in Progress
Dawson County Nebraska Barn Quilt Trail

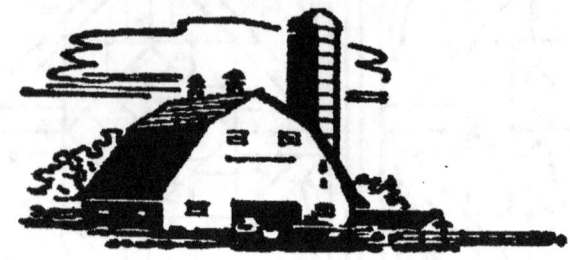

Quilt Block Location
West 8th Street
Cozad, Nebraska

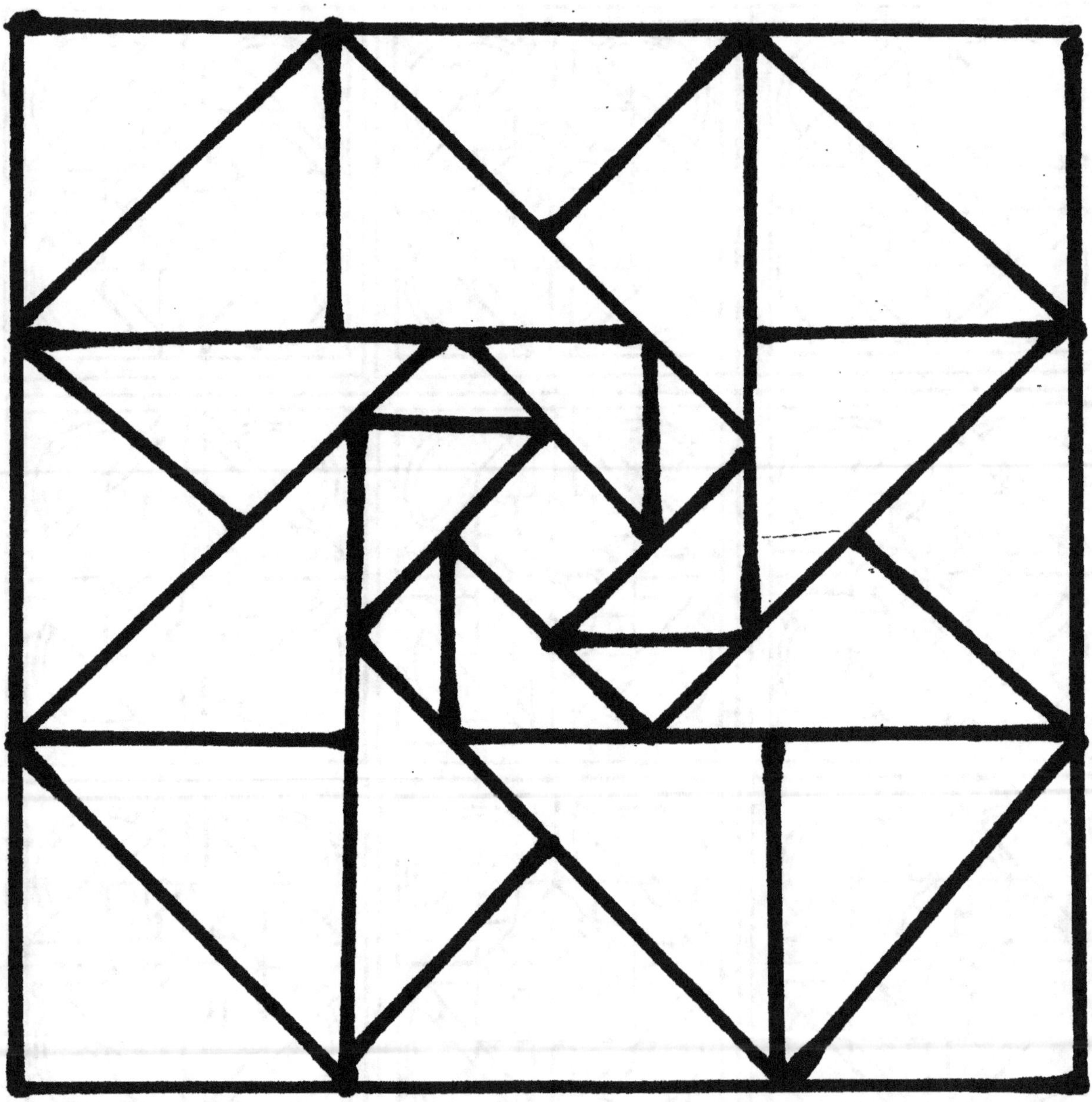

Dawson County Nebraska Barn Quilt Business in Progress

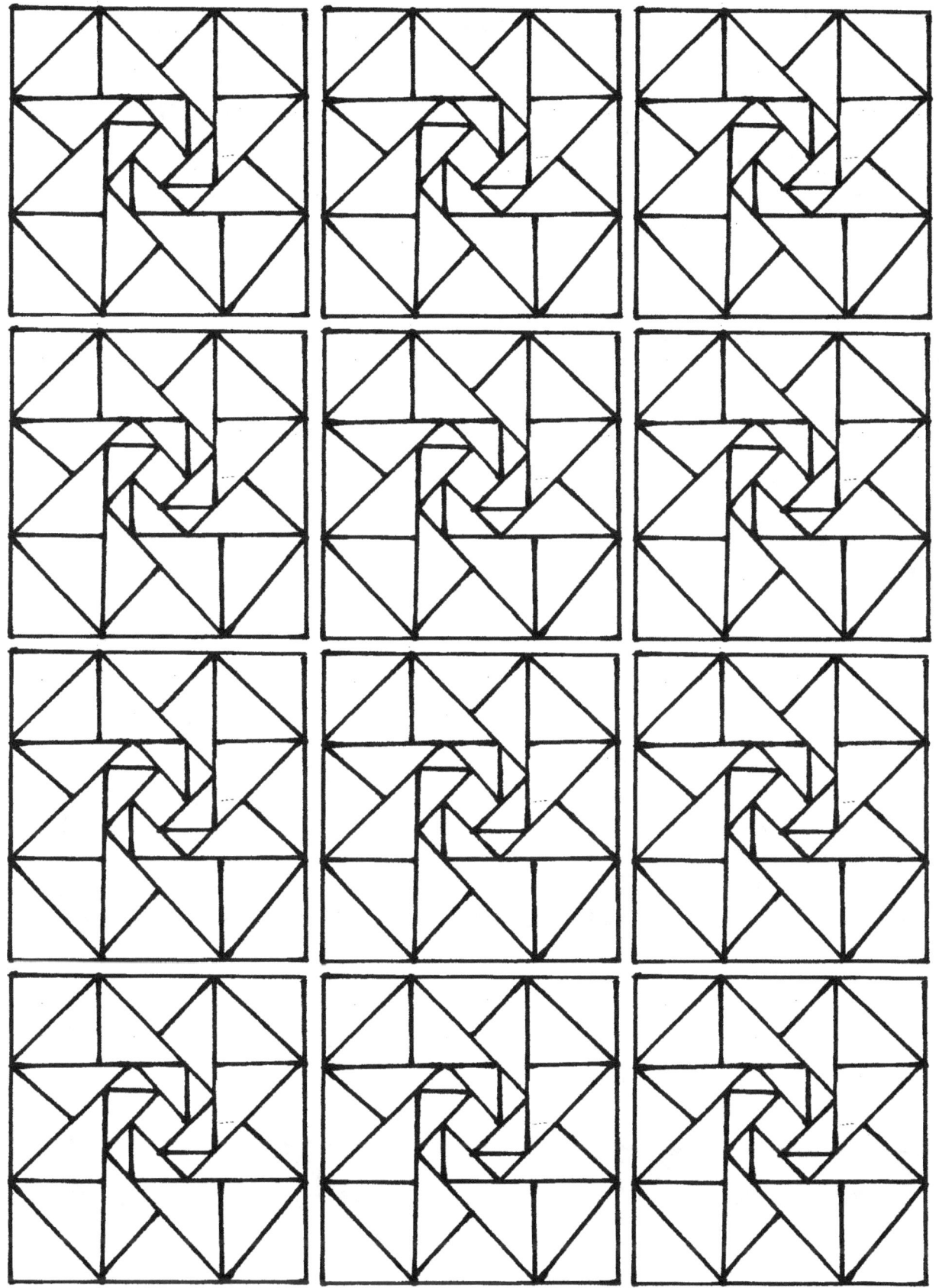

Churn Dash
Dawson County Nebraska Barn Quilt Trail

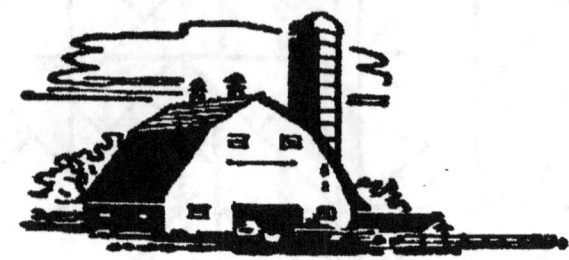

Quilt Block Location
West 13th Street
Cozad, Nebraska

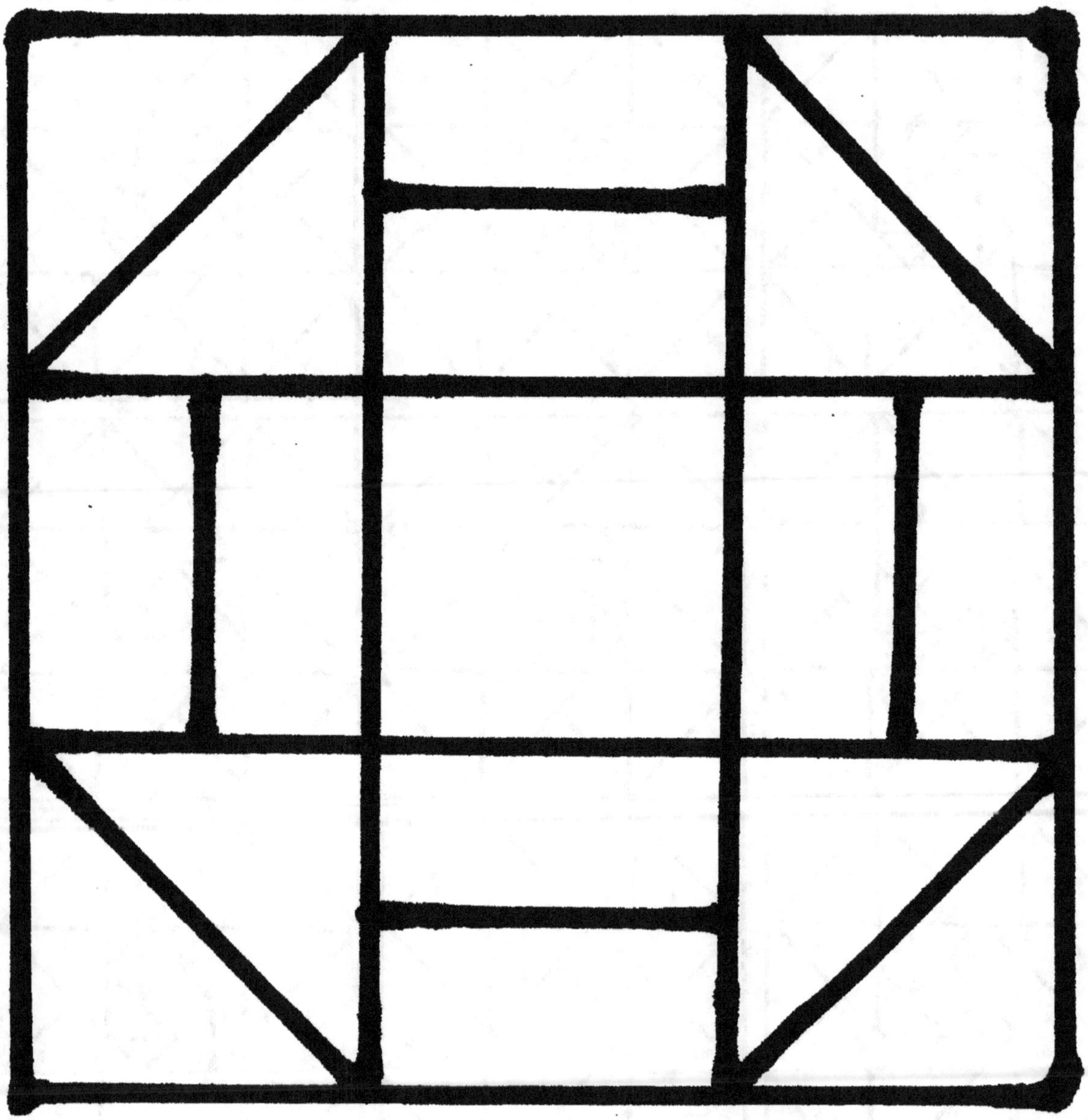

Dawson County Nebraska Barn Quilt Churn Dash

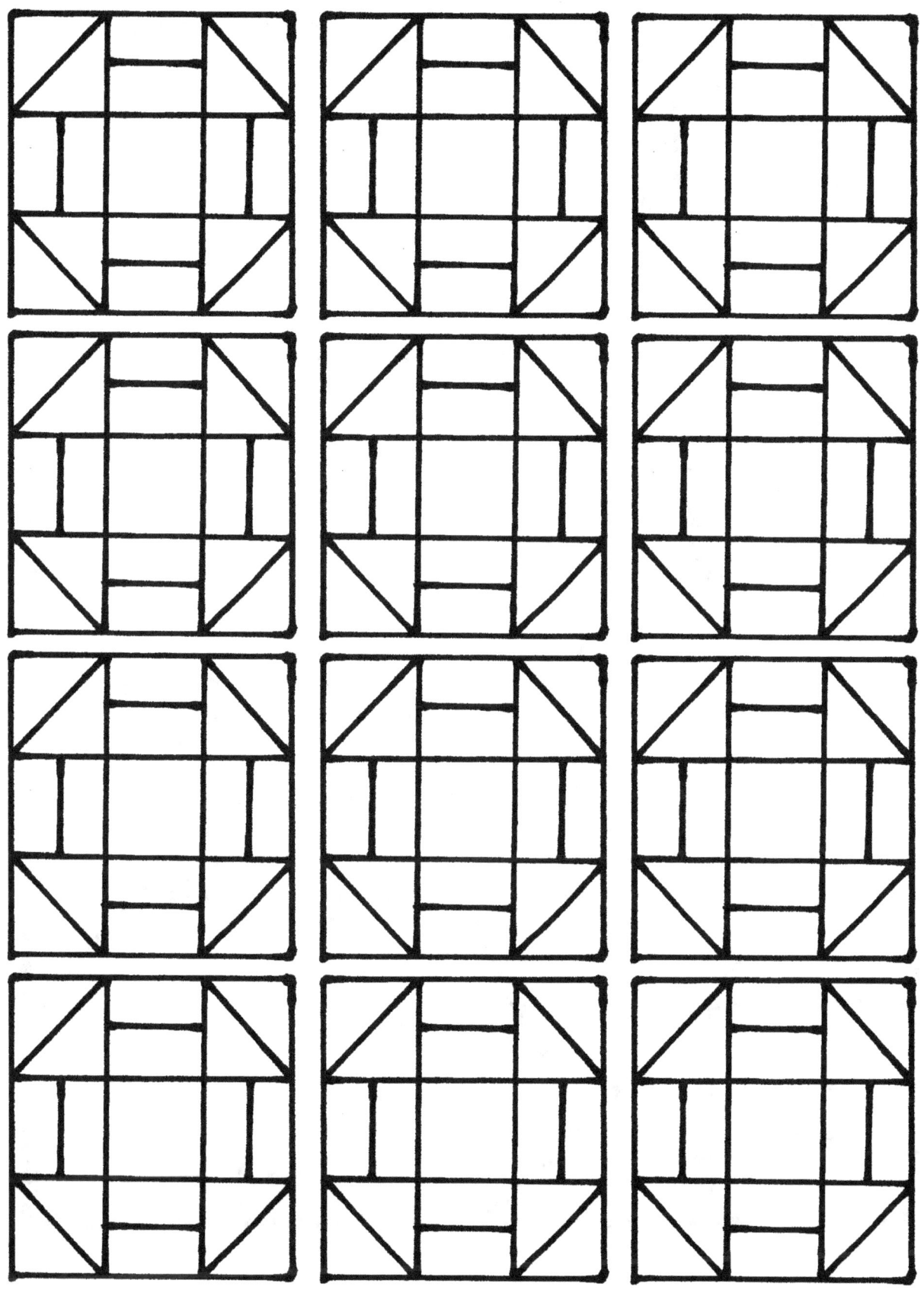

Clipper-Herald
Dawson County Nebraska Barn Quilt Trail

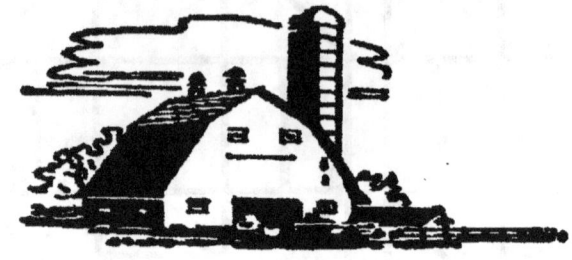

Quilt Block Location
West 5th Street
Cozad, Nebraska

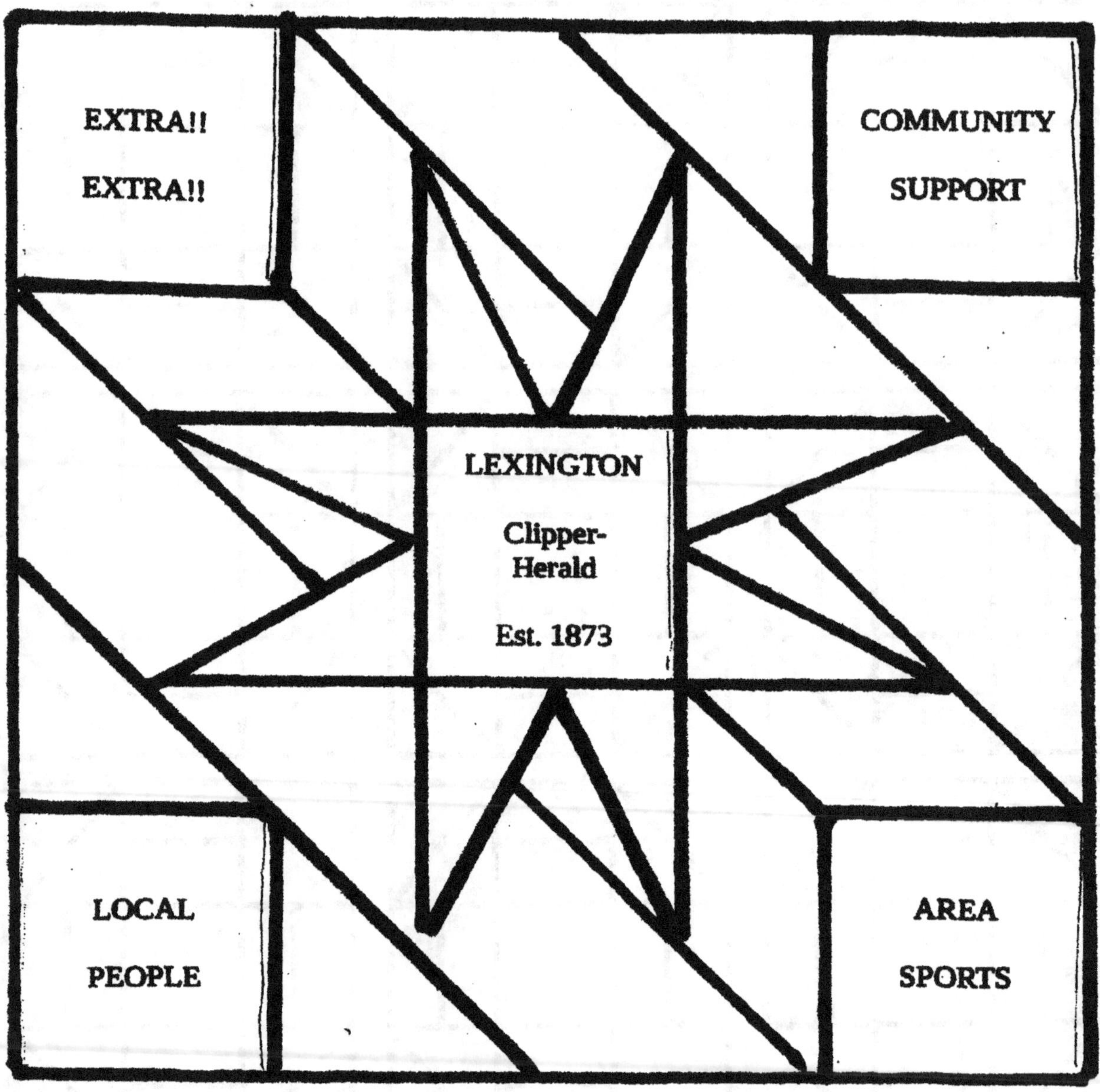

EXTRA!!

EXTRA!!

COMMUNITY

SUPPORT

LEXINGTON

Clipper-
Herald

Est. 1873

LOCAL

PEOPLE

AREA

SPORTS

Dawson County Nebraska Barn Quilt Clipper-Herald

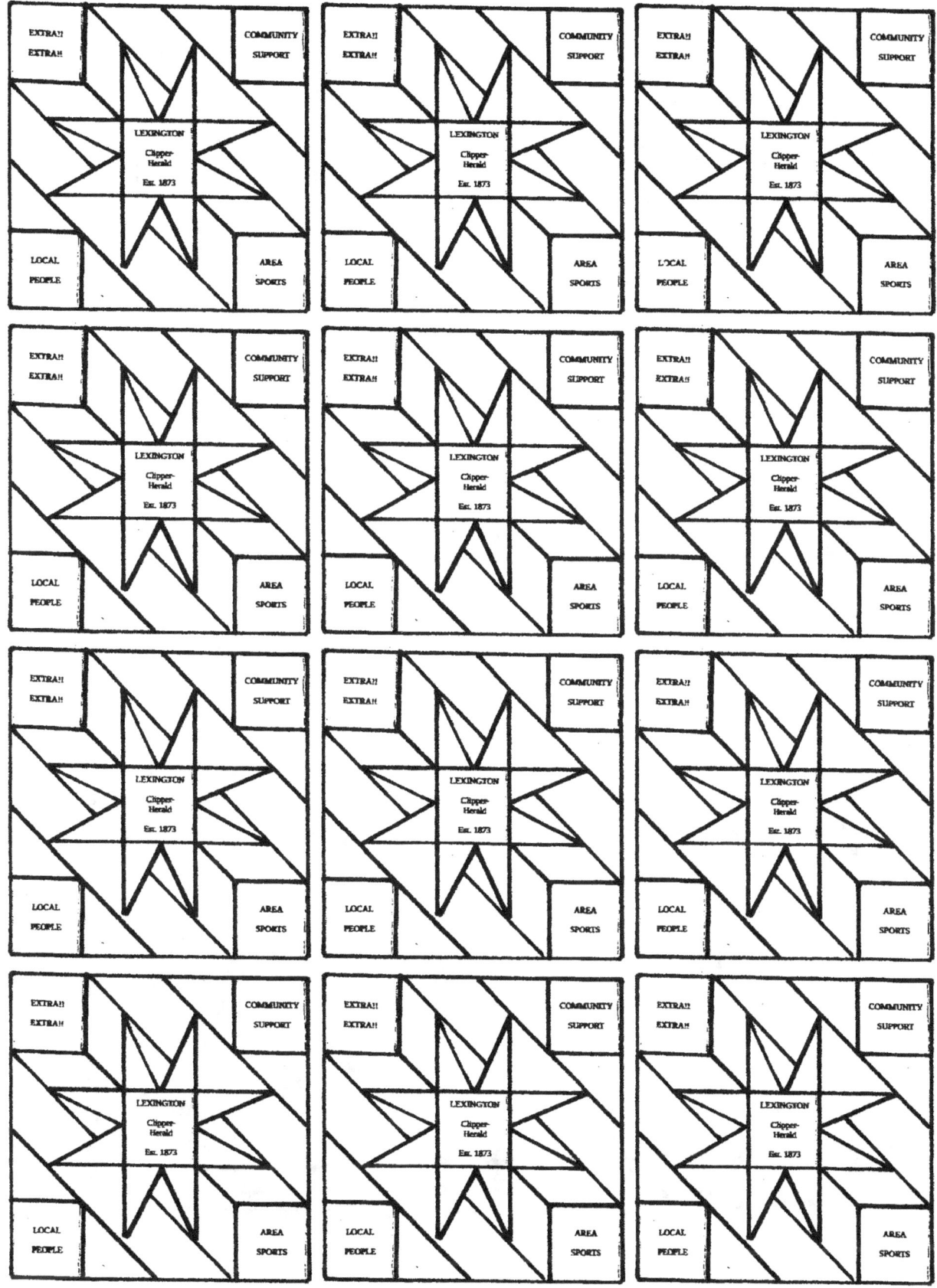

Cross and Stars
Dawson County Nebraska Barn Quilt Trail

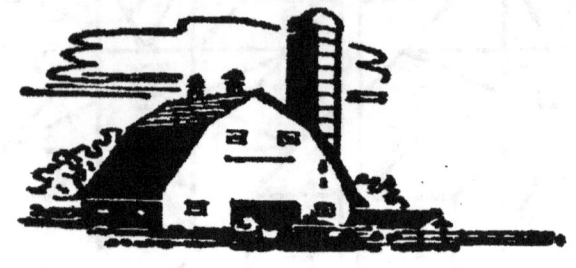

Quilt Block Location
Avenue E & East 10th
Cozad, Nebraska

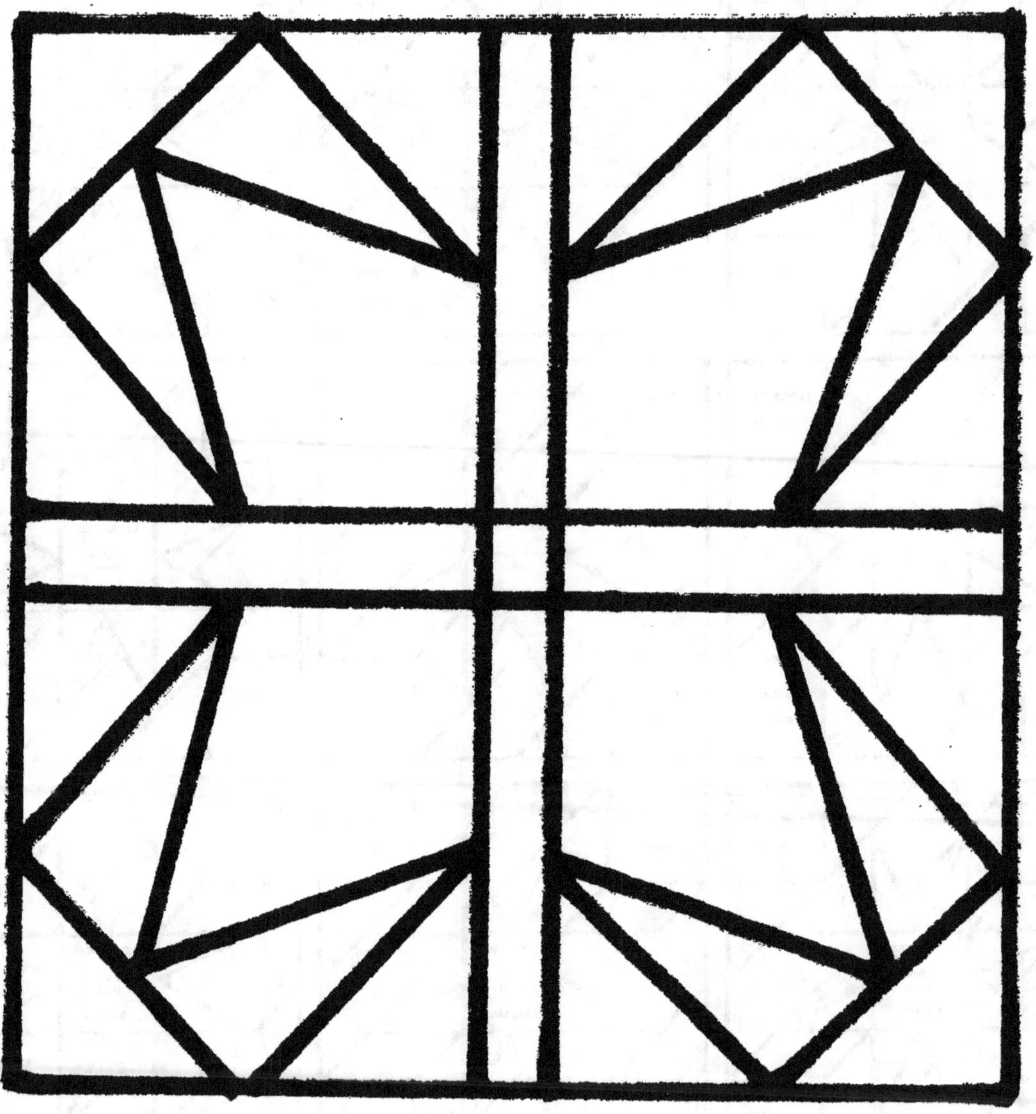

Dawson County Nebraska Barn Quilt Cross & Stars

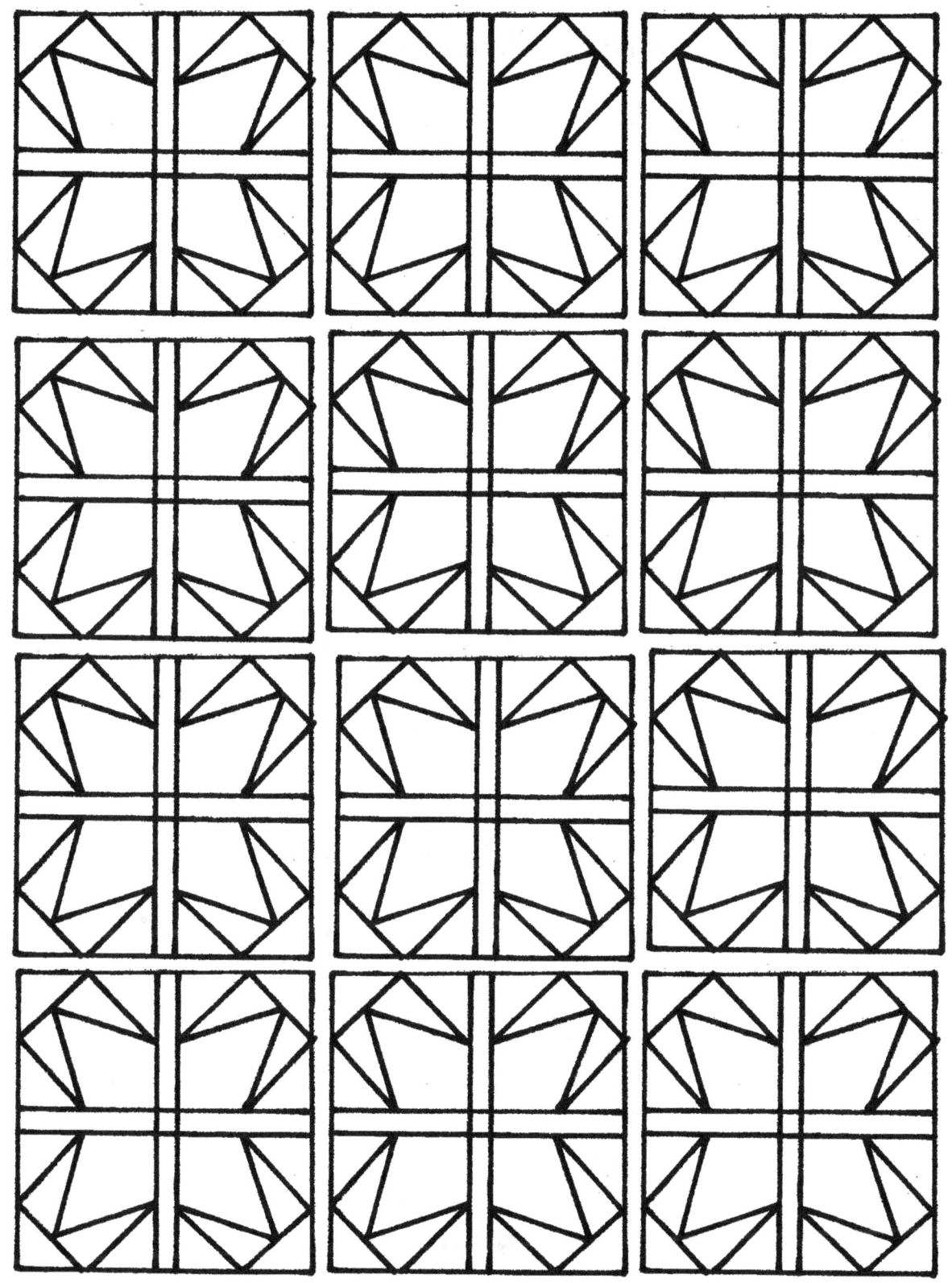

Crossroads
Dawson County Nebraska Barn Quilt Trail

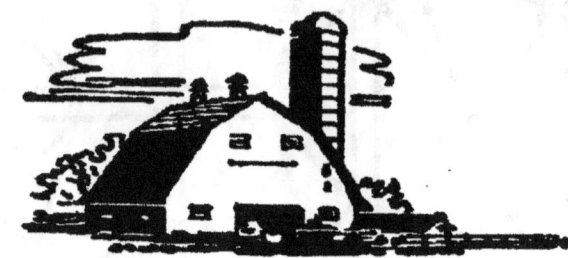

Quilt Block Location
West 10th Street
Cozad, Nebraska

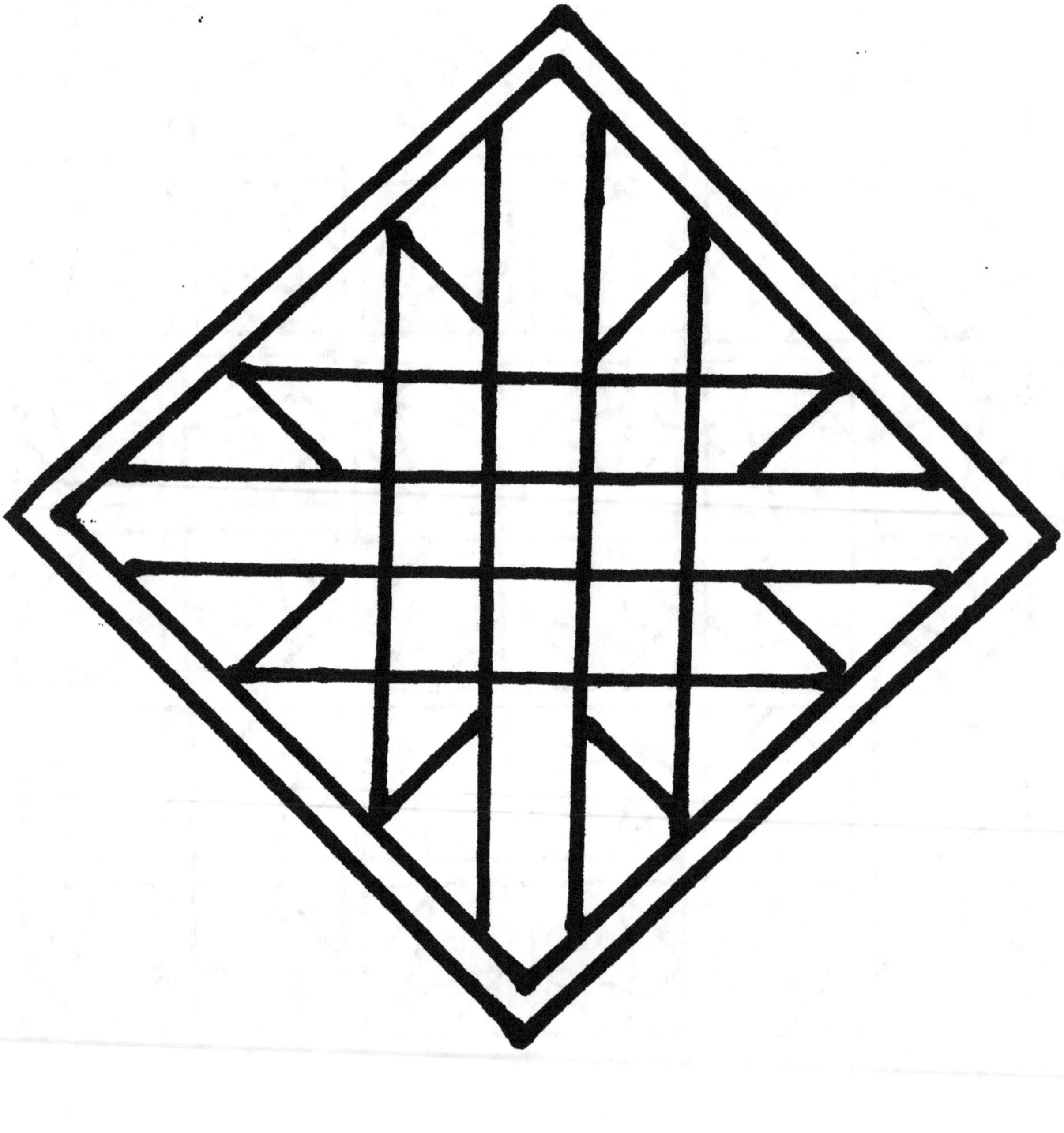

Dawson County Nebraska Barn Quilt Crossroads

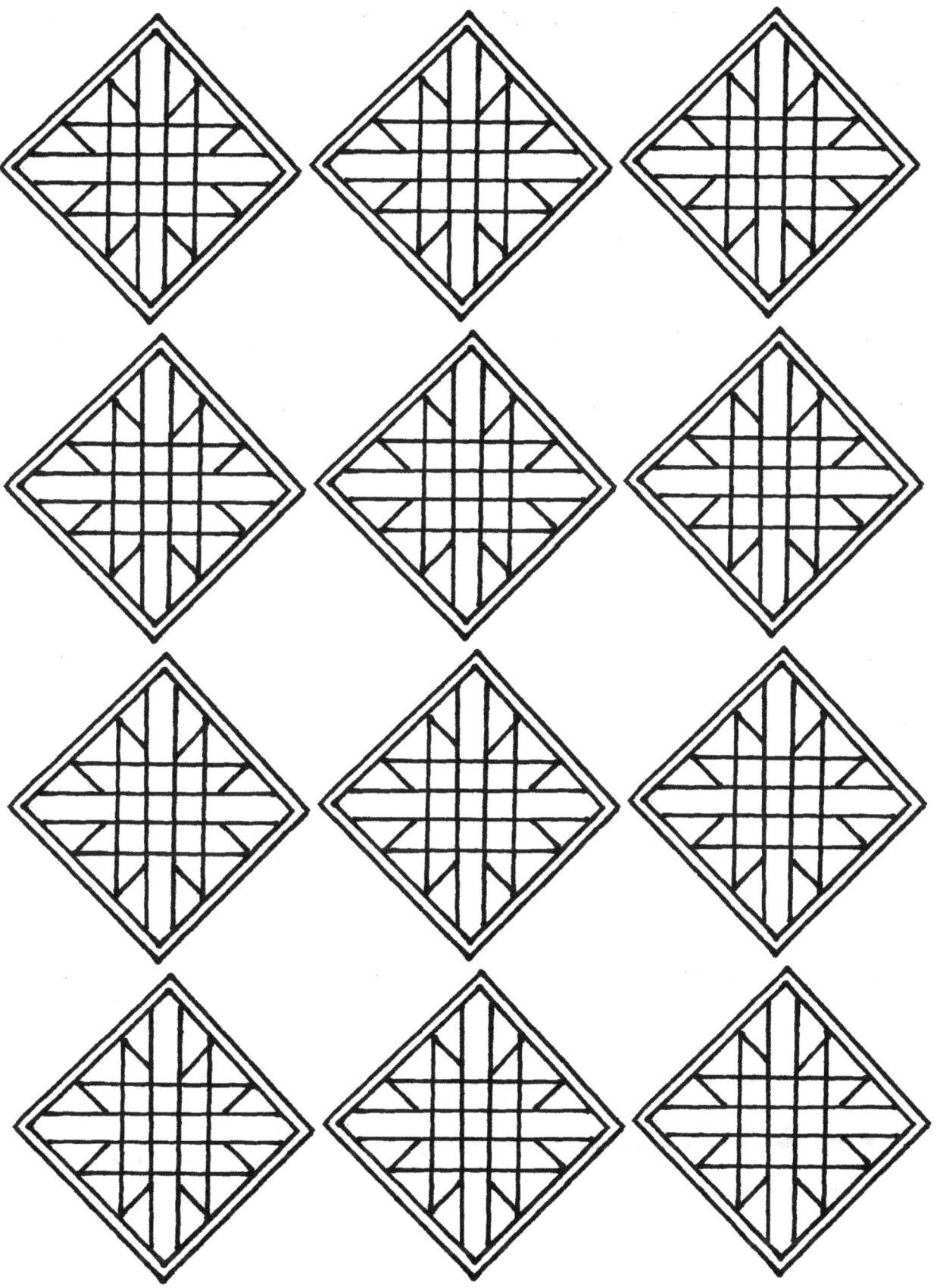

Crown of Thorns
Dawson County Nebraska Barn Quilt Trail

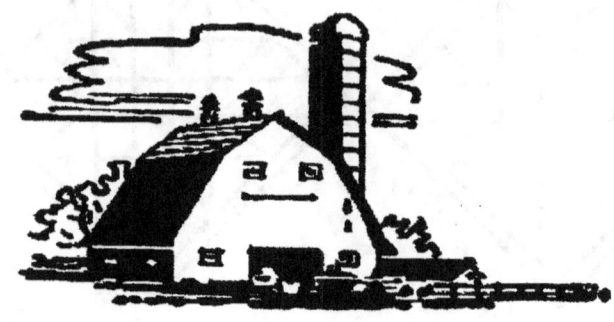

Barn Quilt Location
Avenue E
Cozad, Nebraska

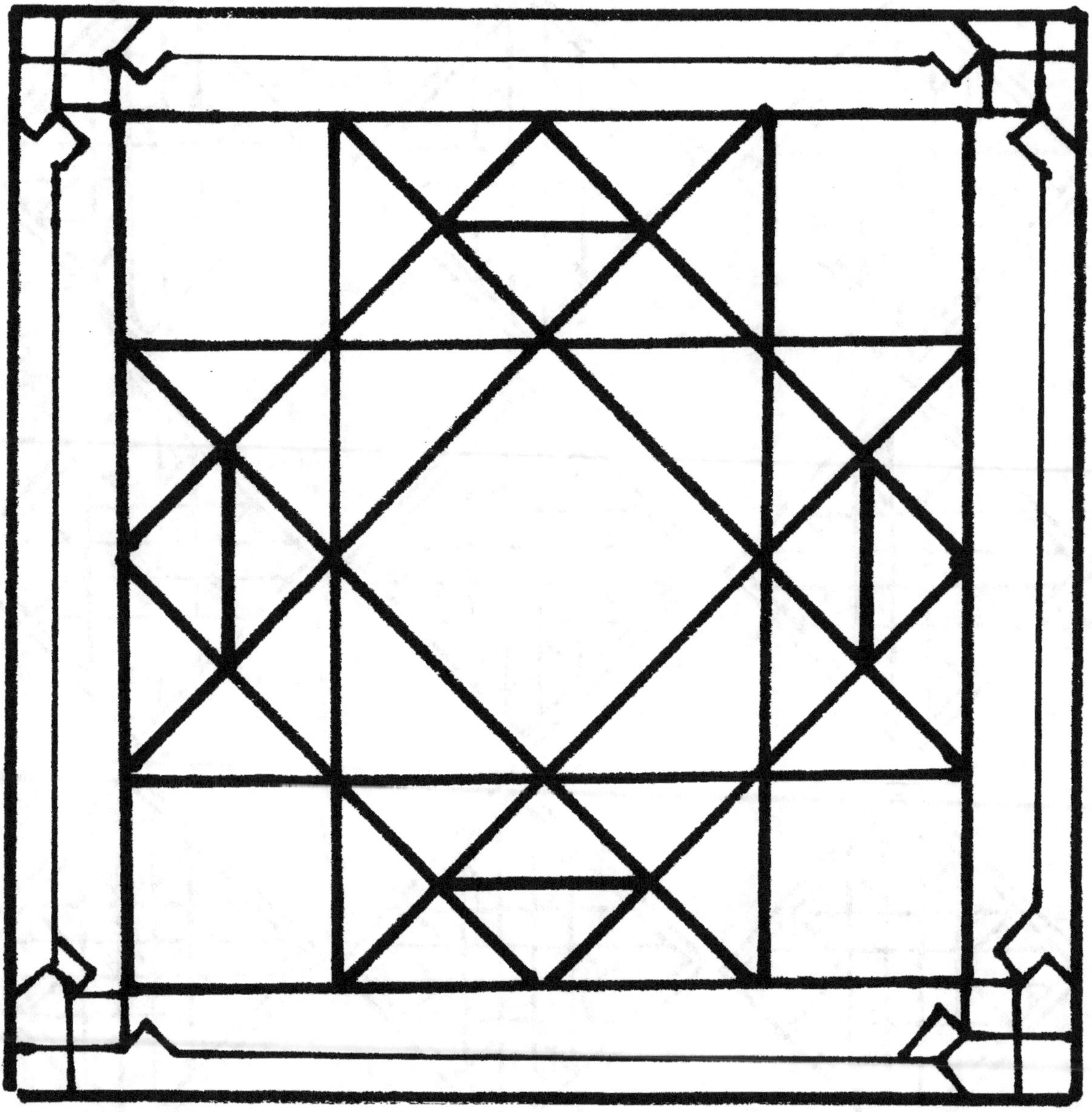

Dawson County Nebraska Barn Quilt Crown of Thorns

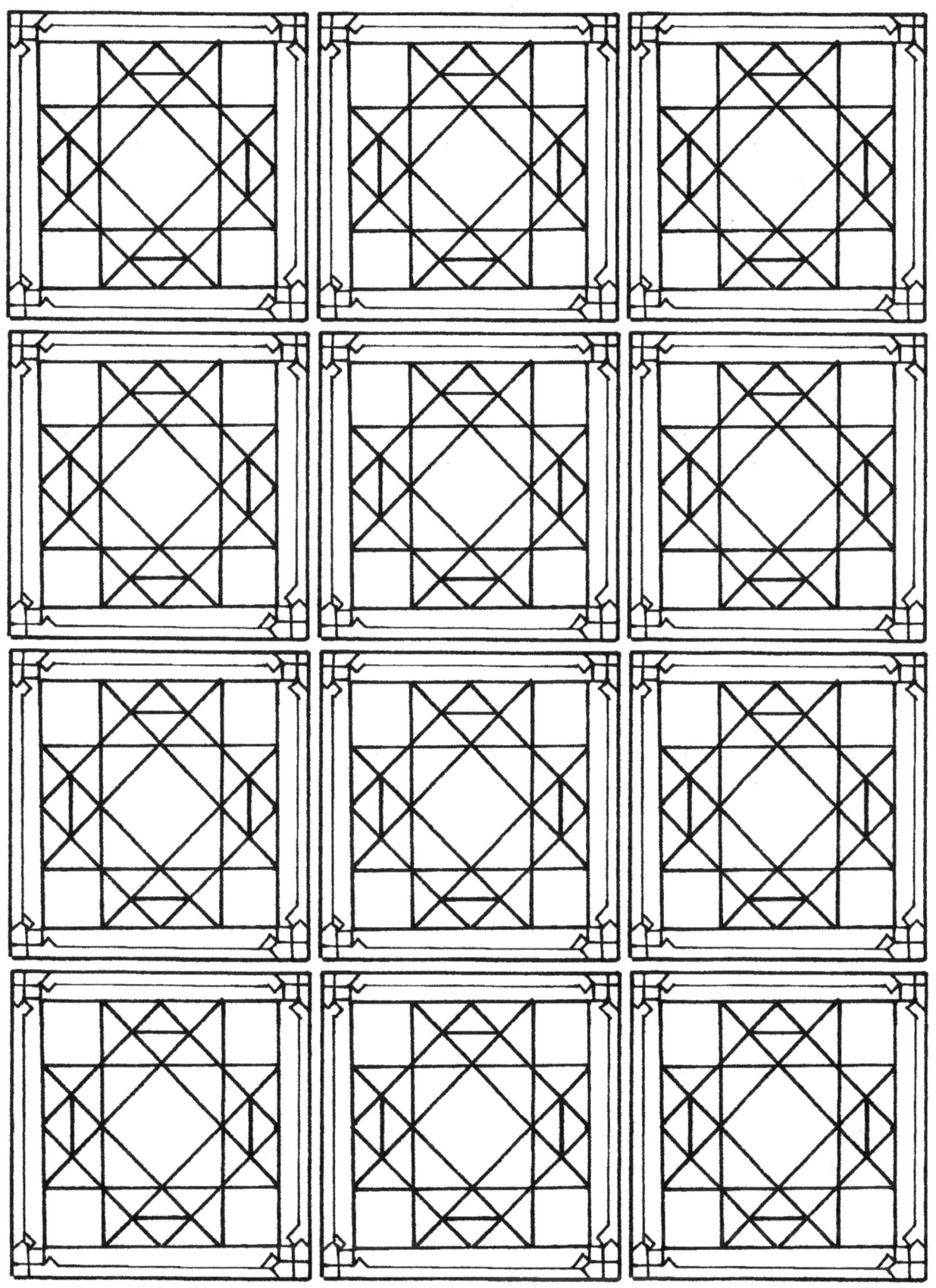

Deconstructed Sunflower
Dawson County Nebraska Barn Quilt Trail

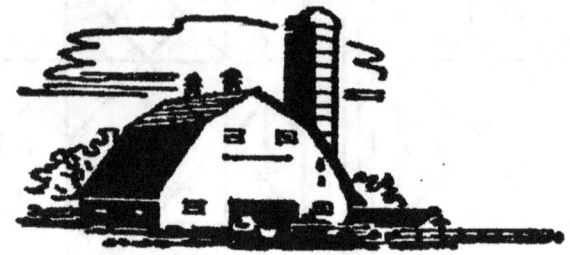

Quilt Block Location
Road 419
Cozad, Nebraska

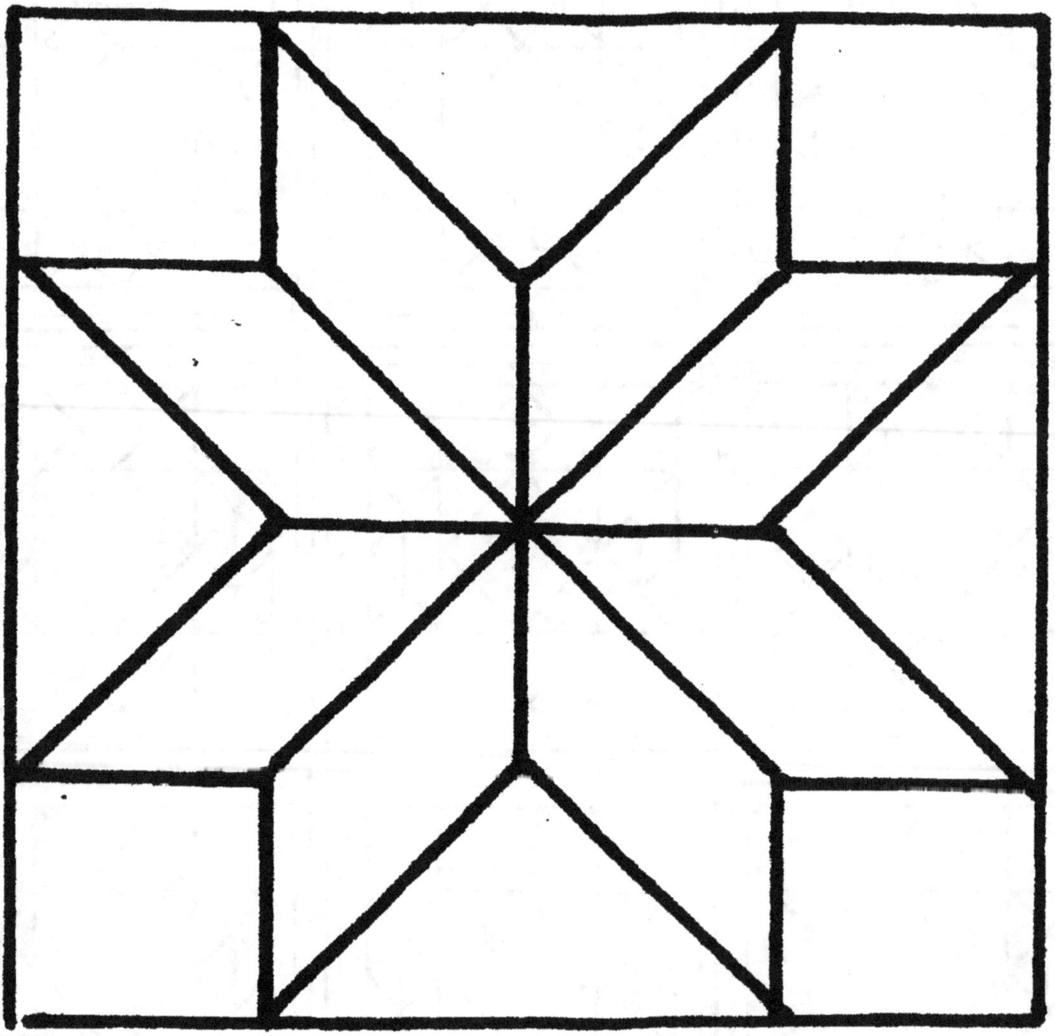

Dawson County Nebraska Barn Quilt Deconstructed Sunflower

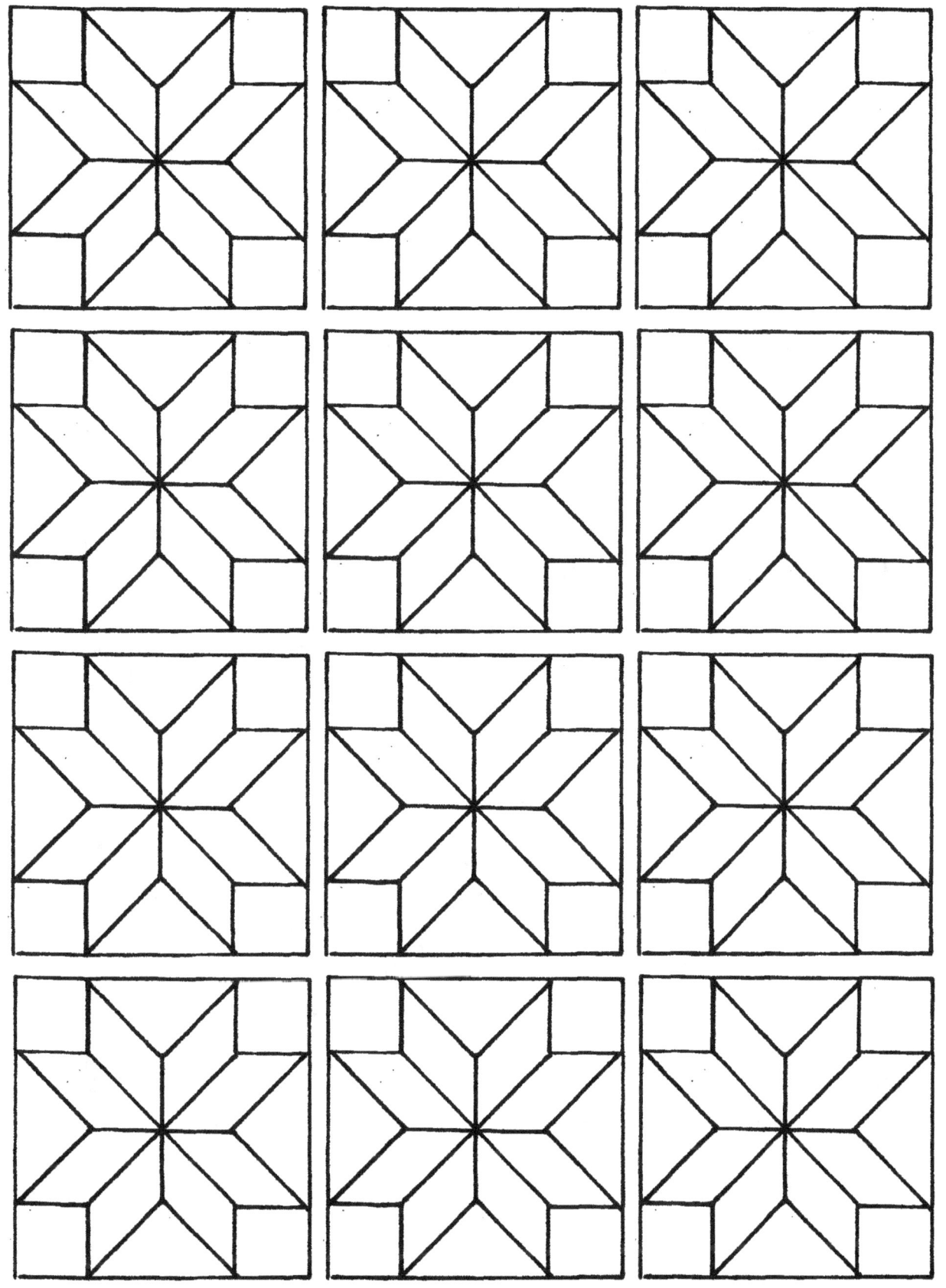

Double Aster
Dawson County Nebraska Barn Quilt Trail

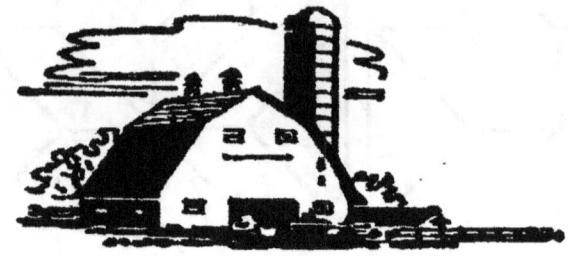

Quilt Block Location
Lincoln Avenue
Cozad, Nebraska

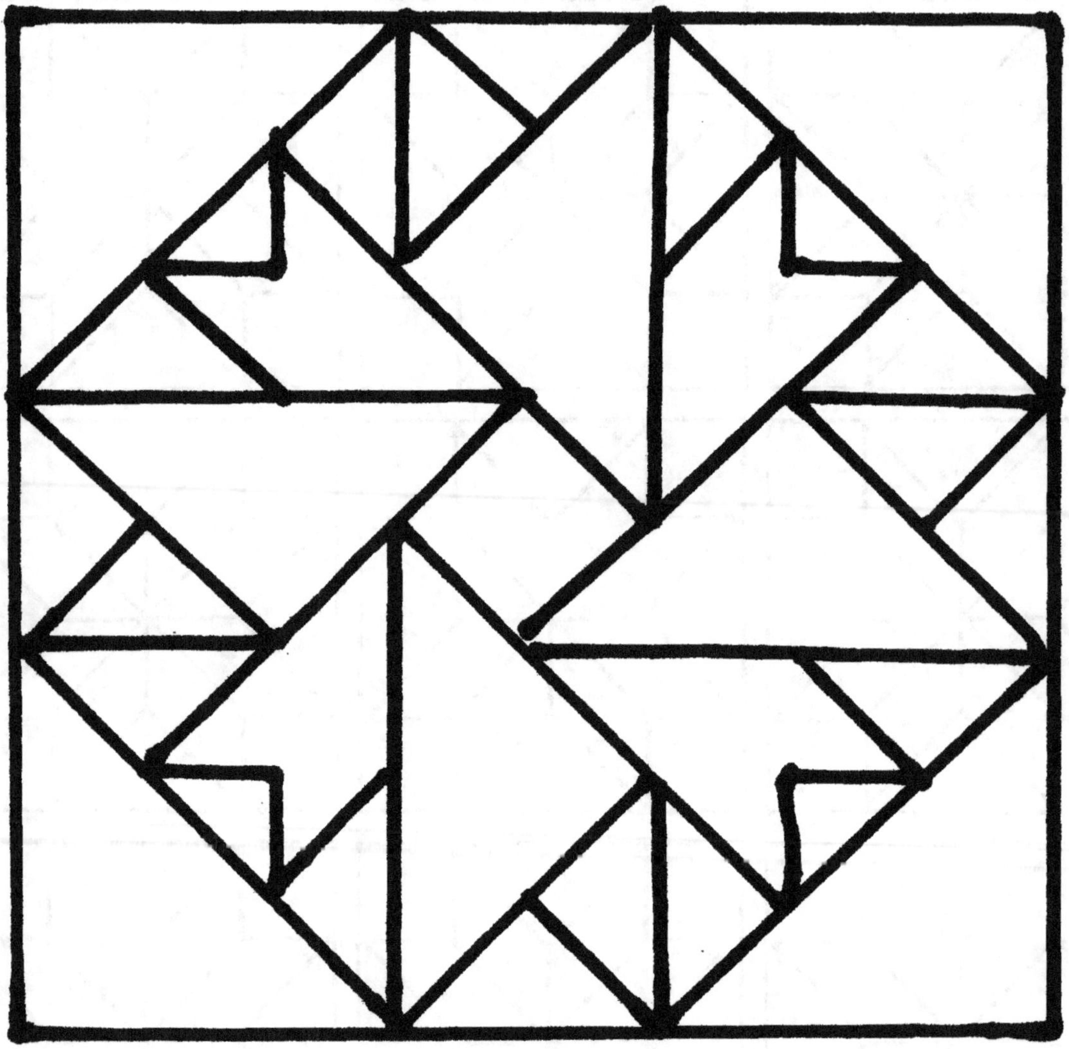

Dawson County Nebraska Barn Quilt Double Aster

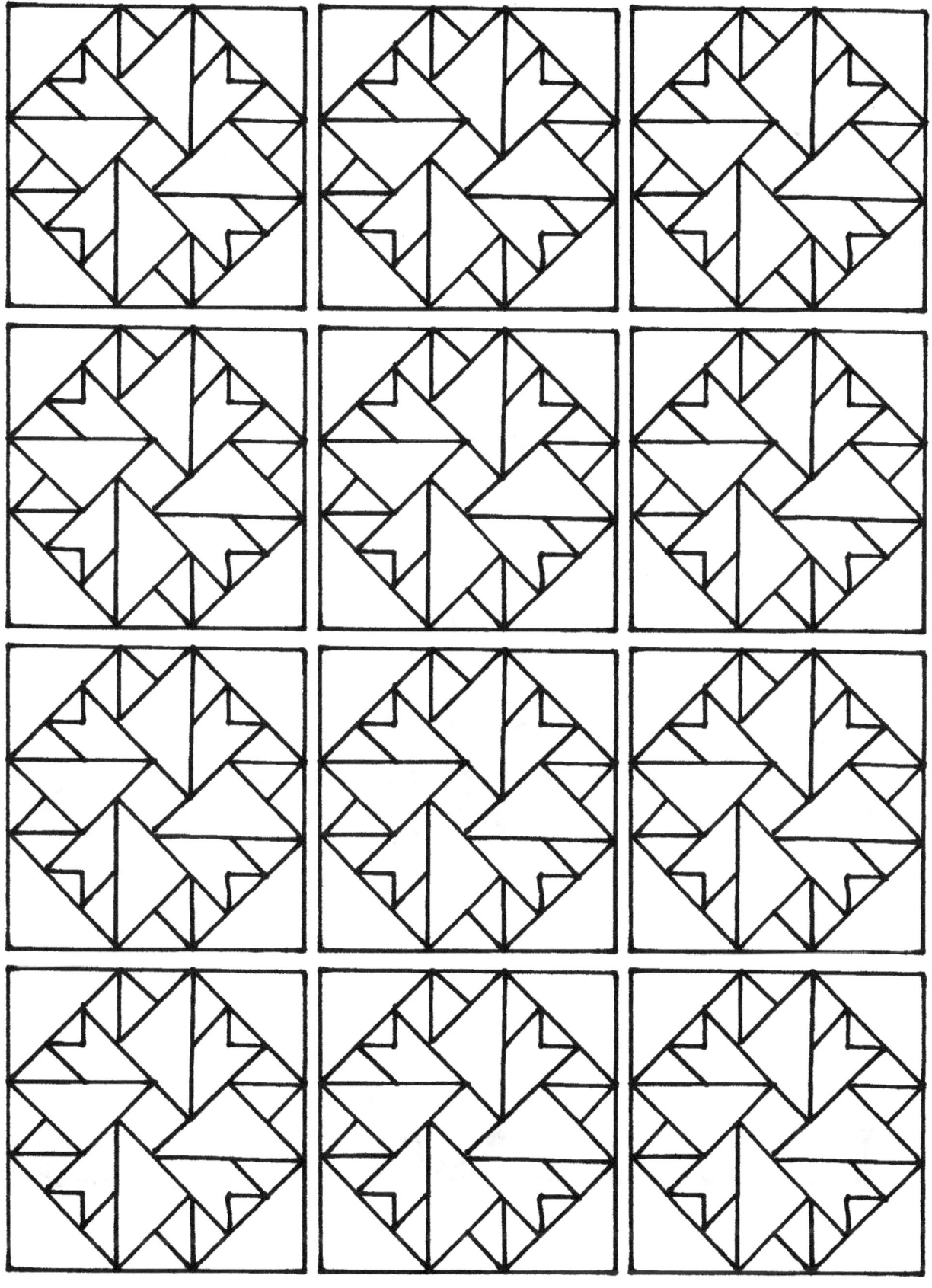

Double Card Trick
Dawson County Nebraska Barn Quilt Trail

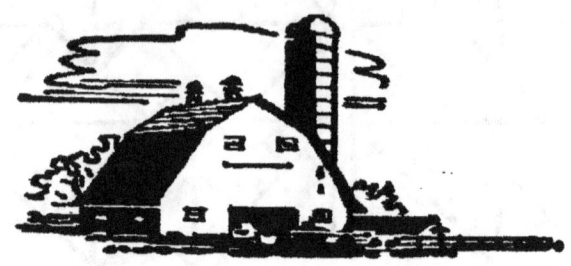

Quilt Block Location
Avenue J
Cozad, Nebraska

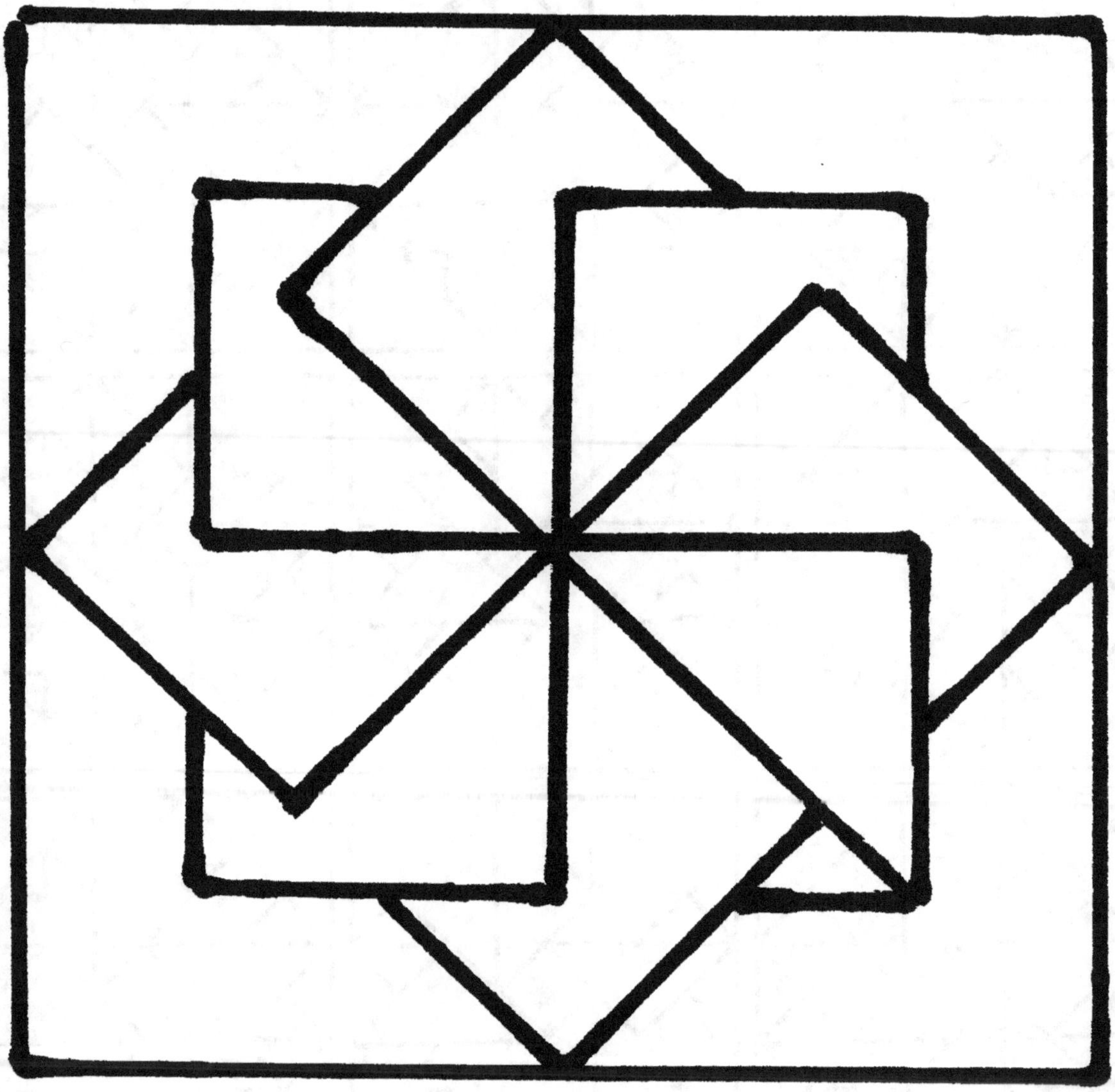

Dawson County Nebraska Barn Quit Double Card Trick

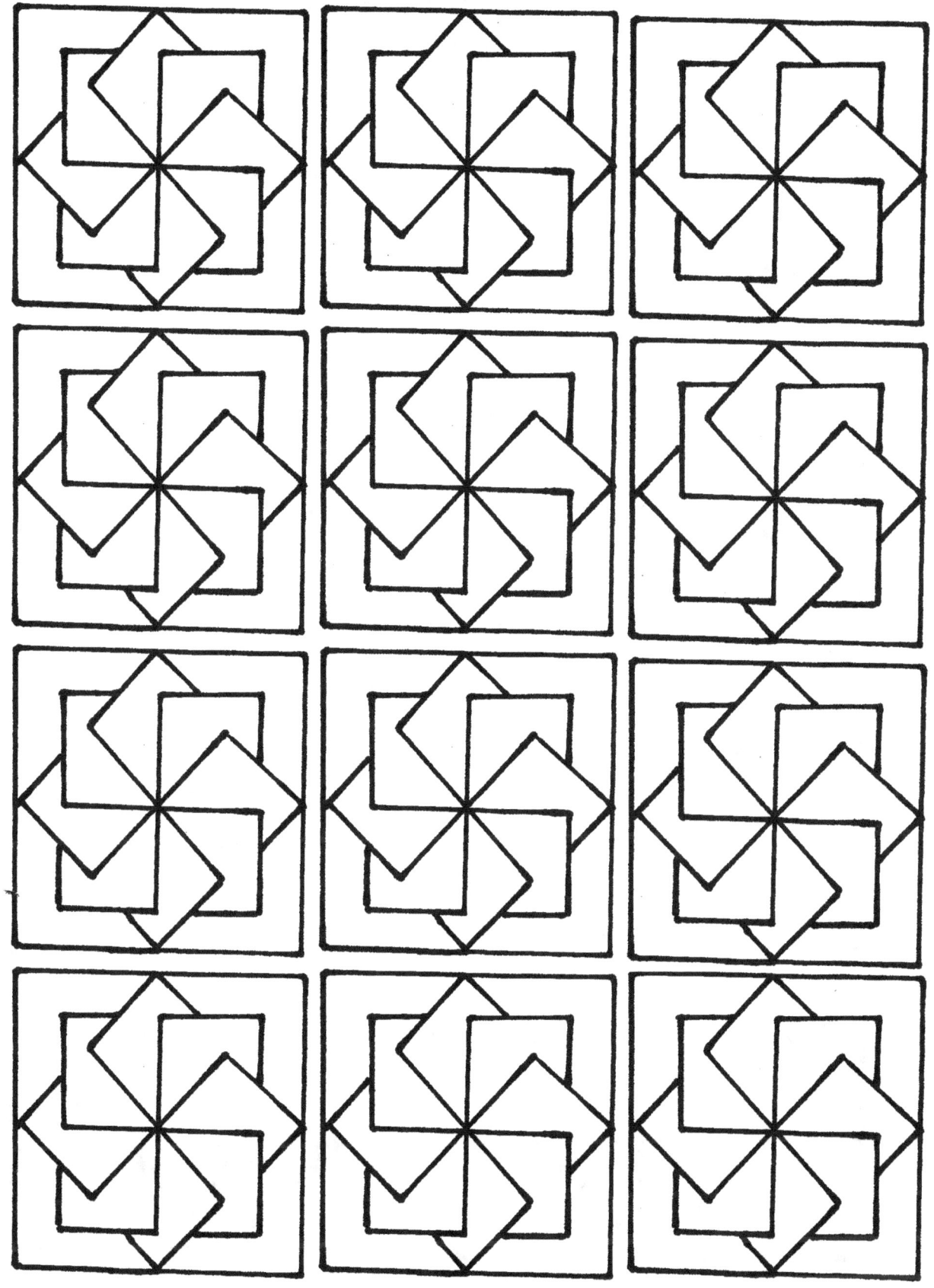

Eclipse
Dawson County Nebraska Barn Quilt Trail

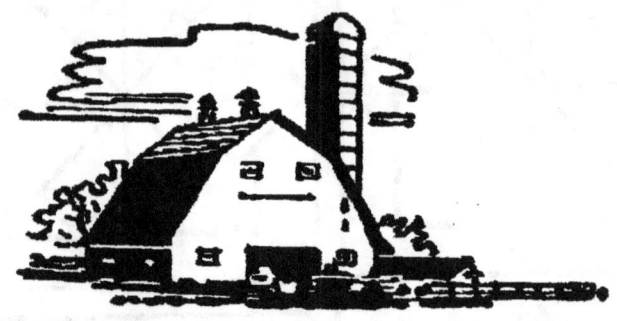

Barn Quilt Location
East 12th Street
Cozad, Nebraska

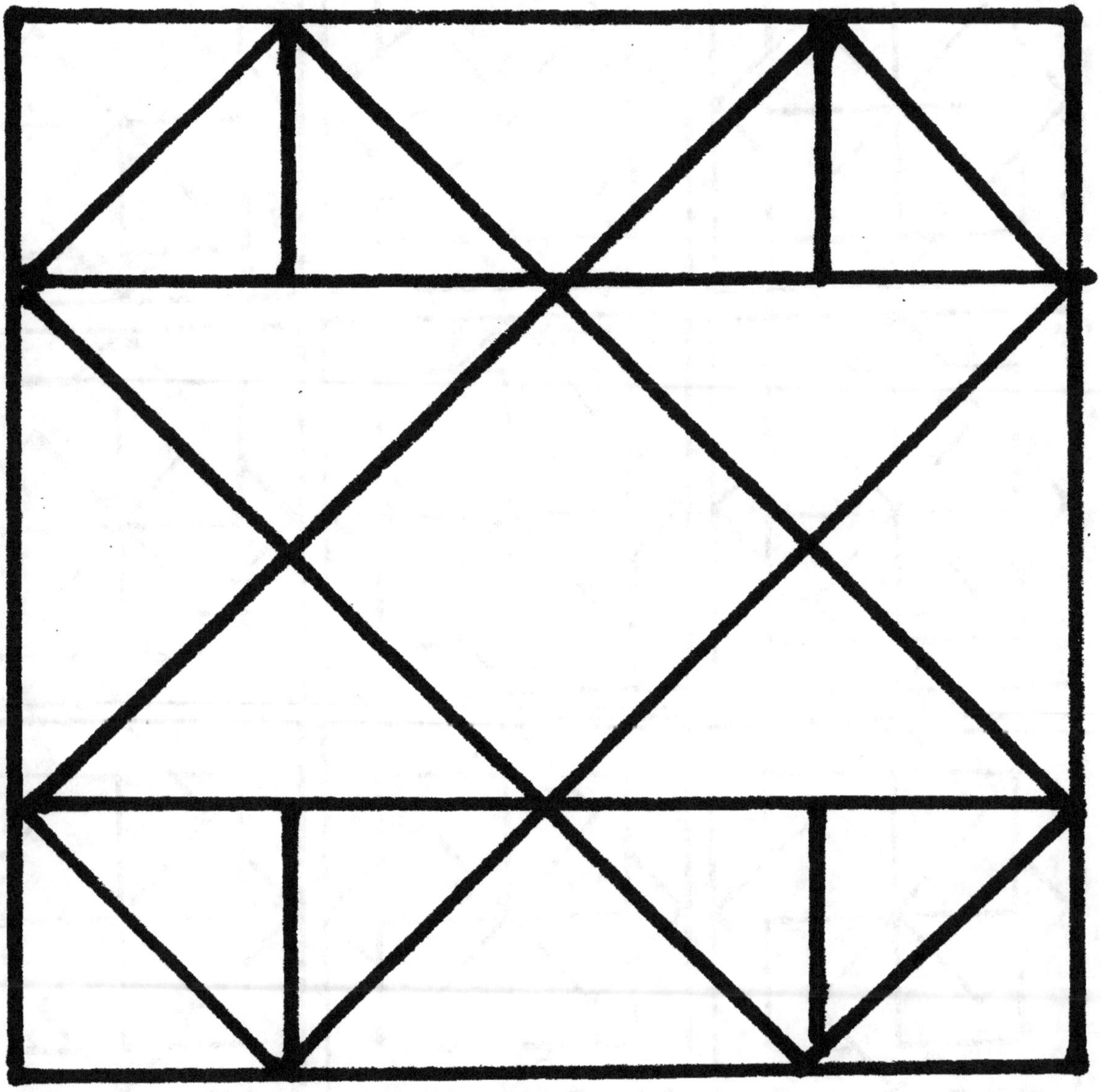

Dawson County Nebraska Barn Quilt Eclipse

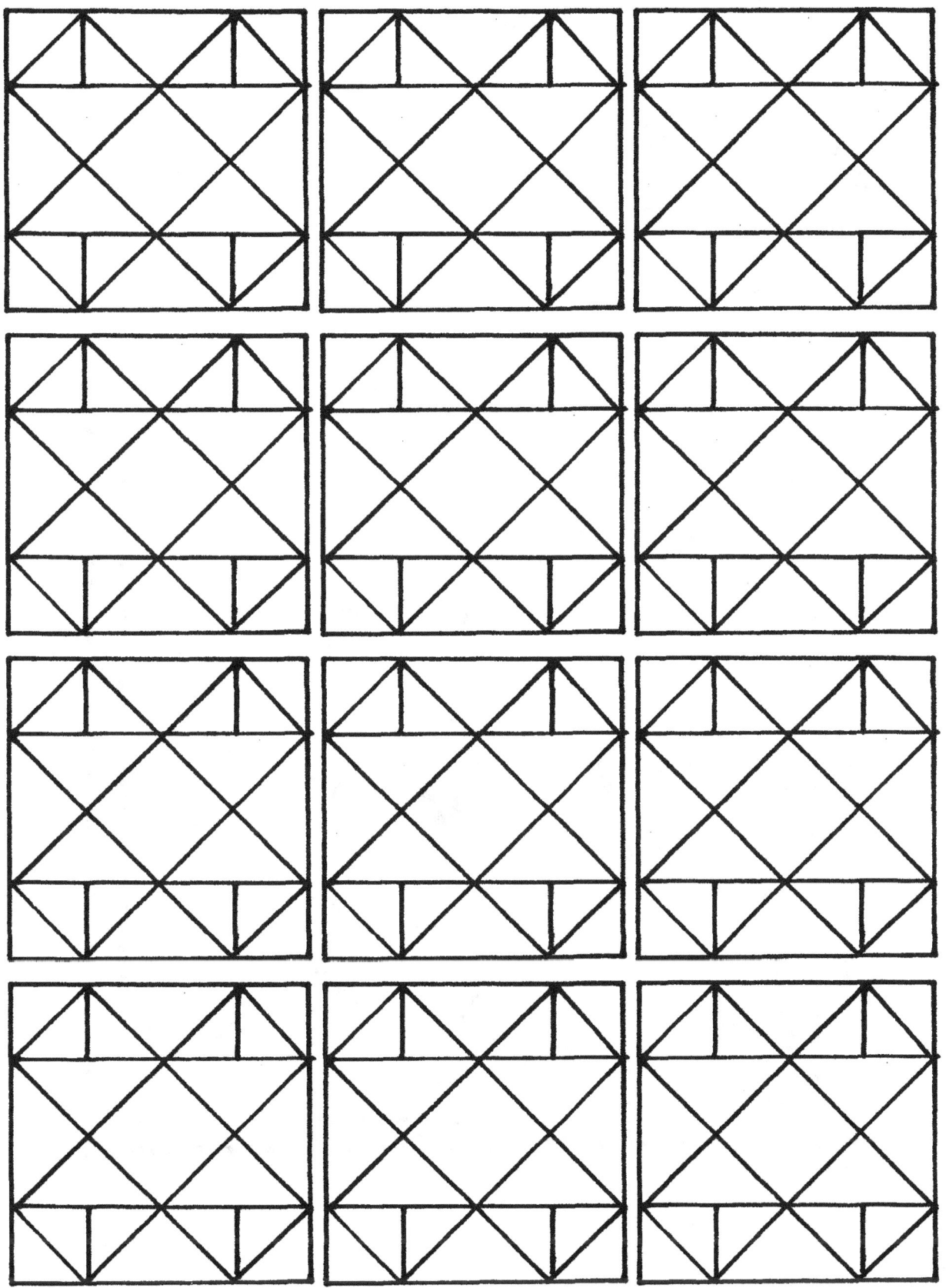

Elks
Dawson County Nebraska Barn Quilt Trail

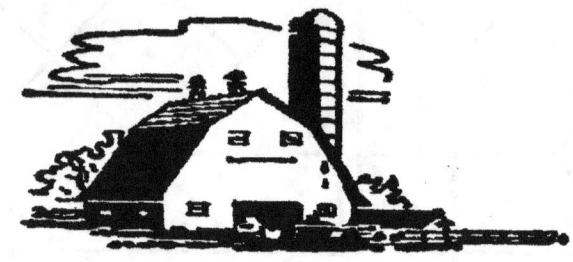

Quilt Block Location
J Street
Cozad, Nebraska

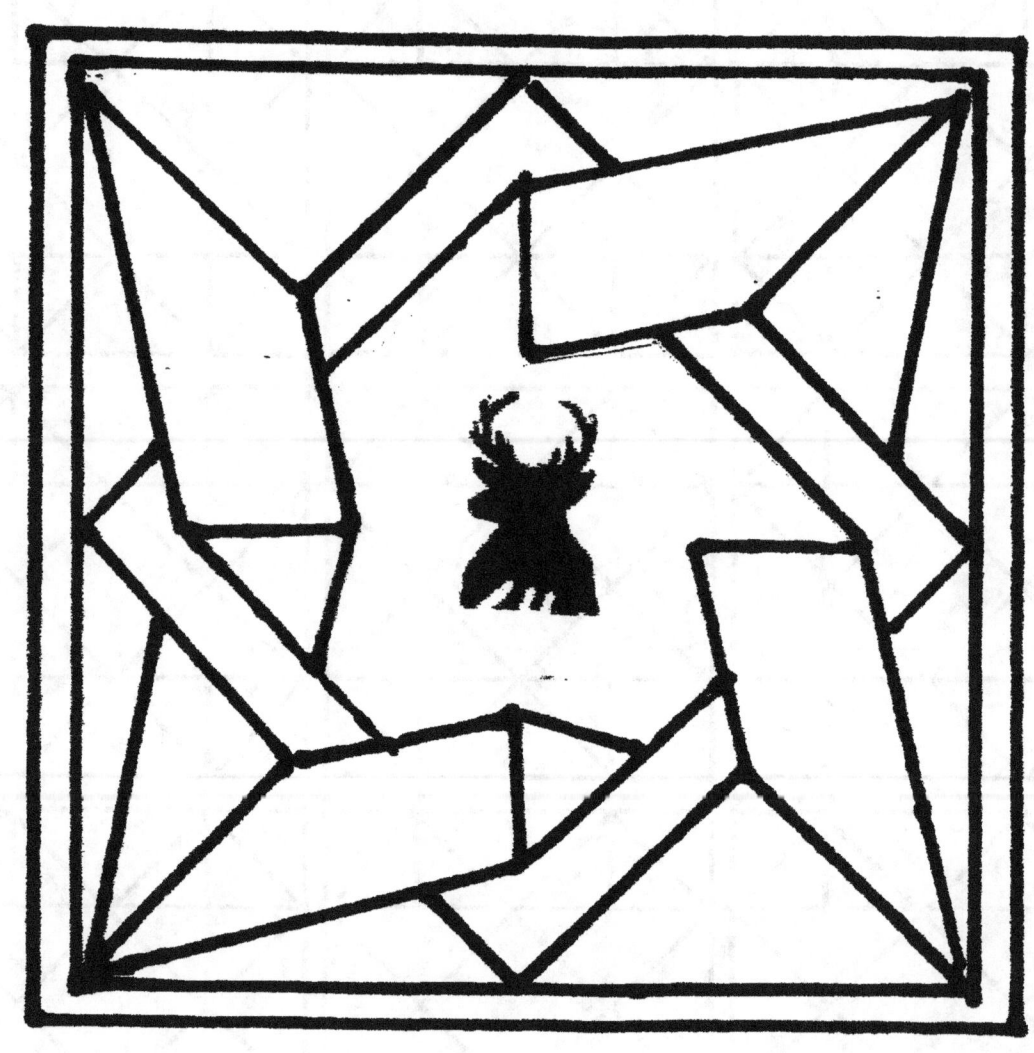

Dawson County Nebraska Barn Quilt Elks

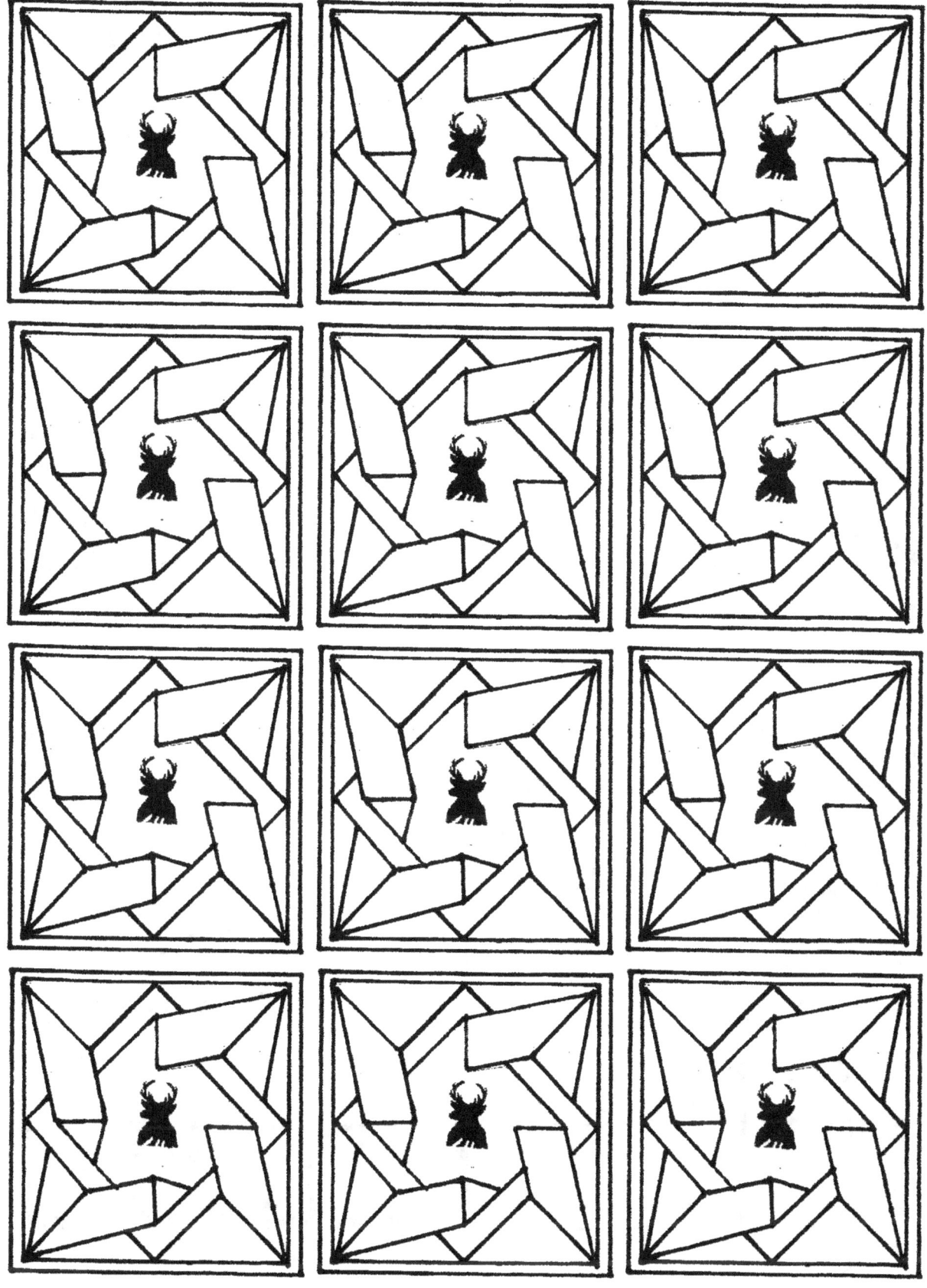

Elks Lodge Flag Colors
Dawson County Nebraska Barn Quilt Trail

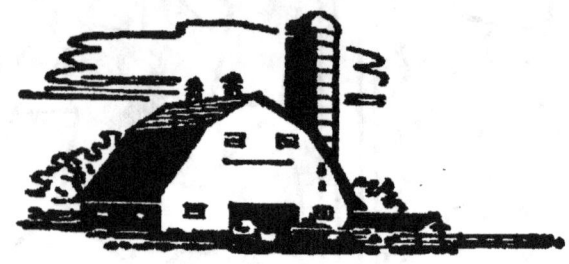

Quilt Block Location
J Street
Cozad, Nebraska

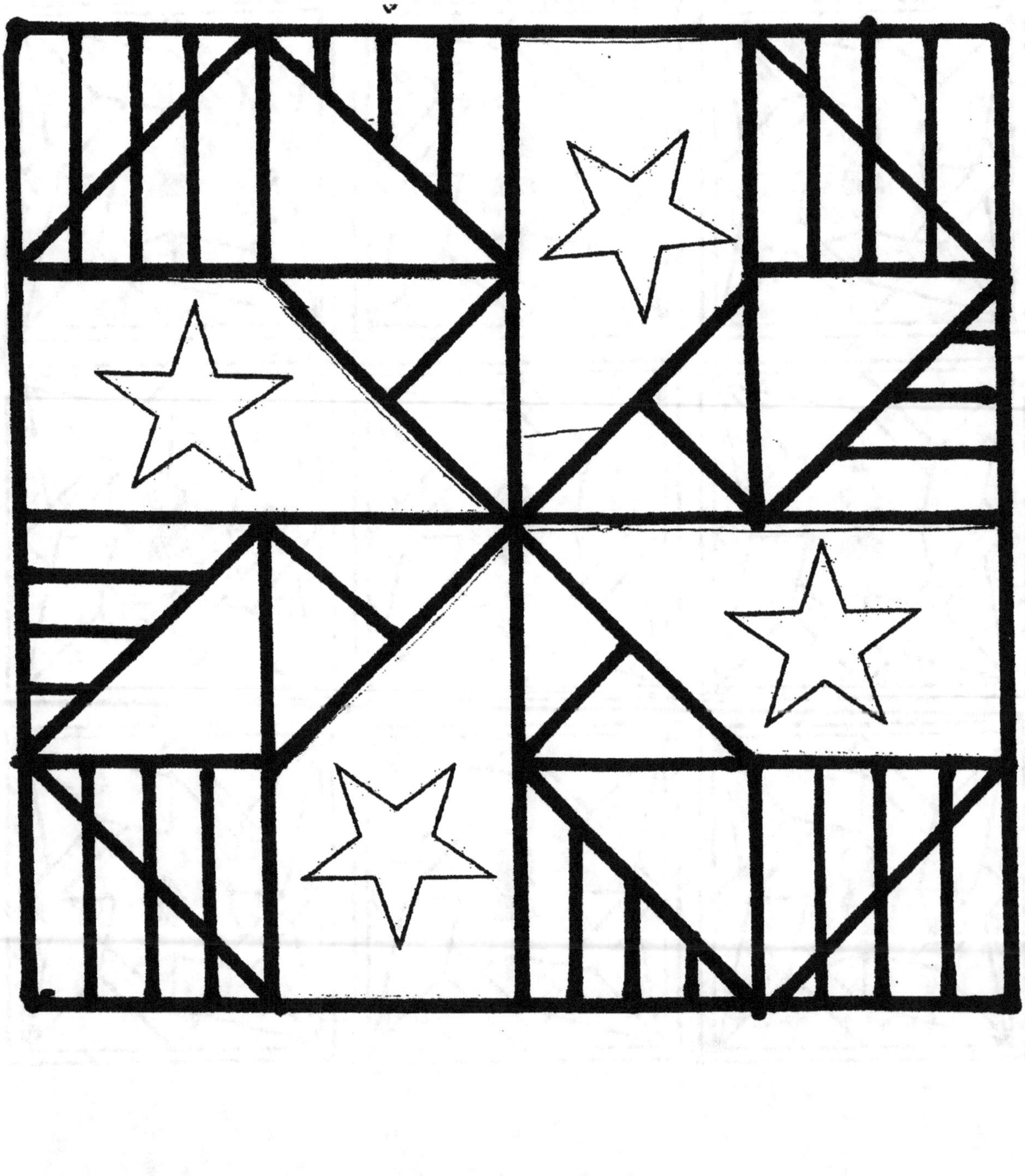

Dawson County Nebraska Barn Quit Elks Lodge Flag Colors

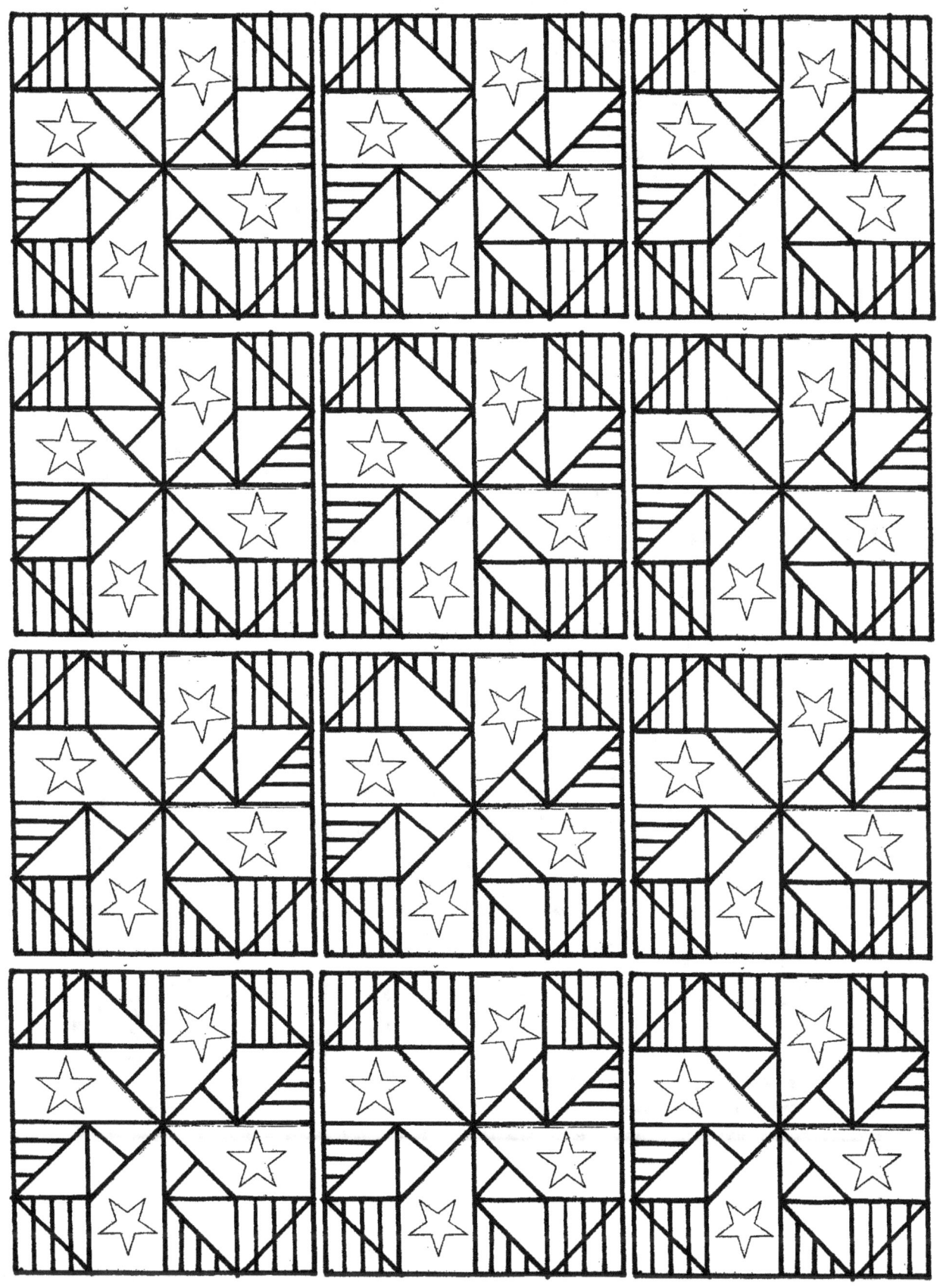

Friendship Star
Dawson County Nebraska Barn Quilt Trail

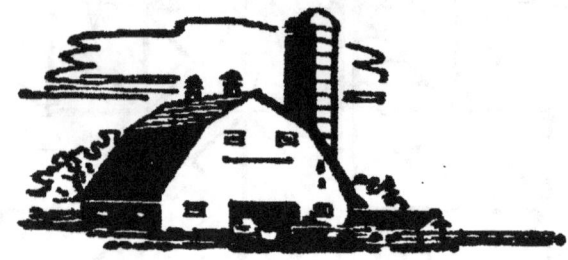

Quilt Block Location
Road 761
Cozad, Nebraska

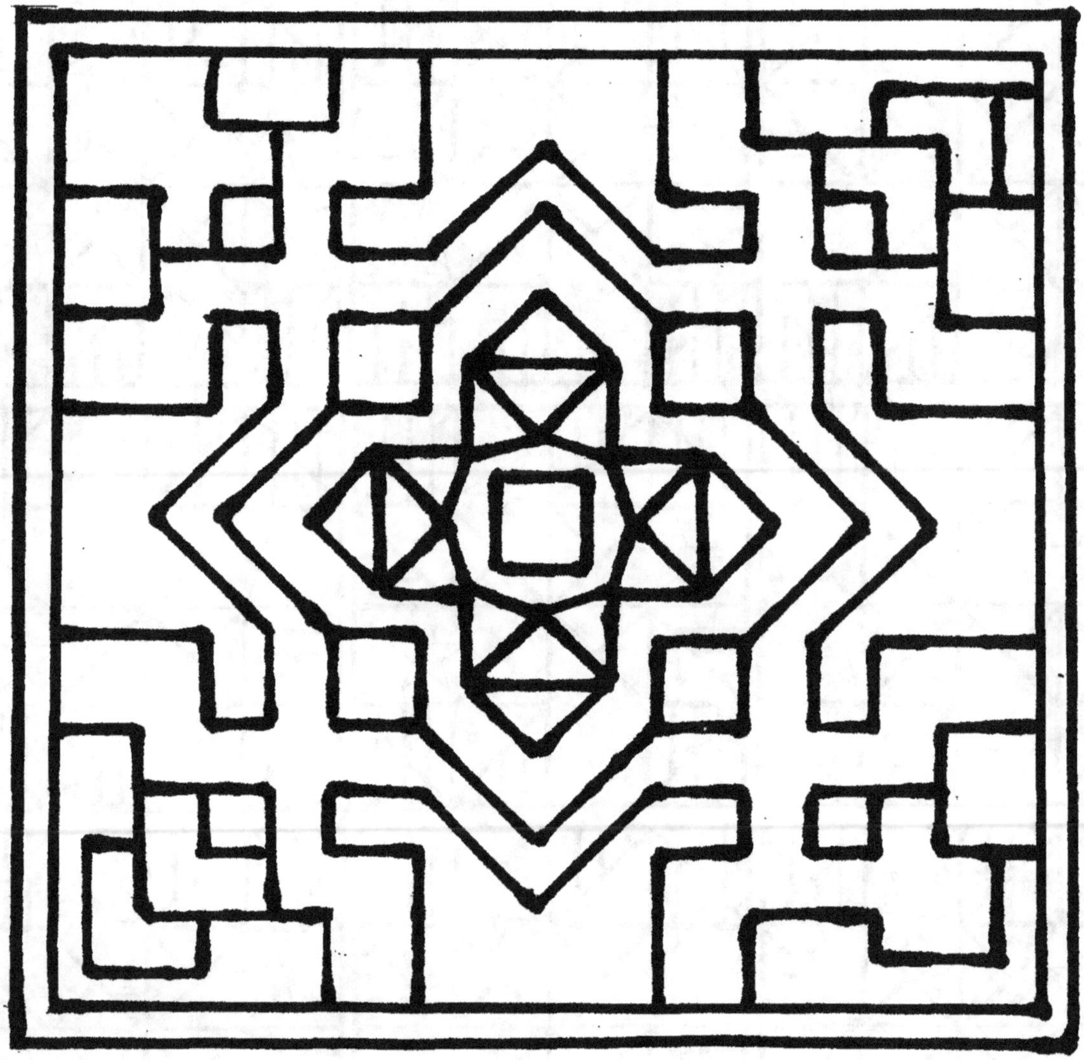

Dawson County Nebraska Barn Quilt Friendship Star

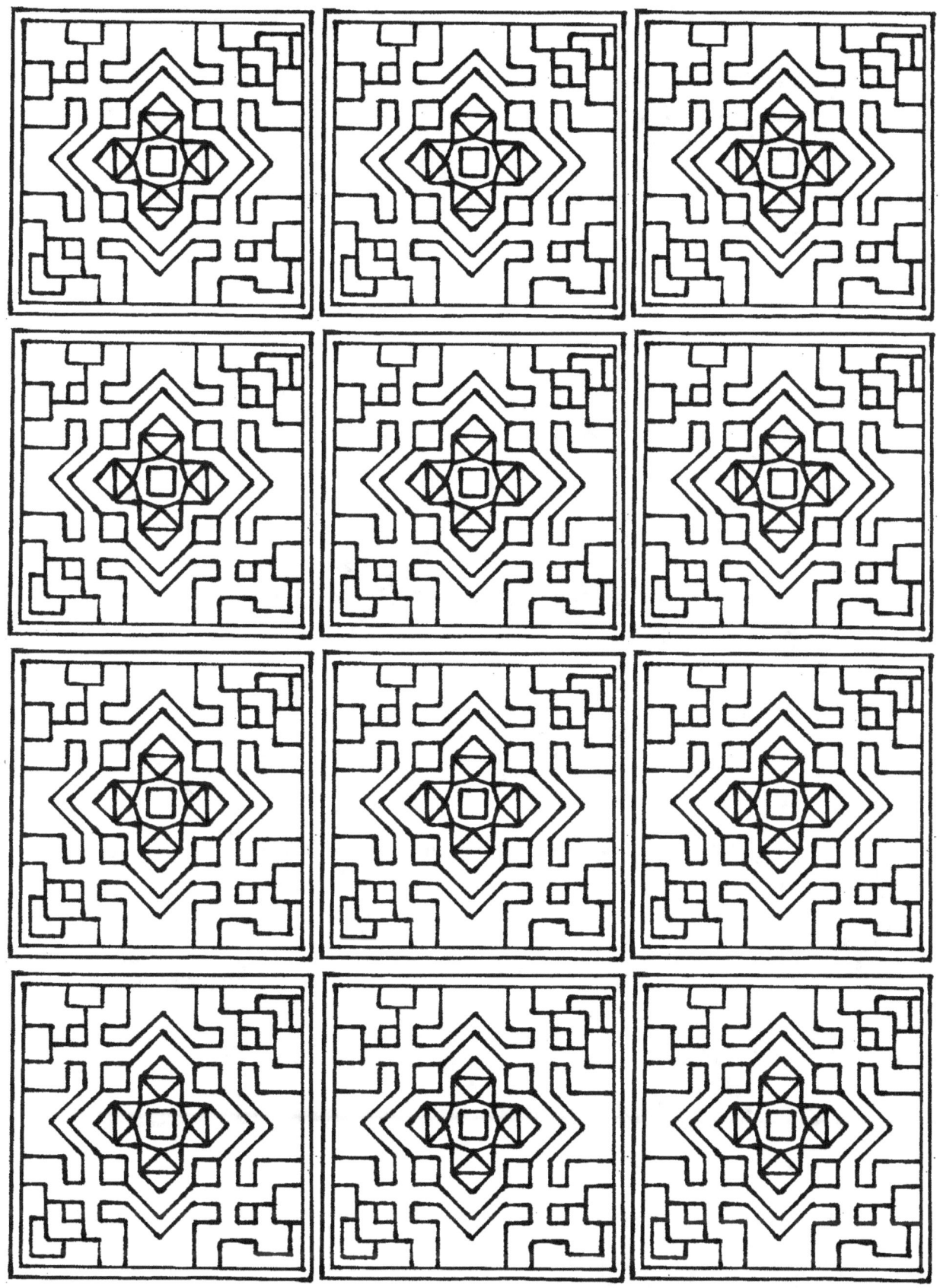

Gensenbach's Creation
Dawson County Nebraska Barn Quilt Trail

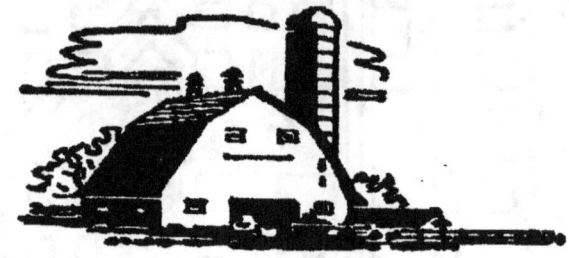

Quilt Block Location
Road 419
Cozad, Nebraska

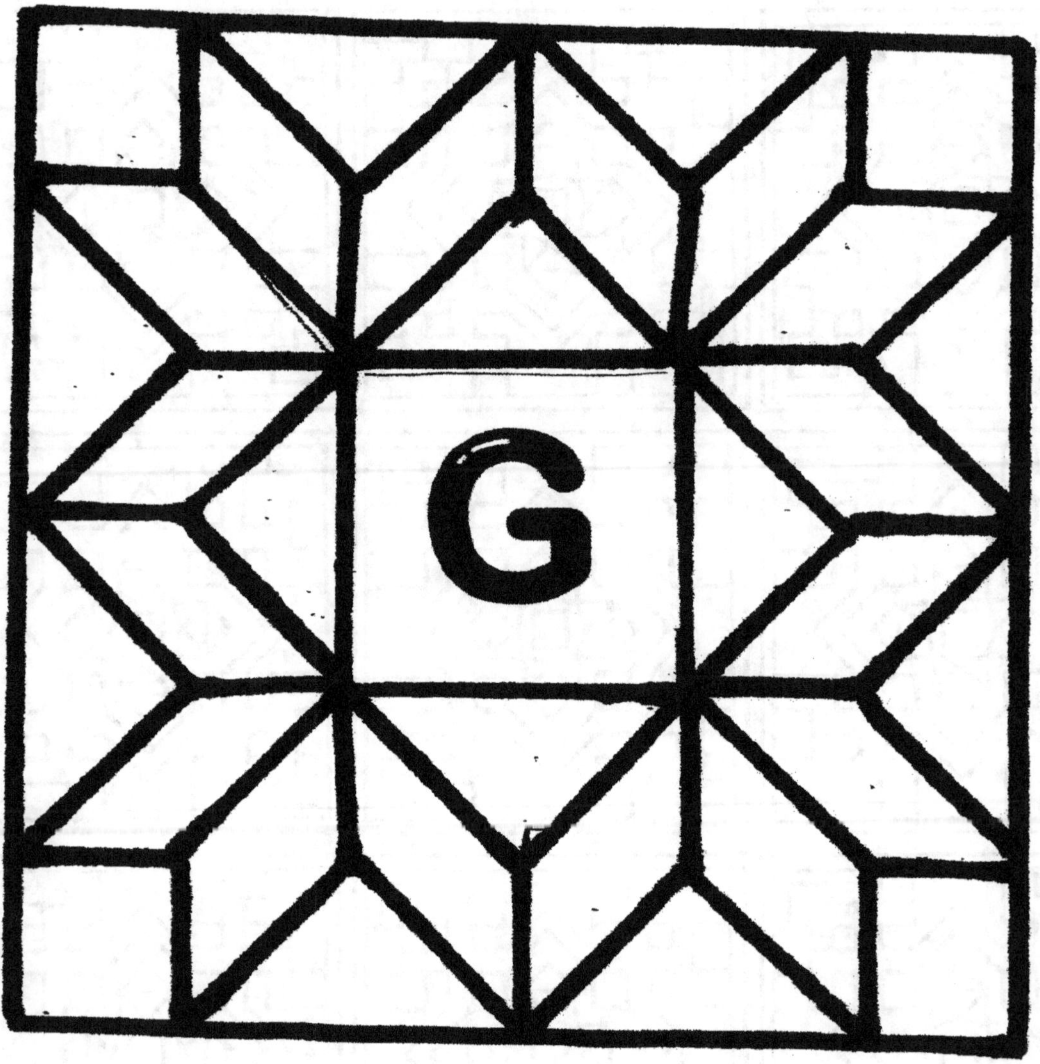

G

Dawson County Nebraska Barn Quilt Gensenbach Creation

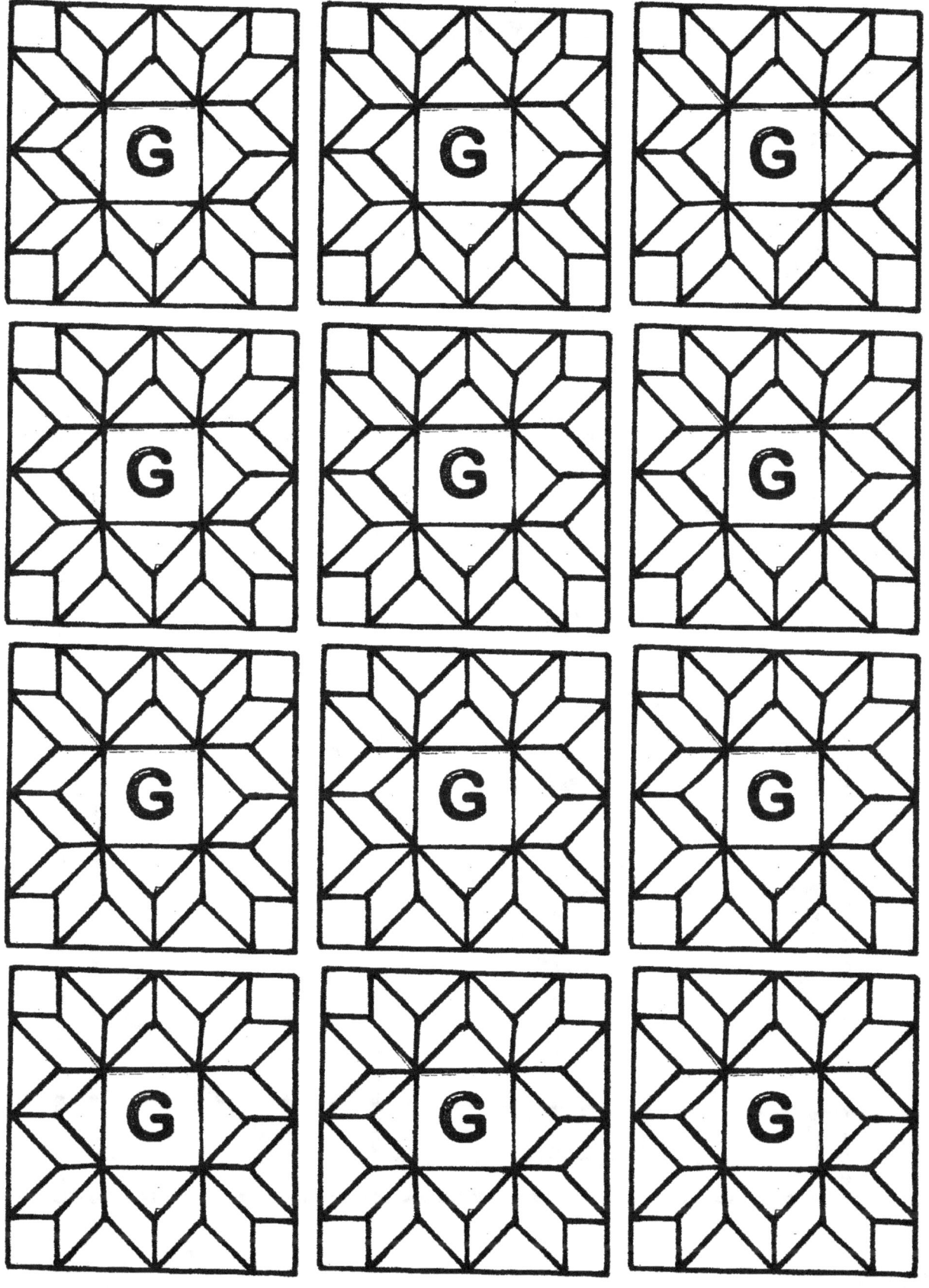

God Bless America
Dawson County Nebraska Barn Quilt Trail

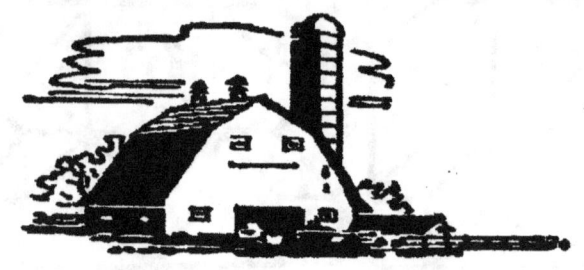

Quilt Block Location
Meridian Avenue
Cozad, Nebraska

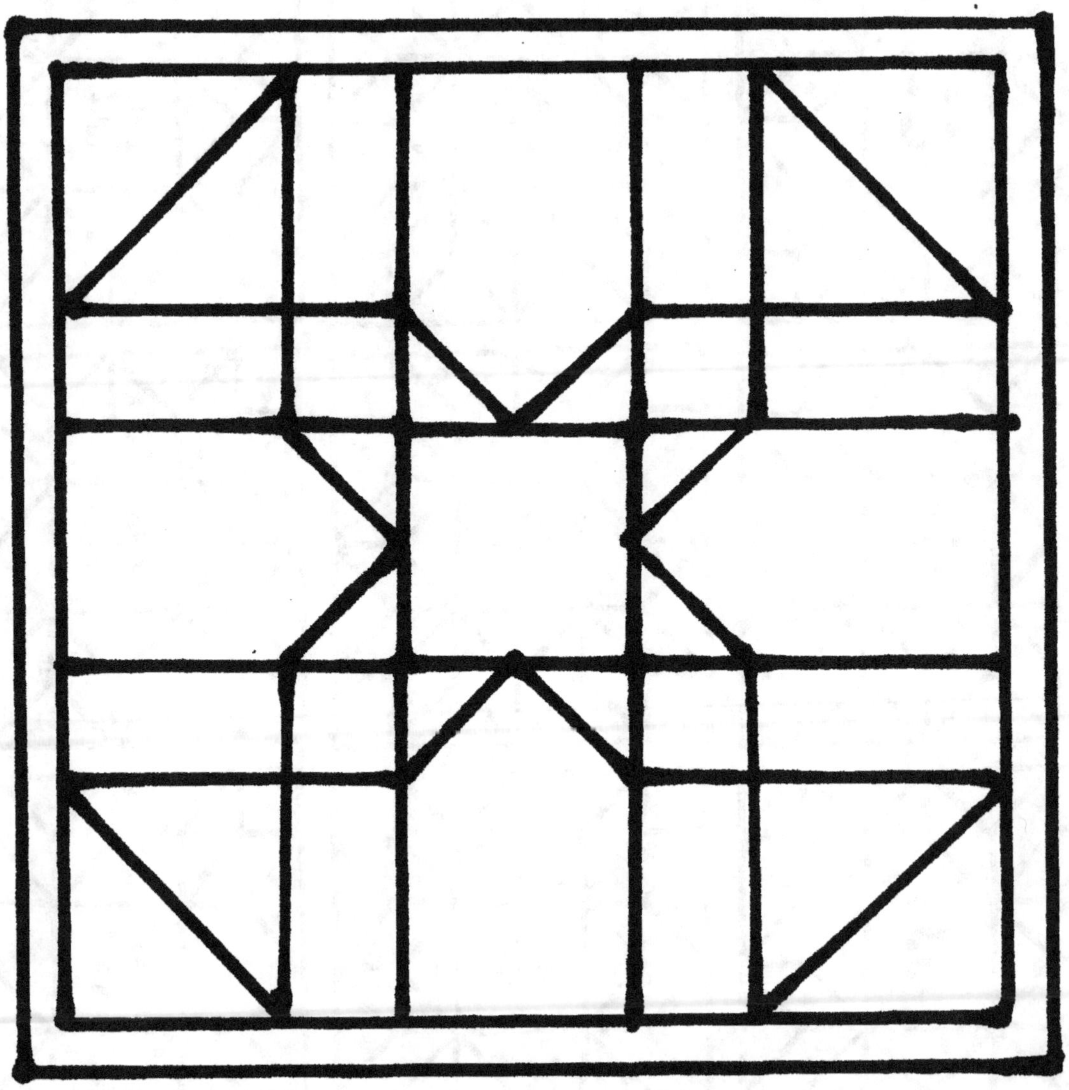

Dawson County Nebraska Barn Quilt God Bless America

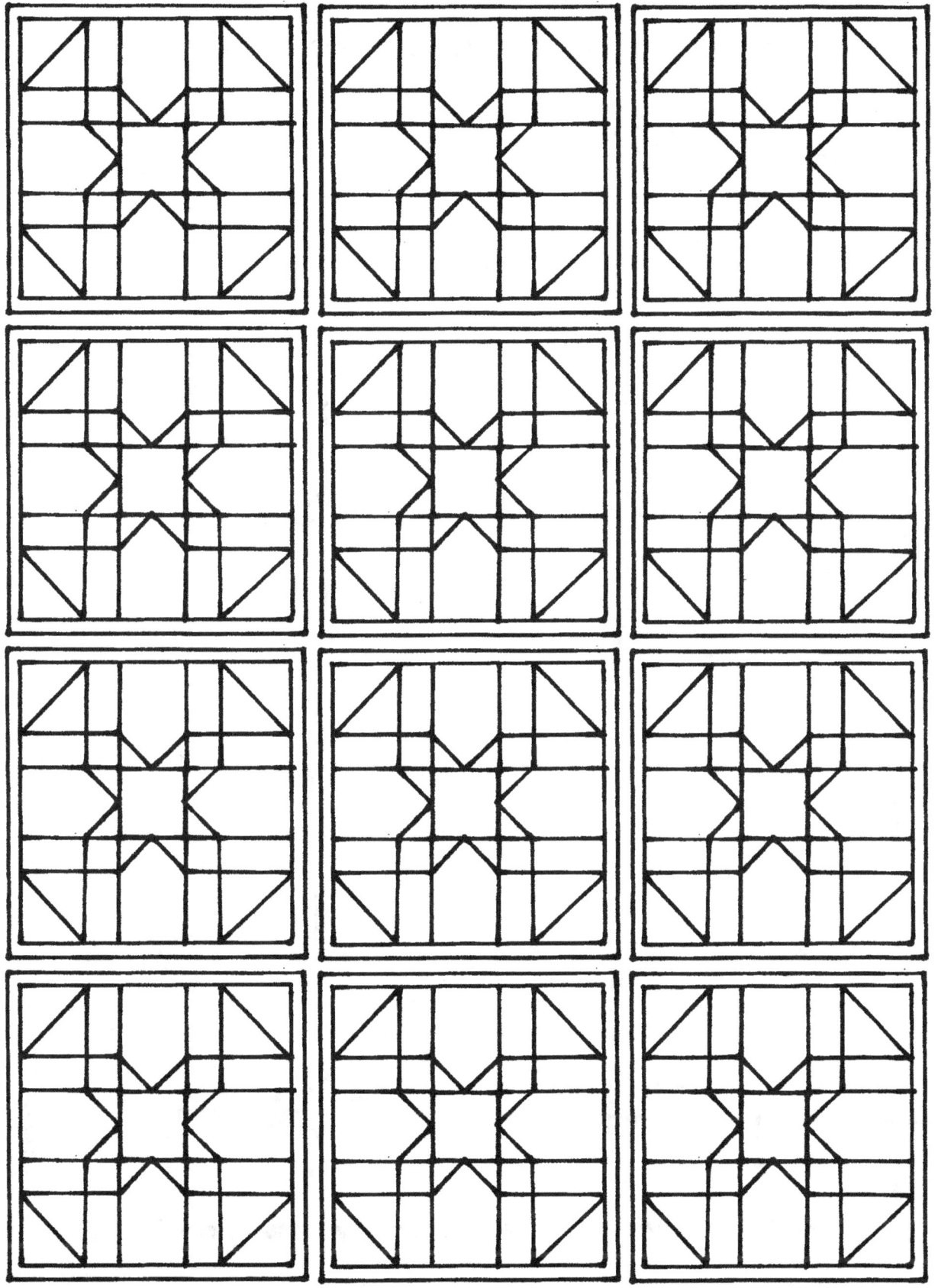

Haymaker Spirit
Dawson County Nebraska Barn Quilt Trail

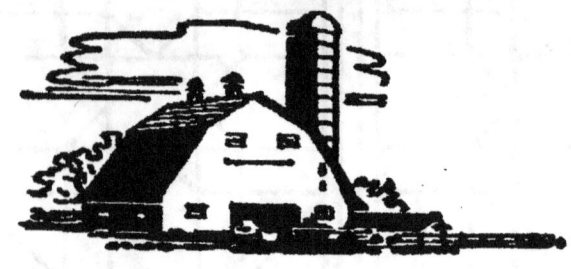

Quilt Block Location
Meridian Avenue
Cozad, Nebraska

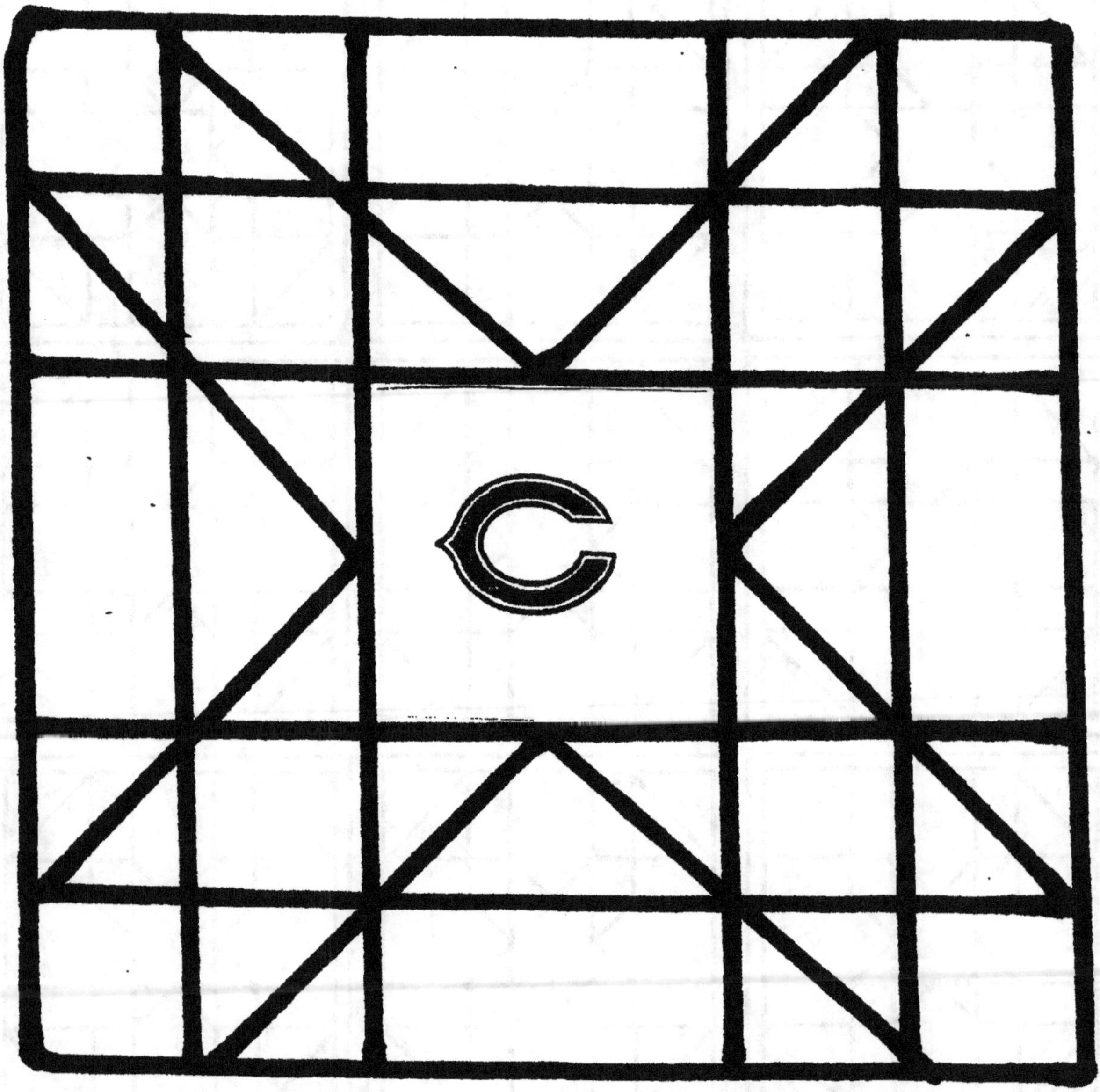

Dawson County Nebraska Barn Quit Haymaker Spirit

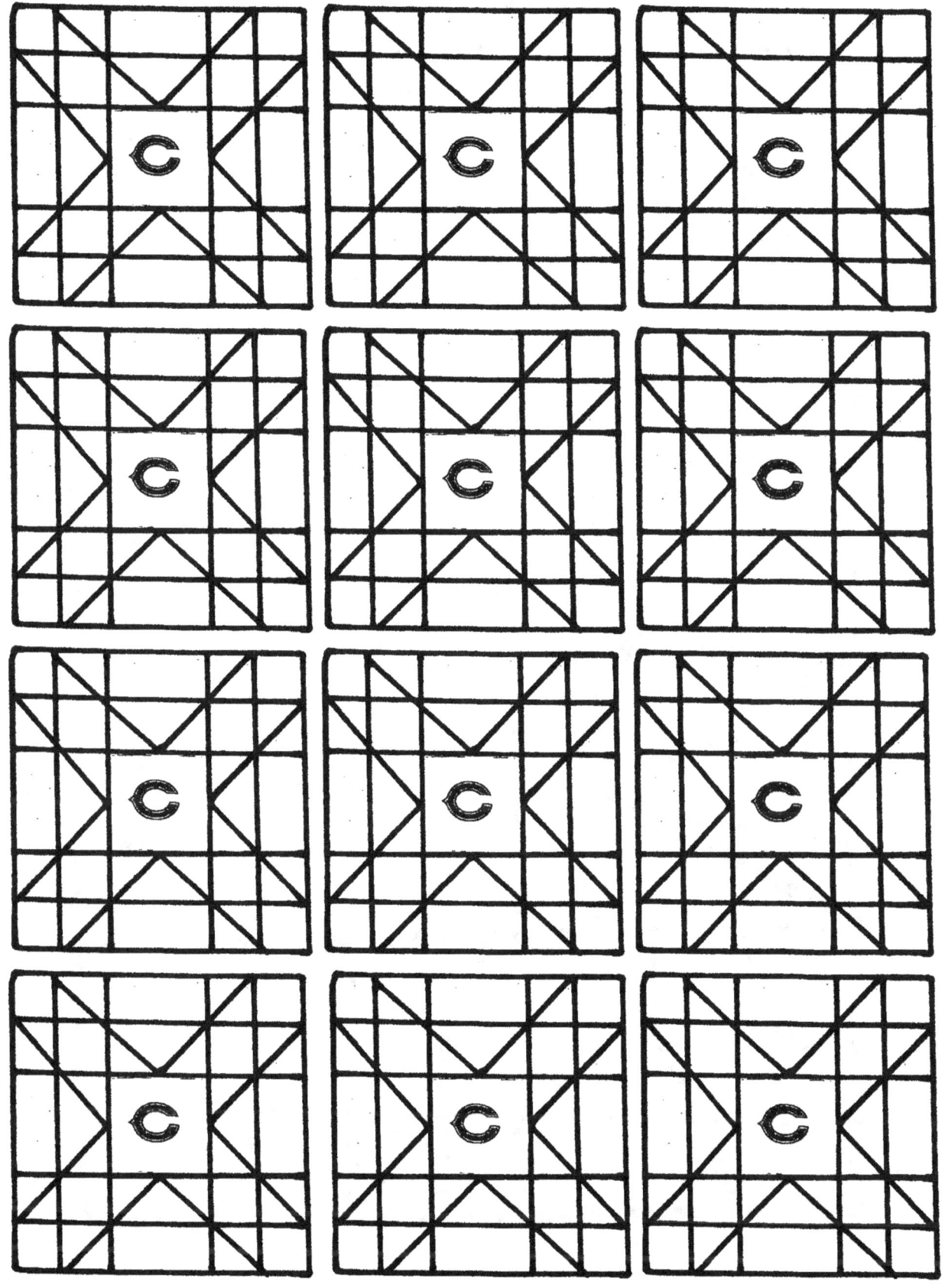

Heavens A Blazin'
Dawson County Nebraska Barn Quilt Trail

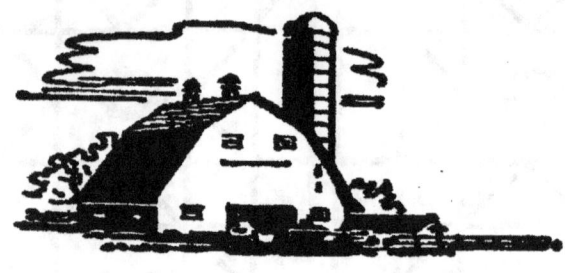

Quilt Block Location
East 12th Street
Cozad, Nebraska

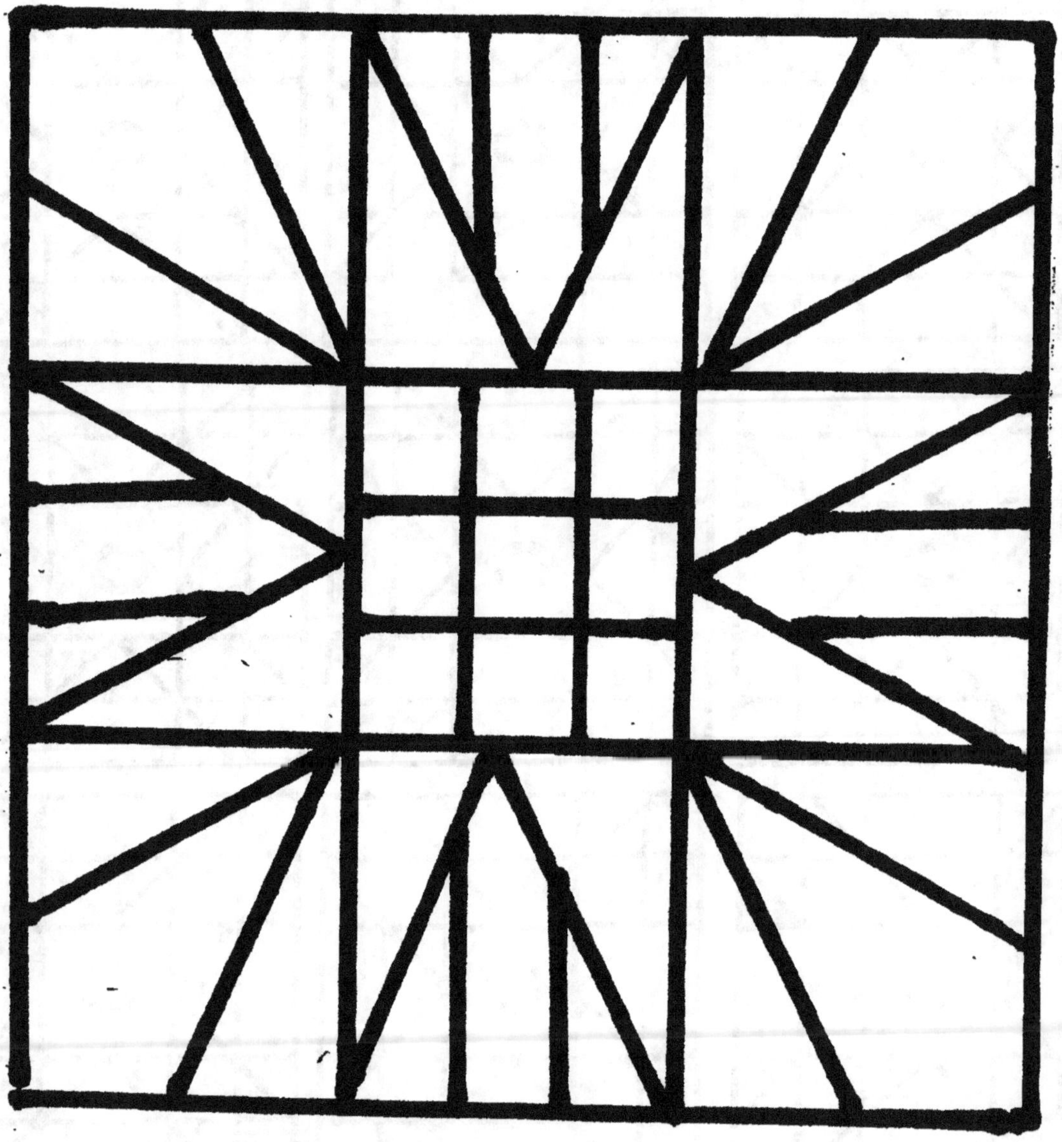

Dawson County Nebraska Barn Quilt Heavens A Blazin'

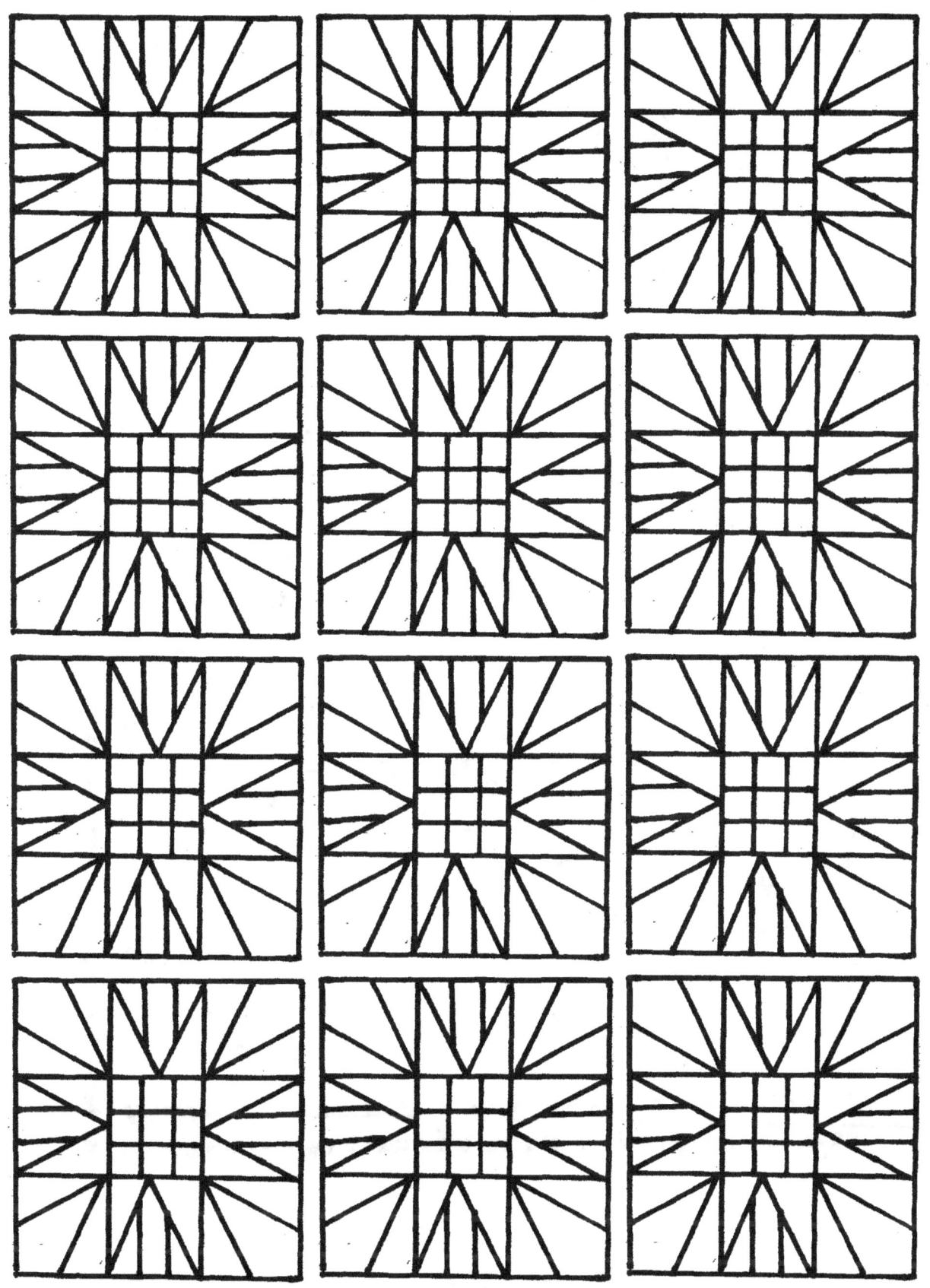

Jane's Place

Dawson County Nebraska Barn Quilt Trail

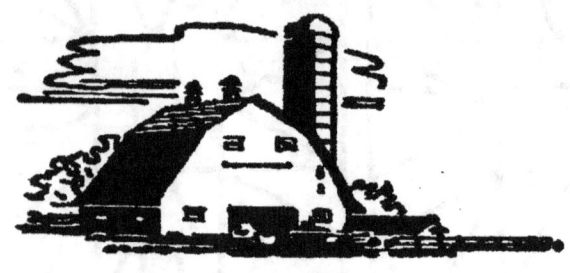

Quilt Block Location
Road 421
Cozad, Nebraska

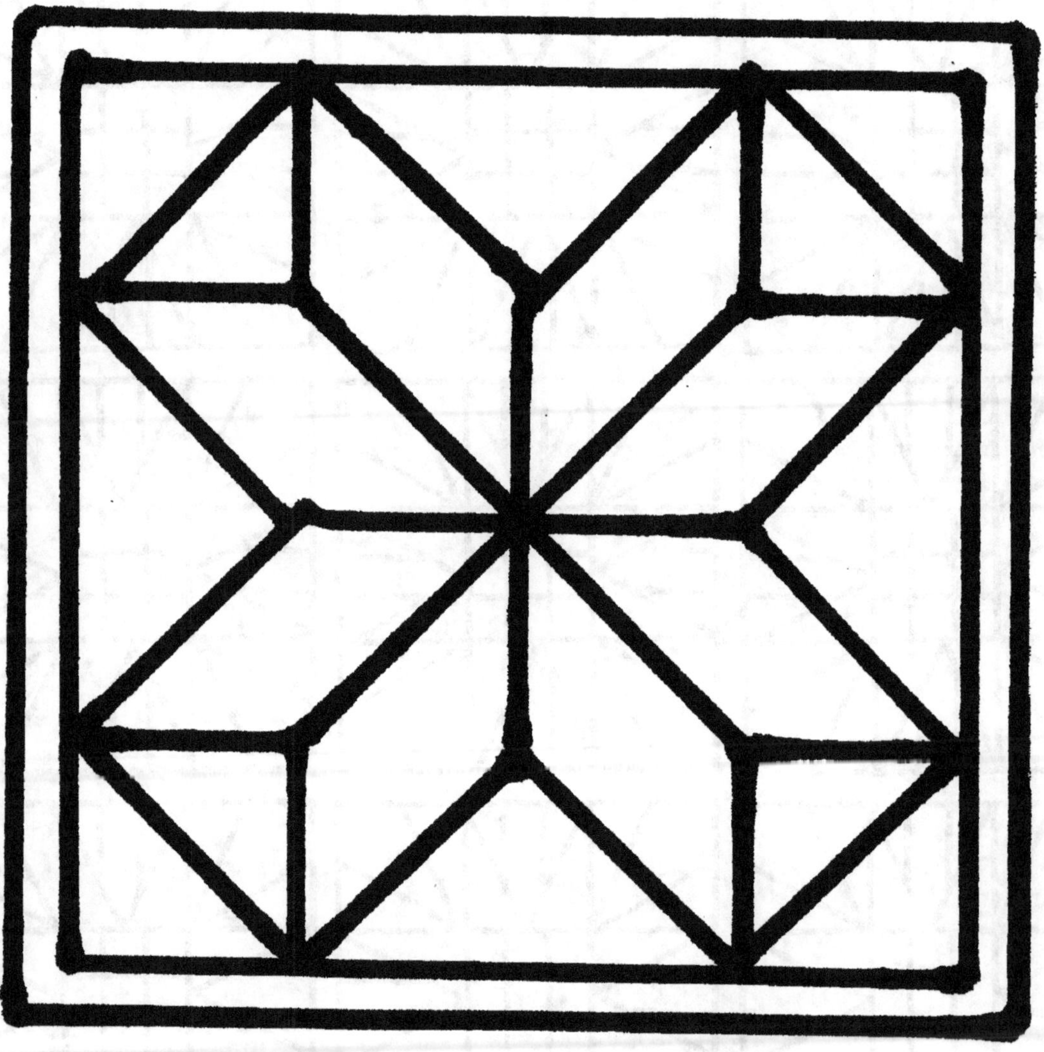

Dawson County Nebraska Barn Quilt Jane's Place

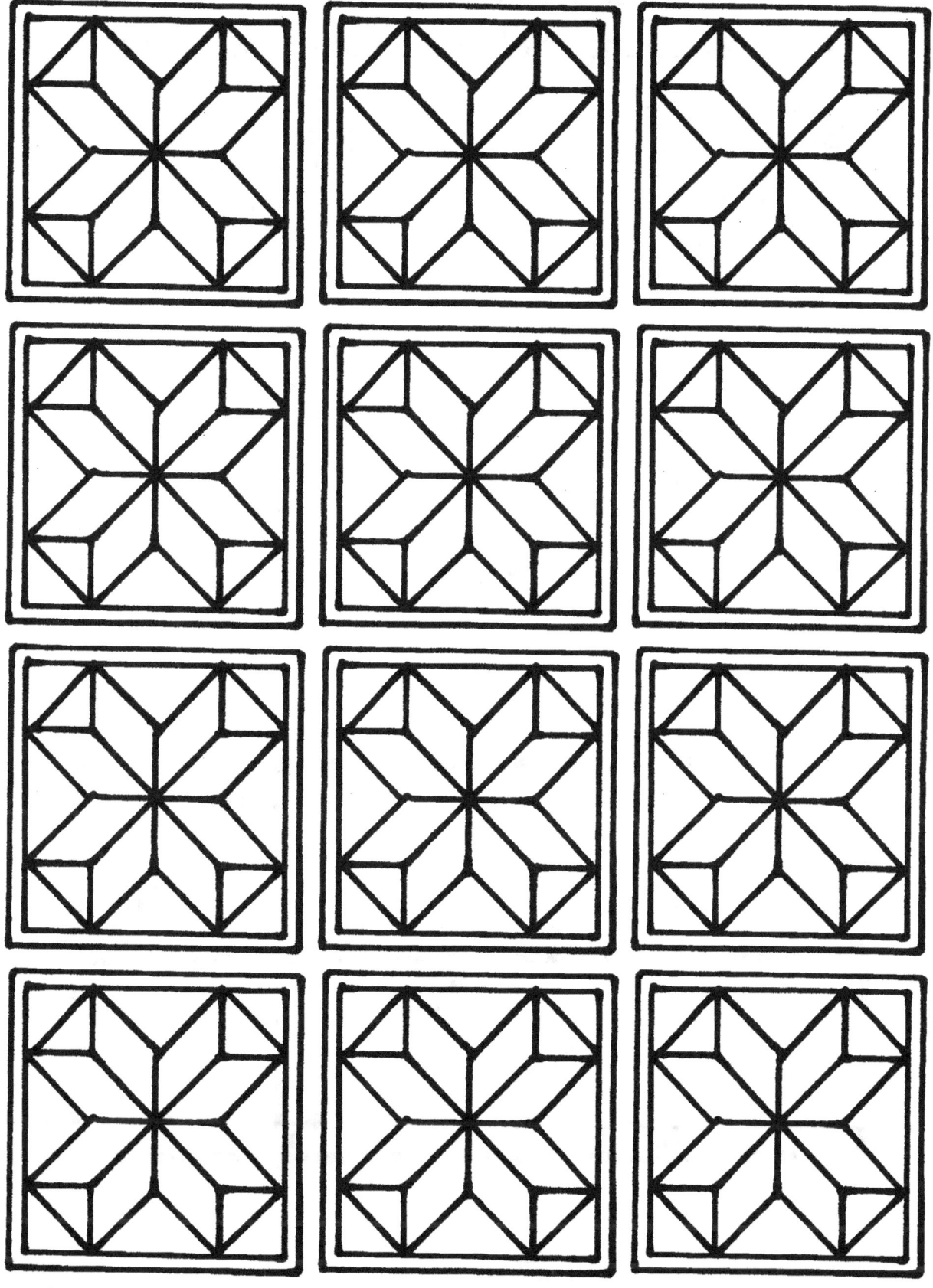

Lots of Fun
Dawson County Nebraska Barn Quilt Trail

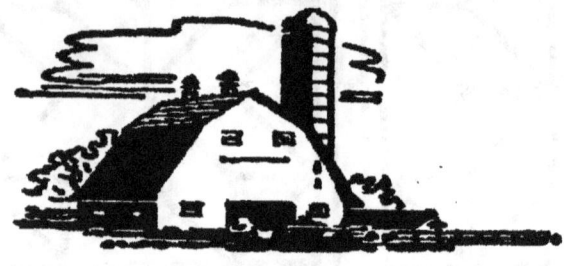

Quilt Block Location
West 8ᵗʰ Street
Cozad, Nebraska

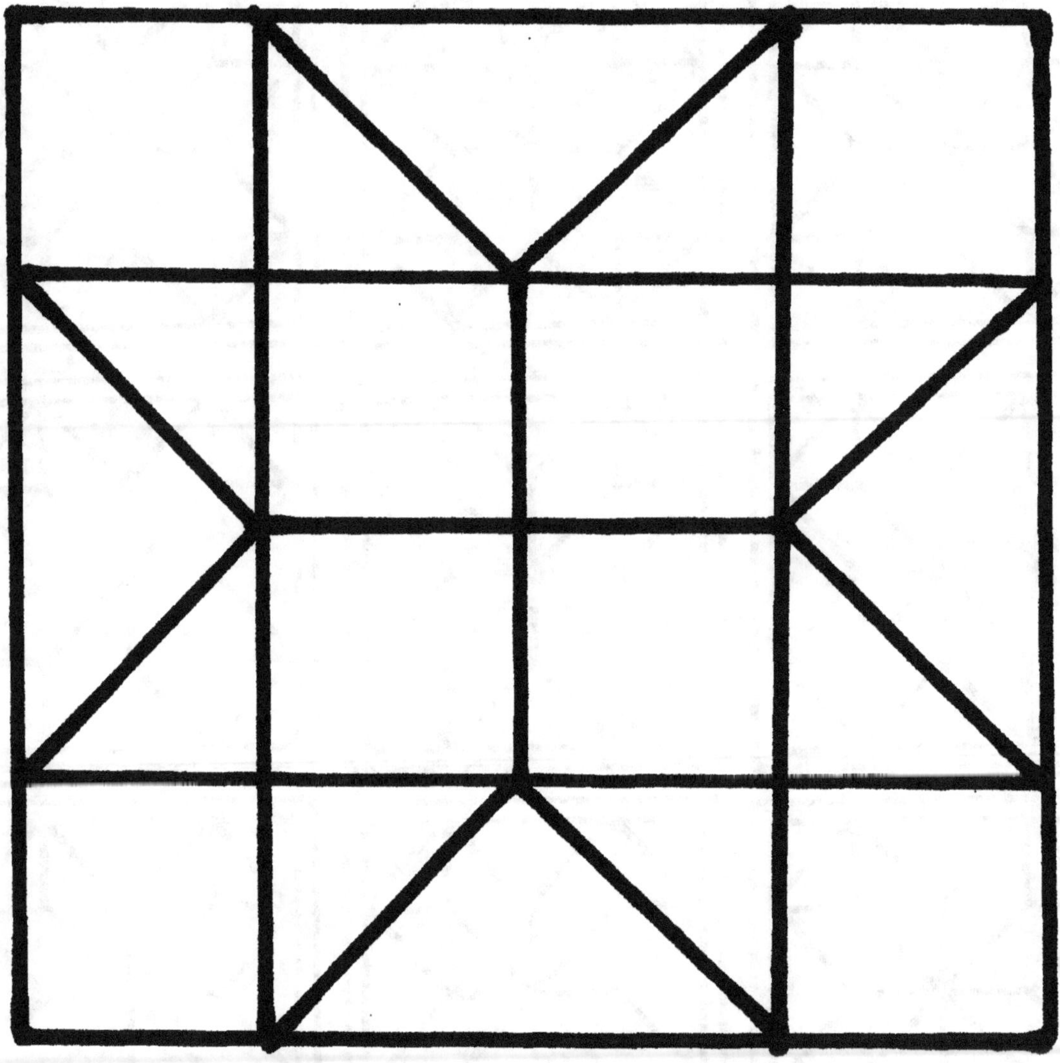

Dawson County Nebraska Barn Quilt Lots of Fun

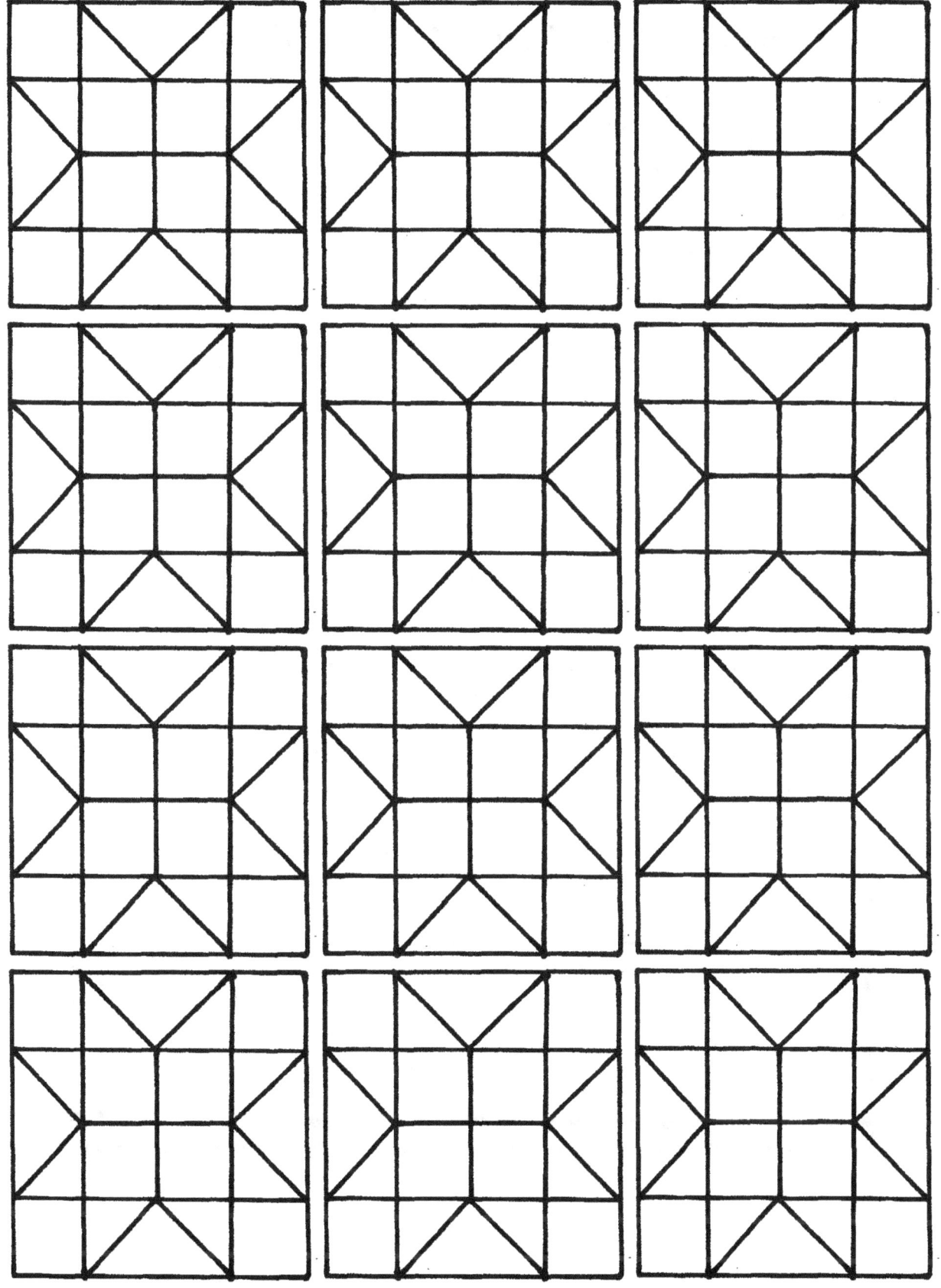

Love Flag
Dawson County Nebraska Barn Quilt Trail

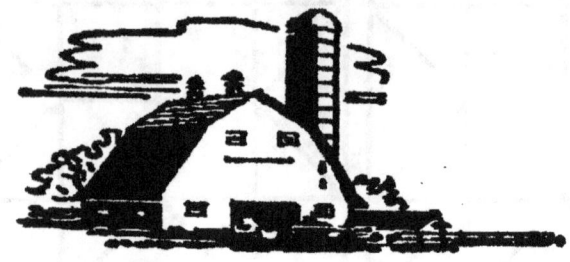

Quilt Block Location
Road 761
Cozad, Nebraska

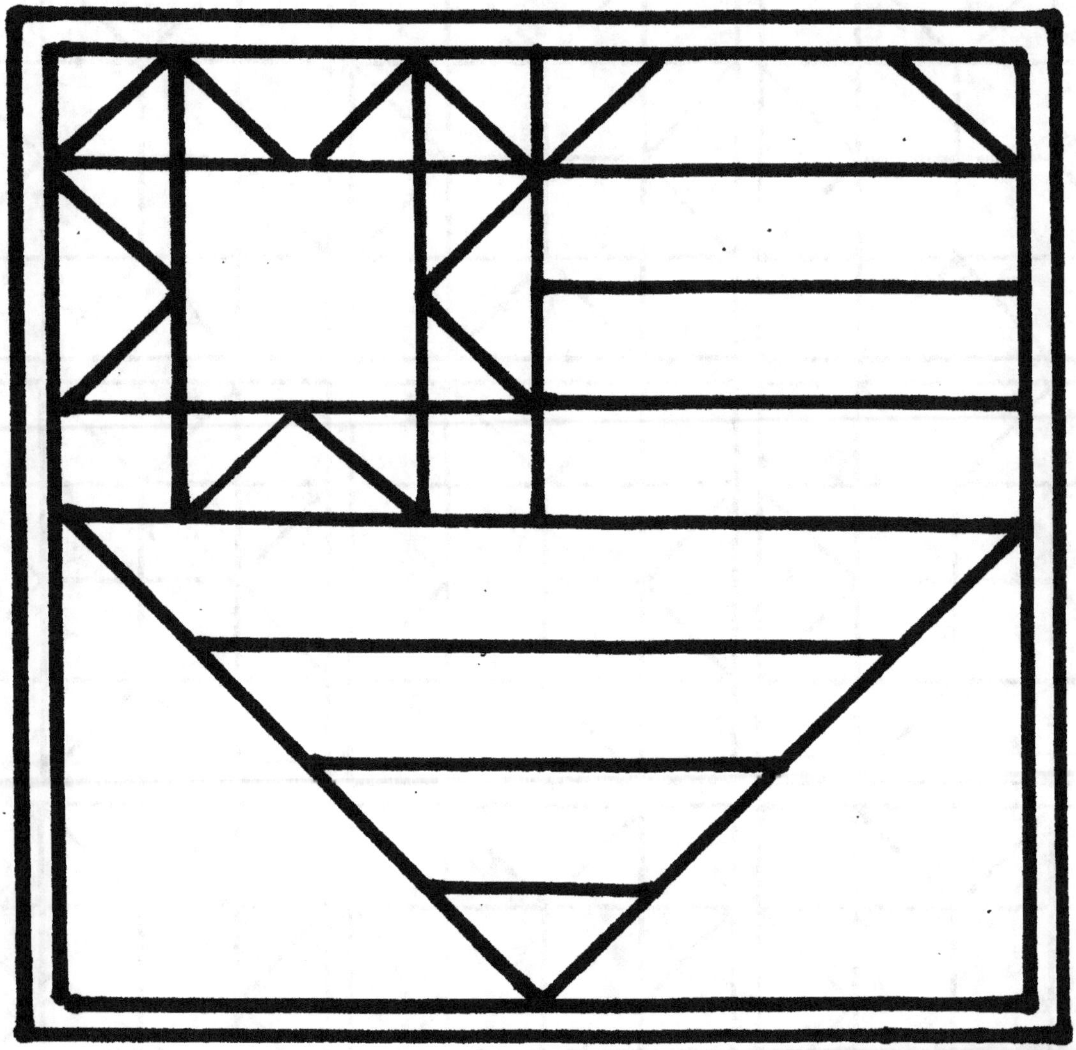

Dawson County Nebraska Barn Quilt Love Flag

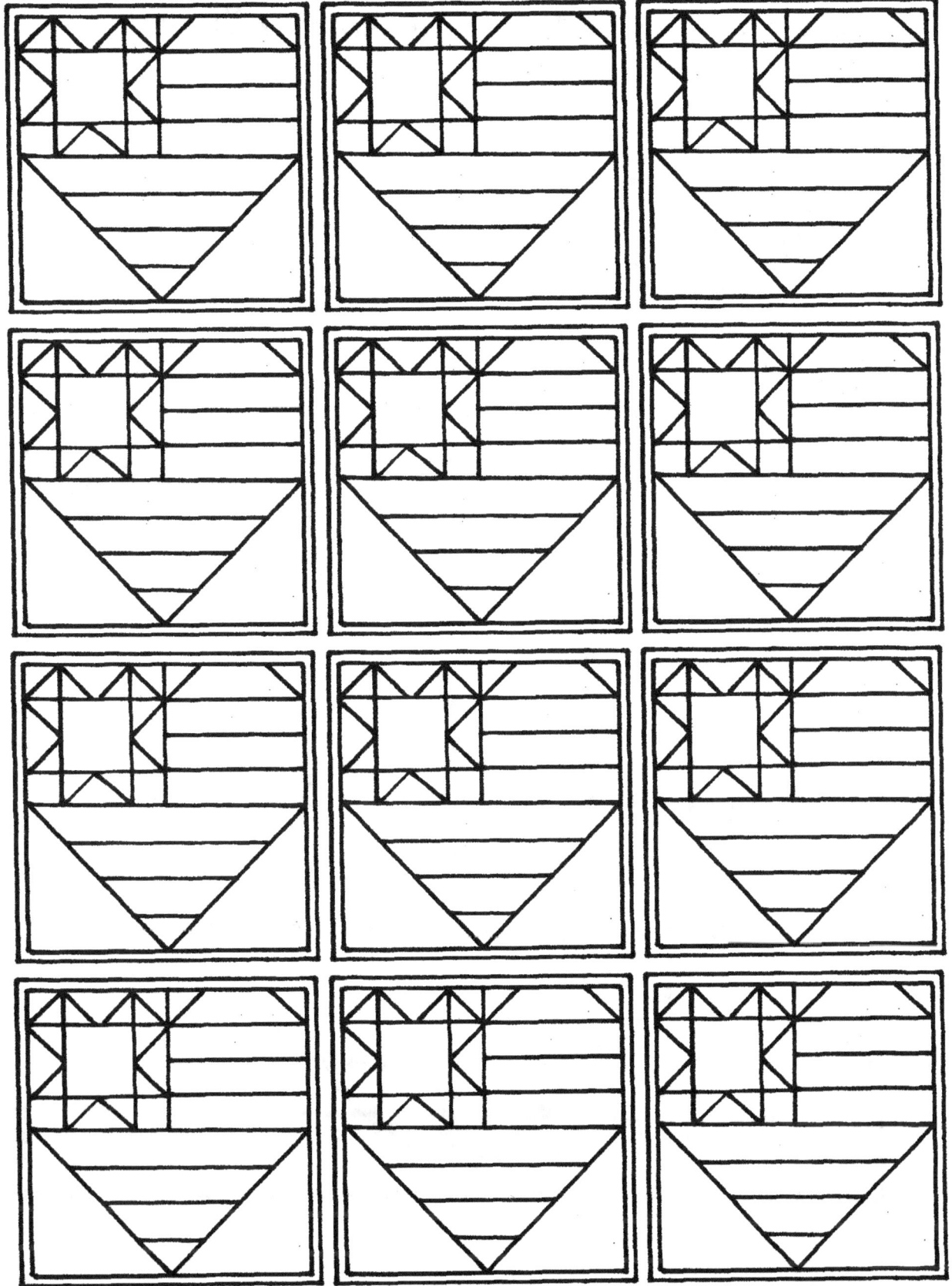

Love of Learning
Dawson County Nebraska Barn Quilt Trail

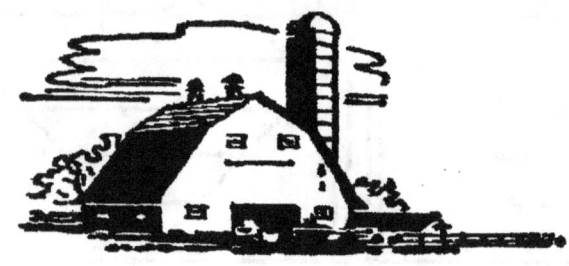

Quilt Block Location
East 14ᵗʰ Street
Cozad, Nebraska

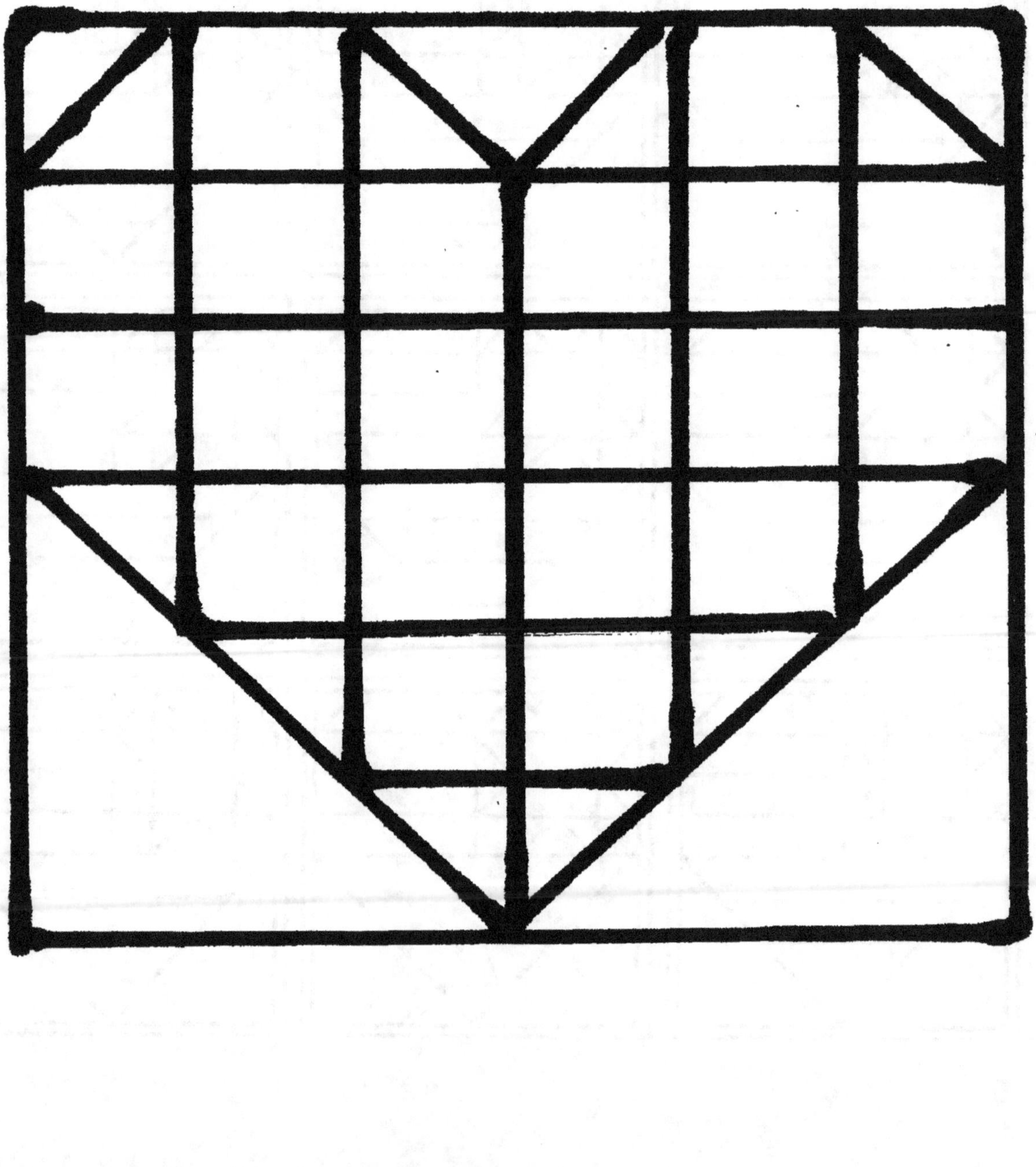

Dawson County Nebraska Barn Quit Love of Learning

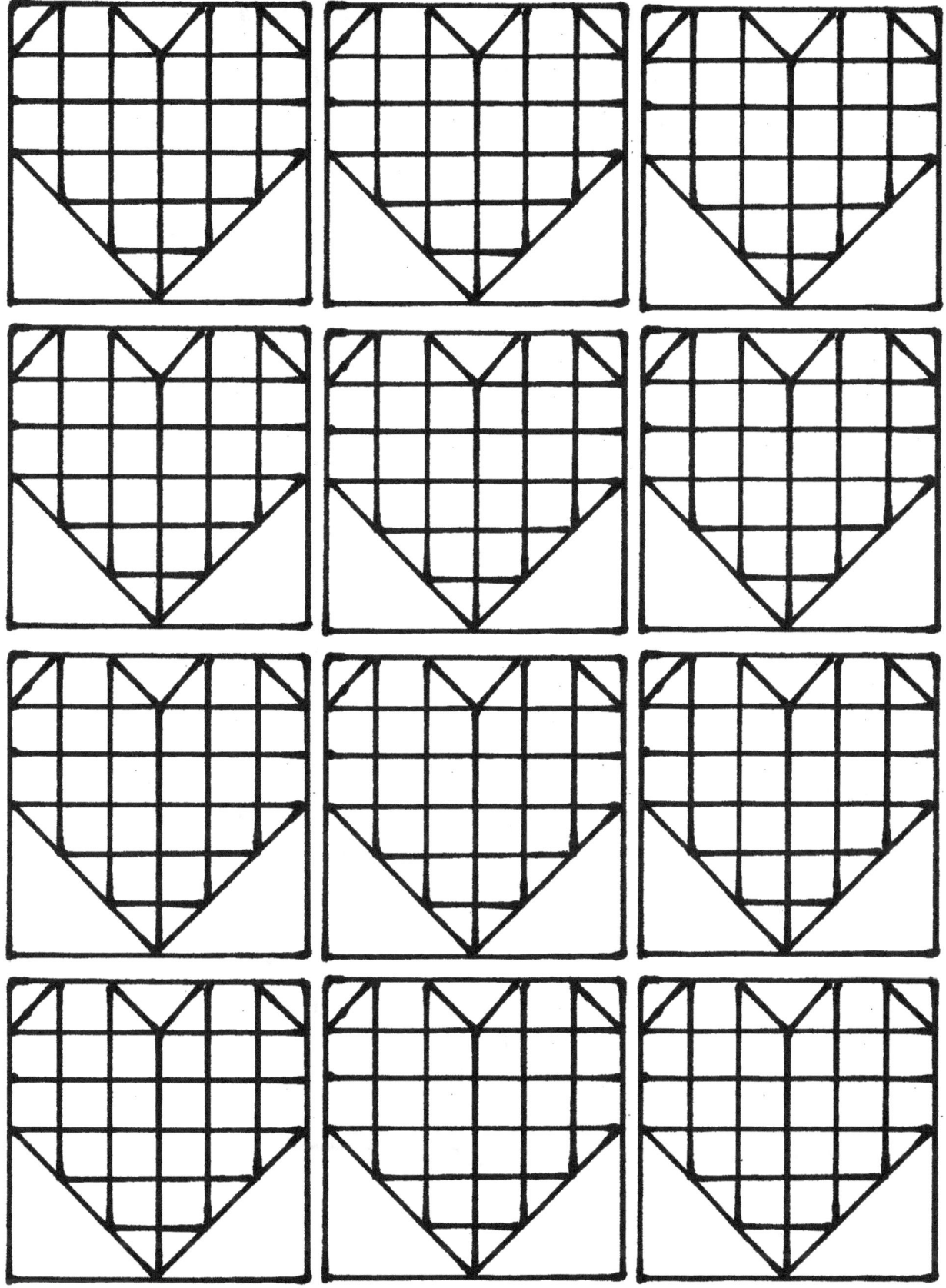

Maple Leaf & Sunshine
Dawson County Nebraska Barn Quilt Trail

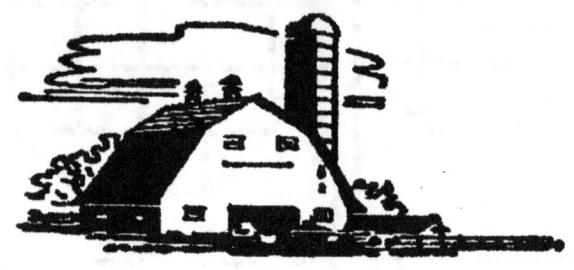

Quilt Block Location
East 8th Street
Cozad, Nebraska

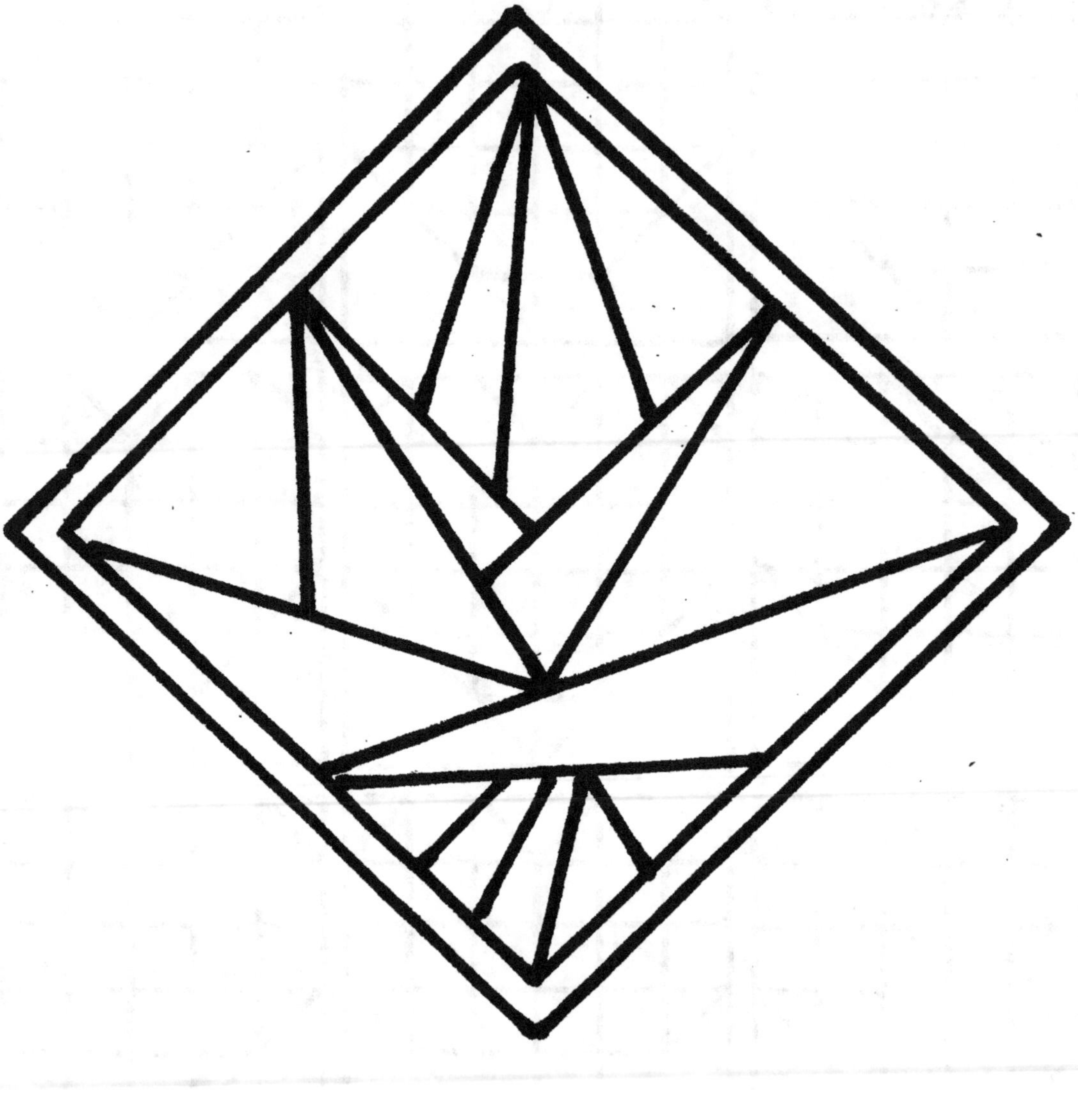

Dawson County Nebraska Barn Quilt Maple Leaf & Sunshine

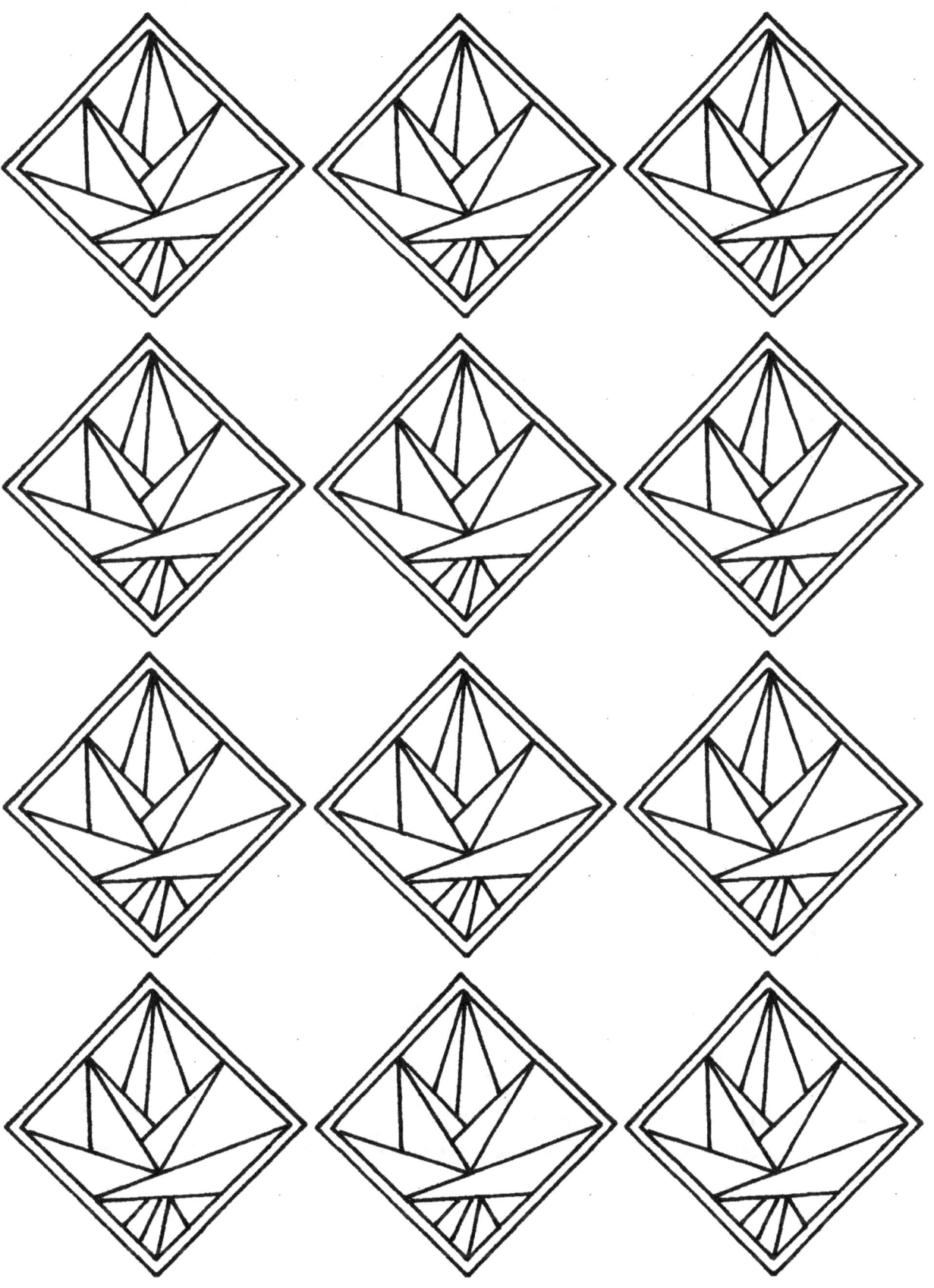

Meridian Museum Quilt
Dawson County Nebraska Barn Quilt Trail

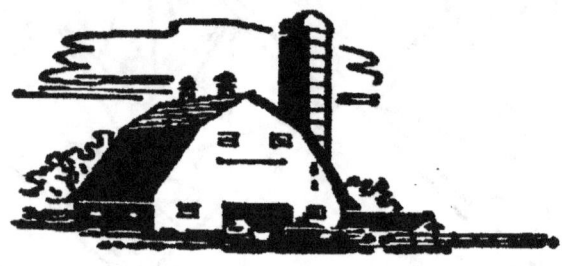

Quilt Block Location
East 8th Street
Cozad, Nebraska

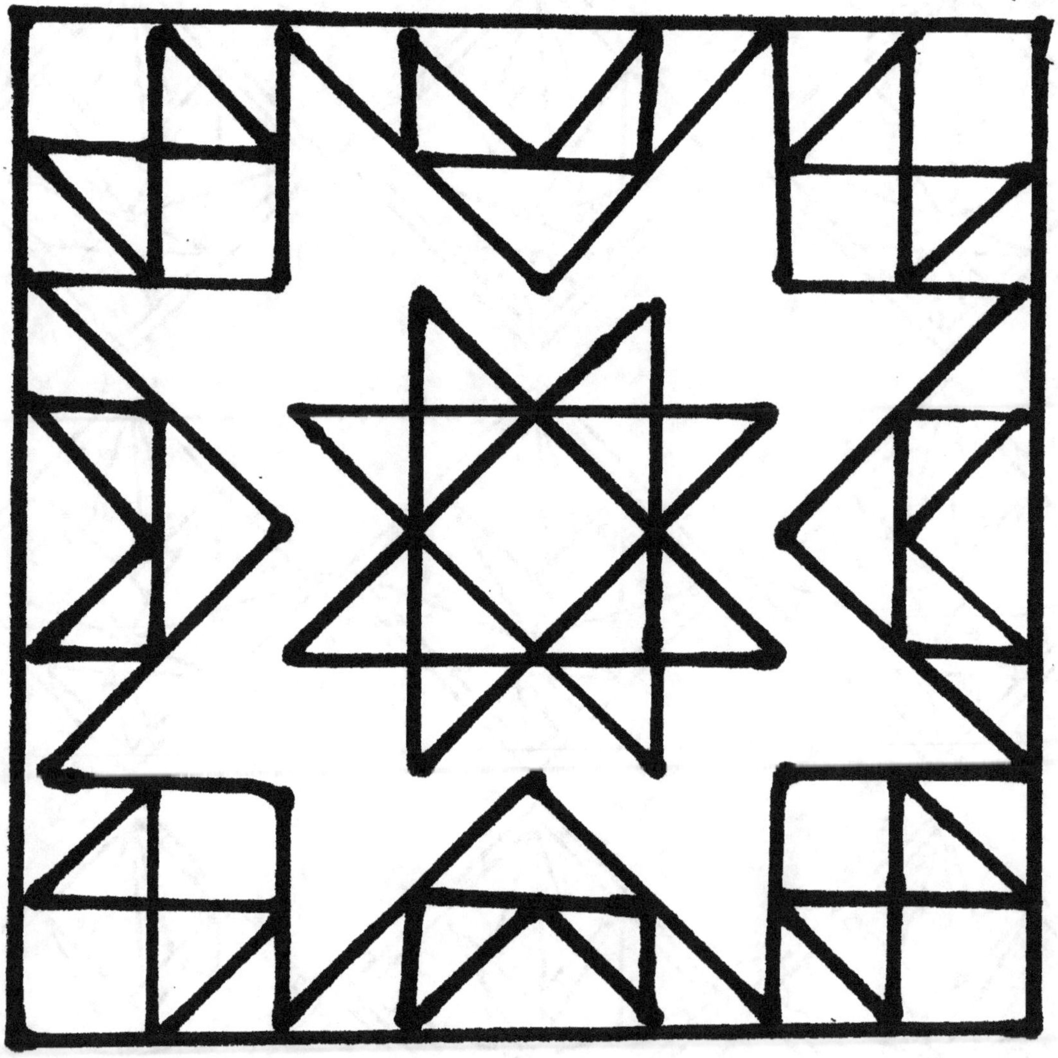

Dawson County Nebraska Barn Quilt Meridian Museum Quilt

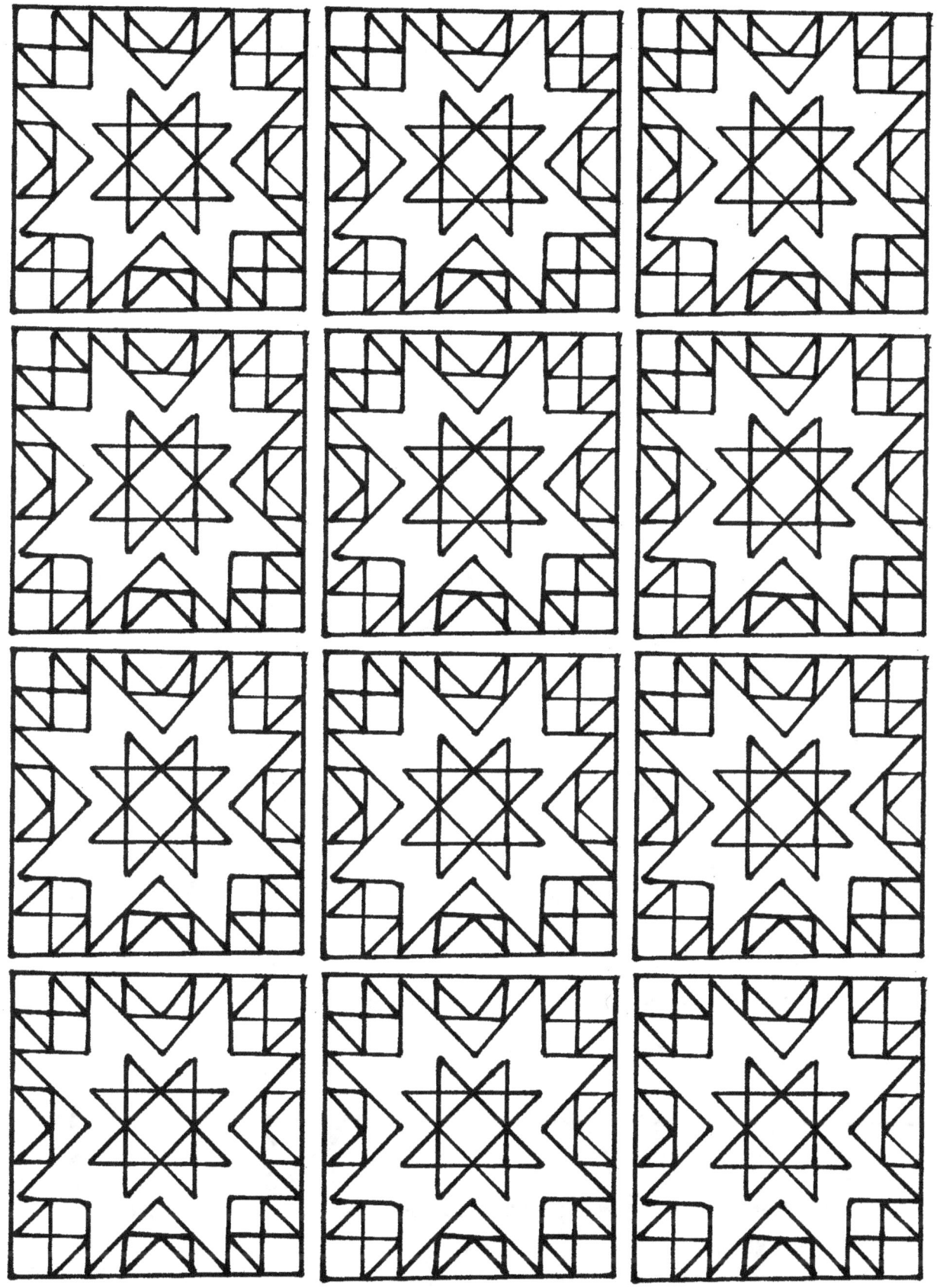

Missouri Star
Dawson County Nebraska Barn Quilt Trail

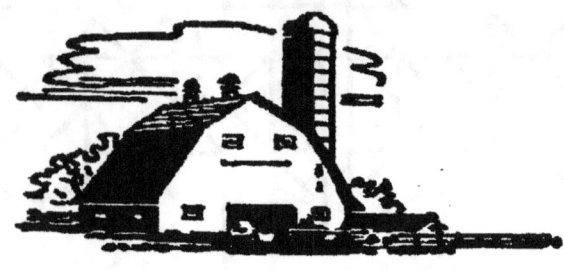

Quilt Block Location
Lincoln Avenue
Cozad, Nebraska

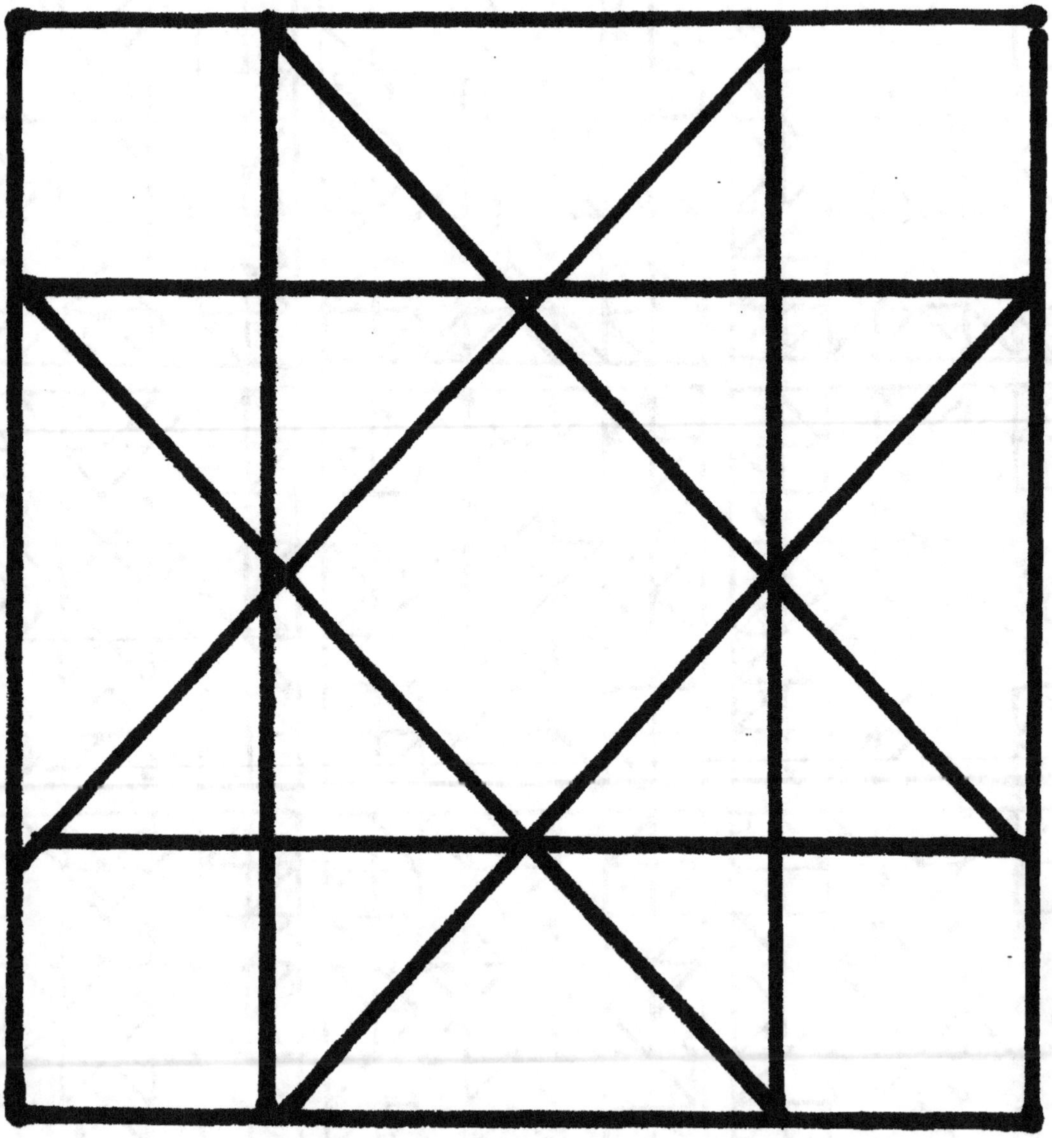

Dawson County Nebraska Barn Quilt Missouri Star

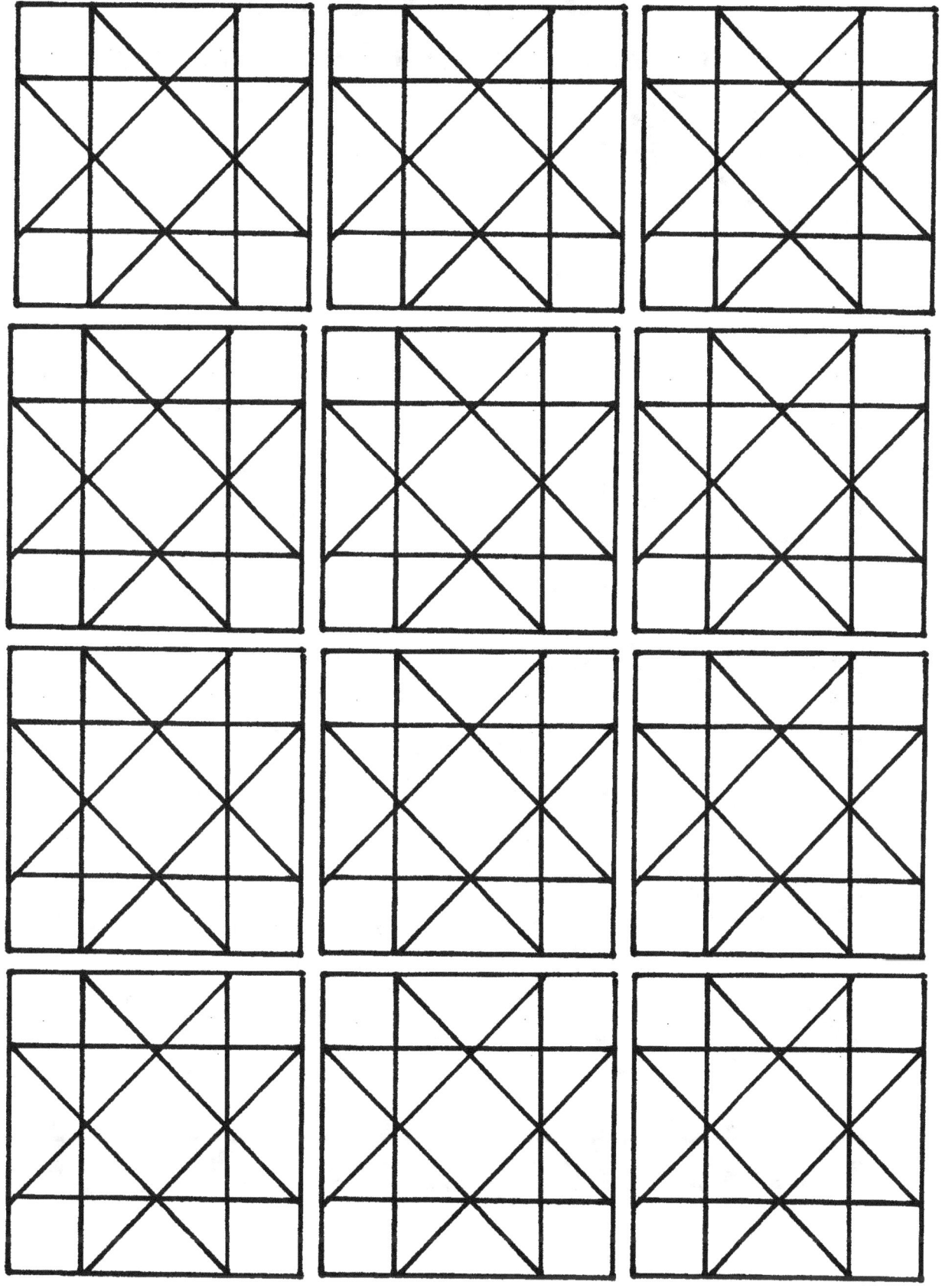

Nebraska 4-H Star
Dawson County Nebraska Barn Quilt Trail

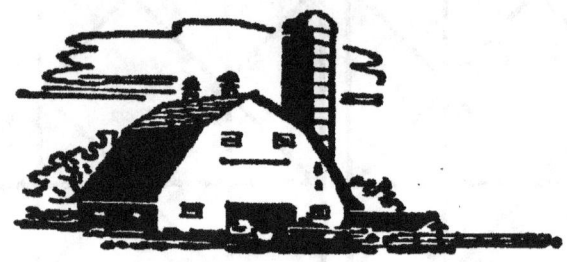

Quilt Block Location
Plum Creek Parkway
Cozad, Nebraska

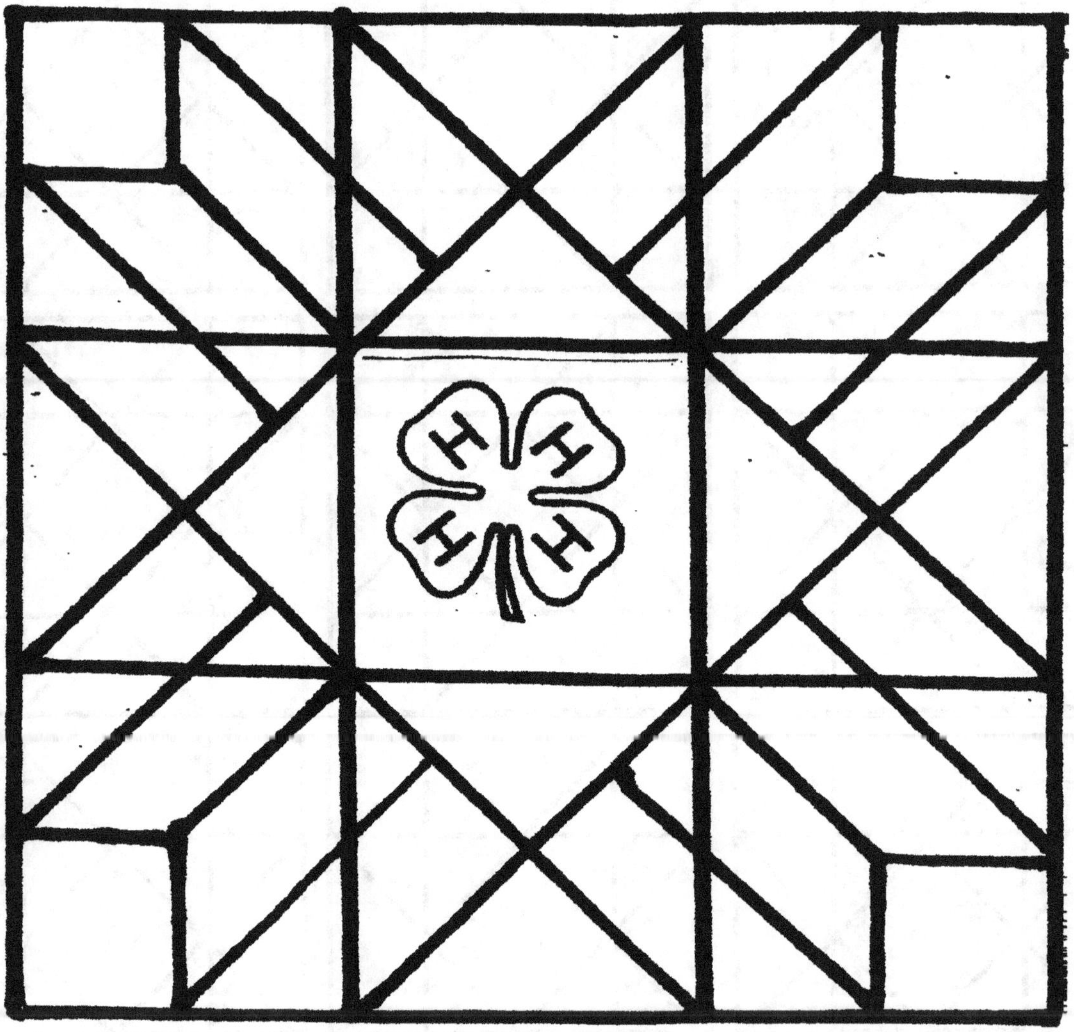

Dawson County Nebraska Barn Quilt Nebraska 4-H Star

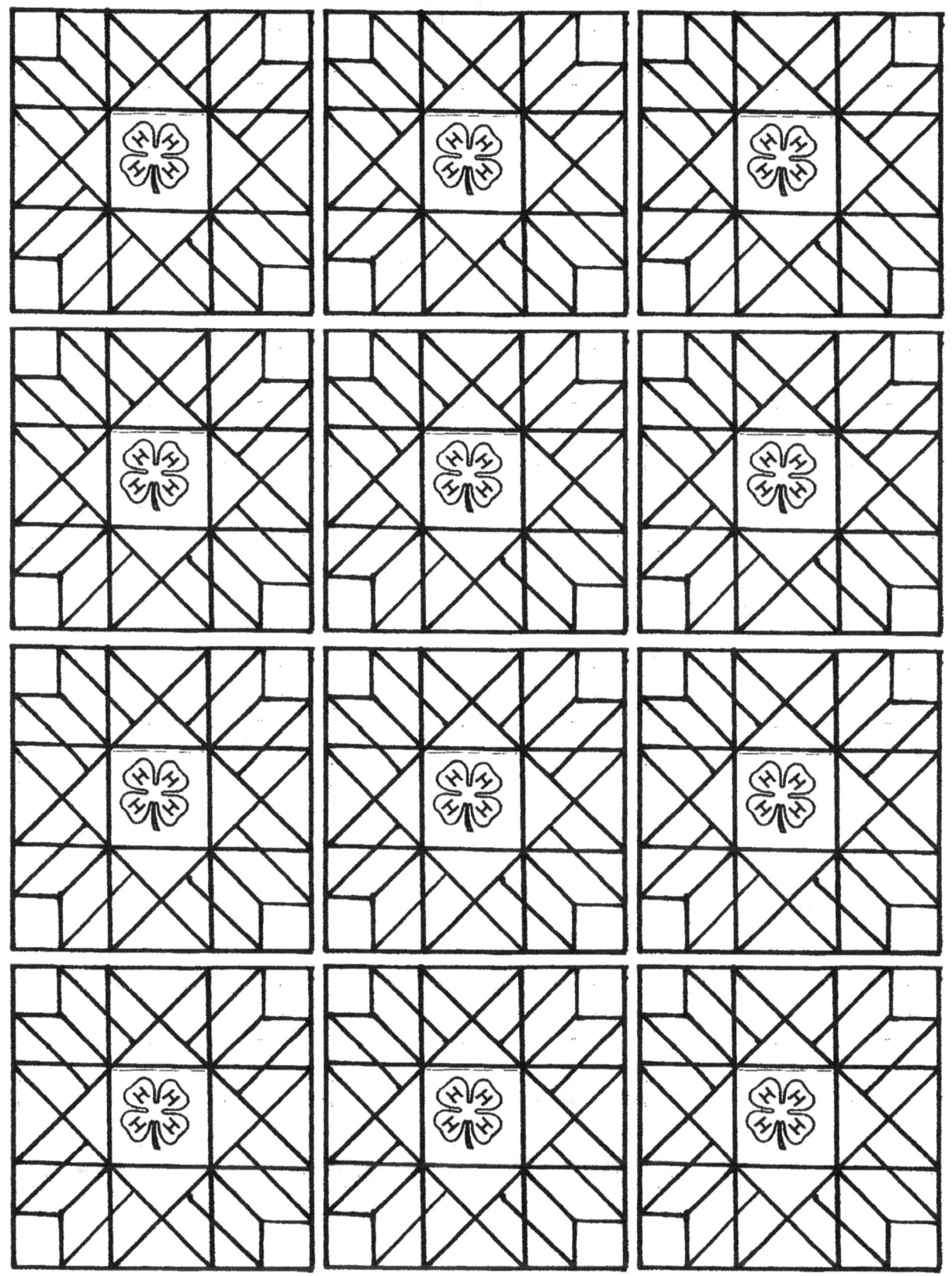

Nebraska National Forest
Dawson County Nebraska Barn Quilt Trail

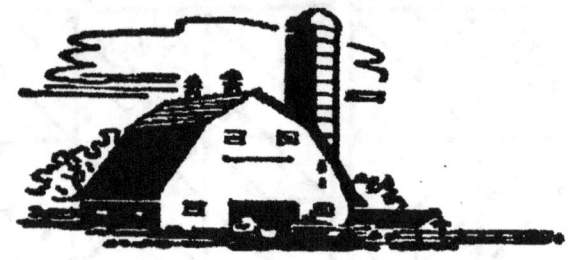

Quilt Block Location
West 17ᵗʰ Street
Cozad, Nebraska

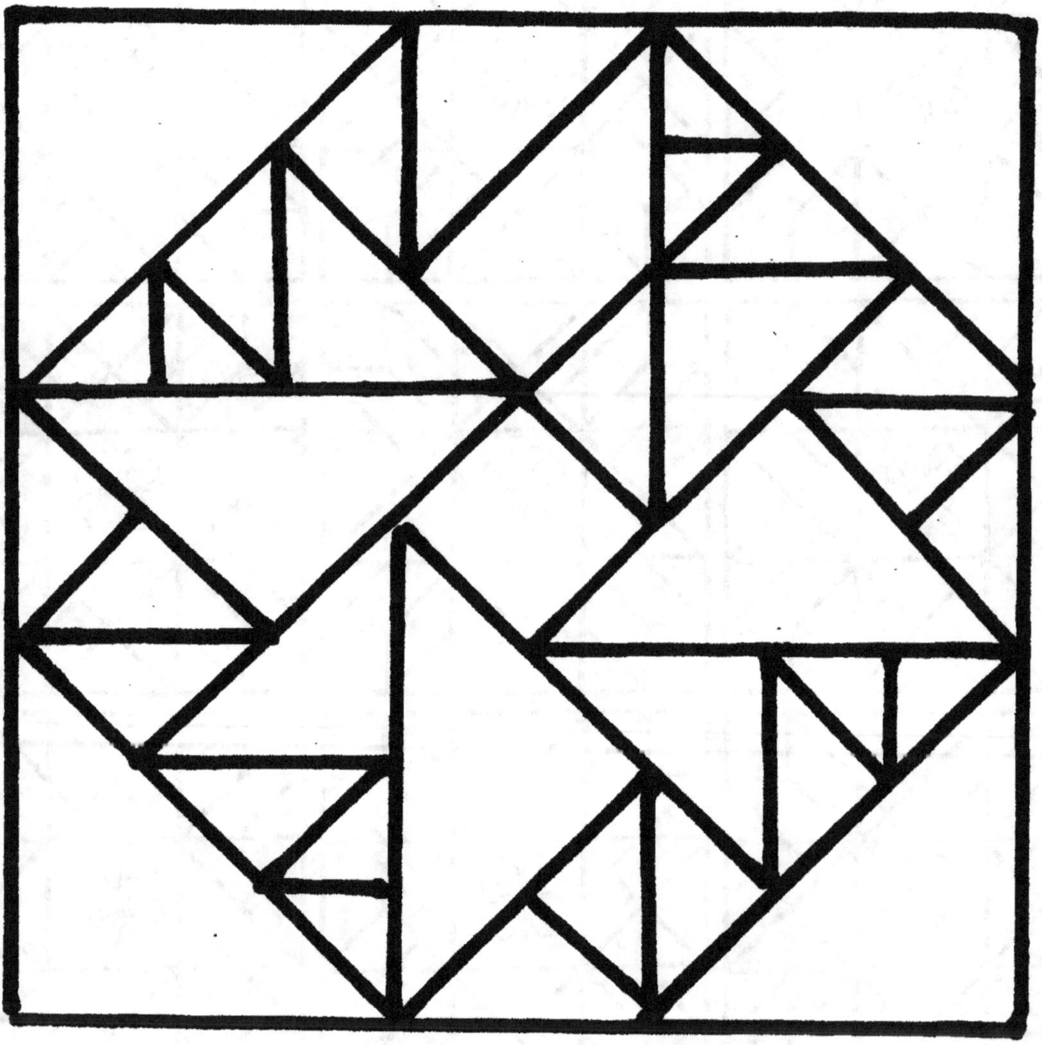

Dawson County Nebraska Barn Quilt Nebraska National Forest

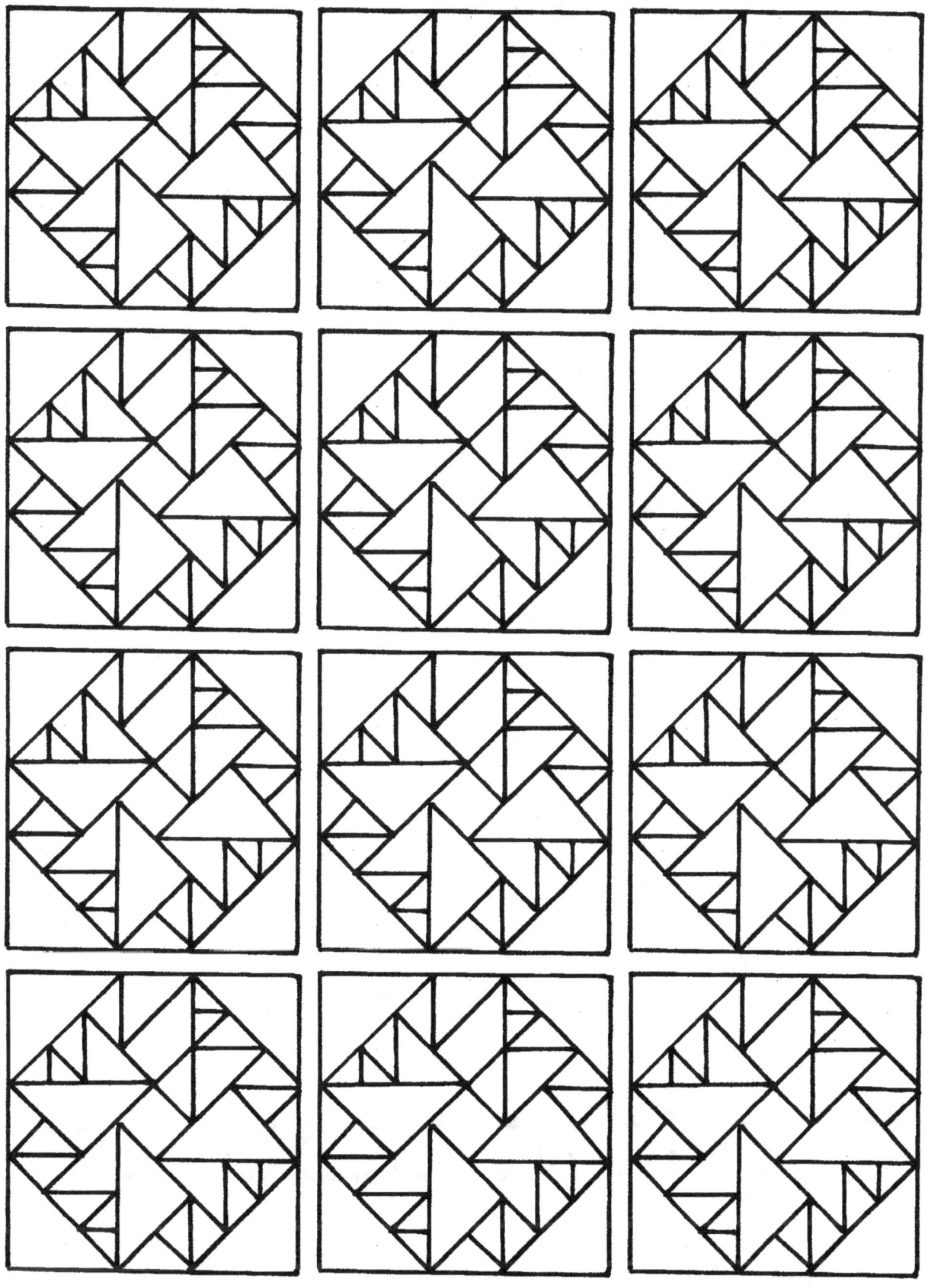

Our Version of Sunflower
Dawson County Nebraska Barn Quilt Trail

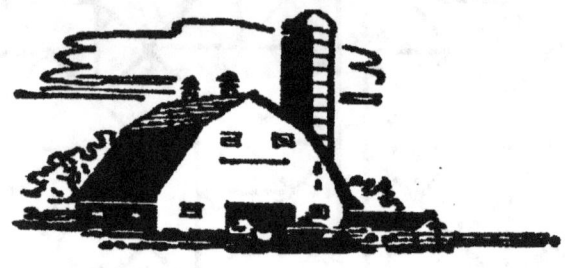

Quilt Block Location
East 22nd Street
Cozad, Nebraska

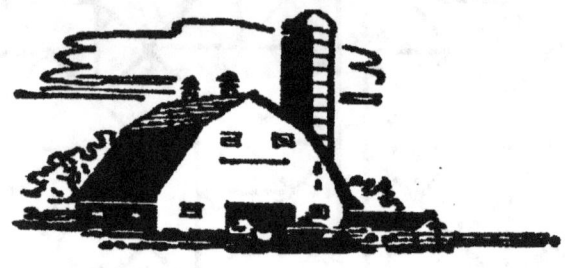

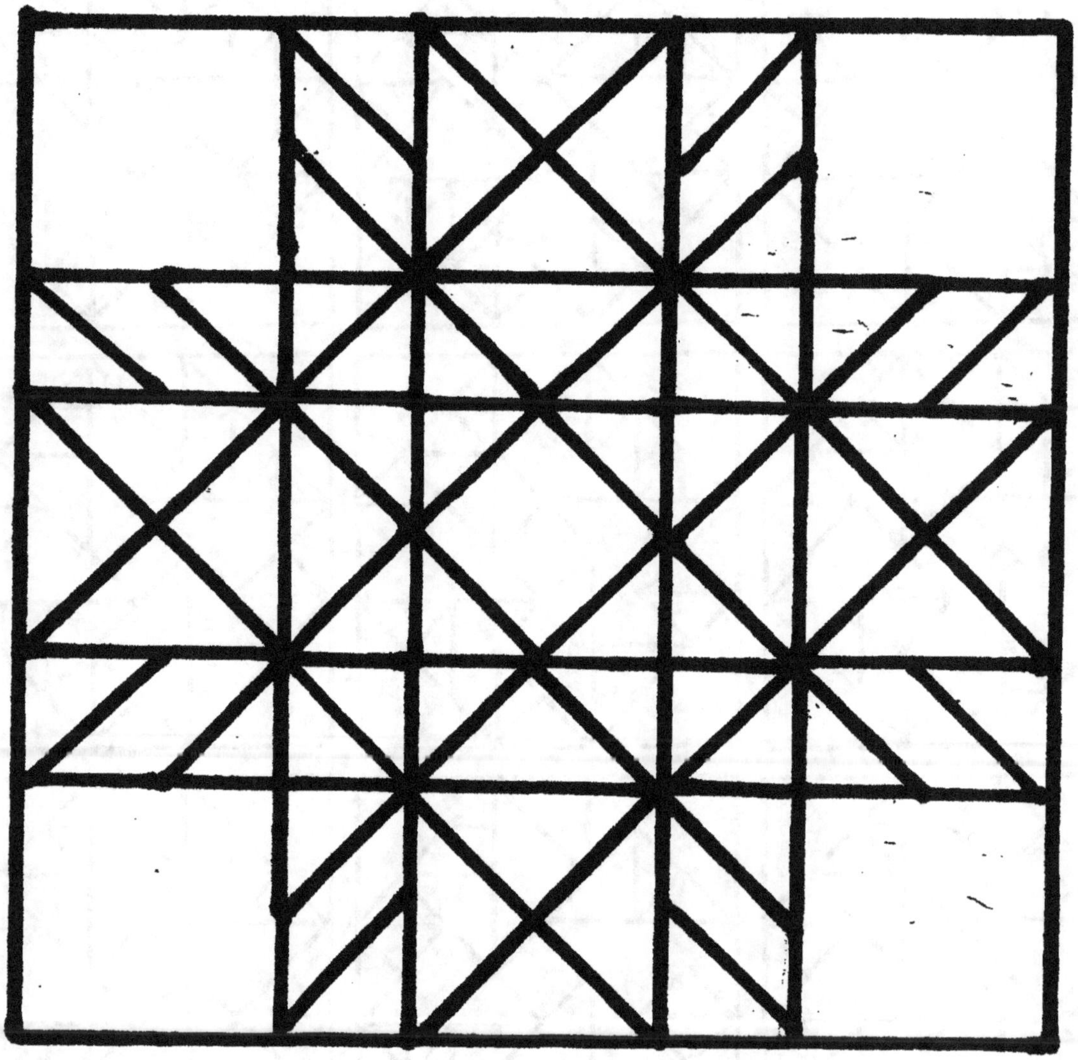

Dawson County Nebraska Barn Quilt Our Version of Sunflower

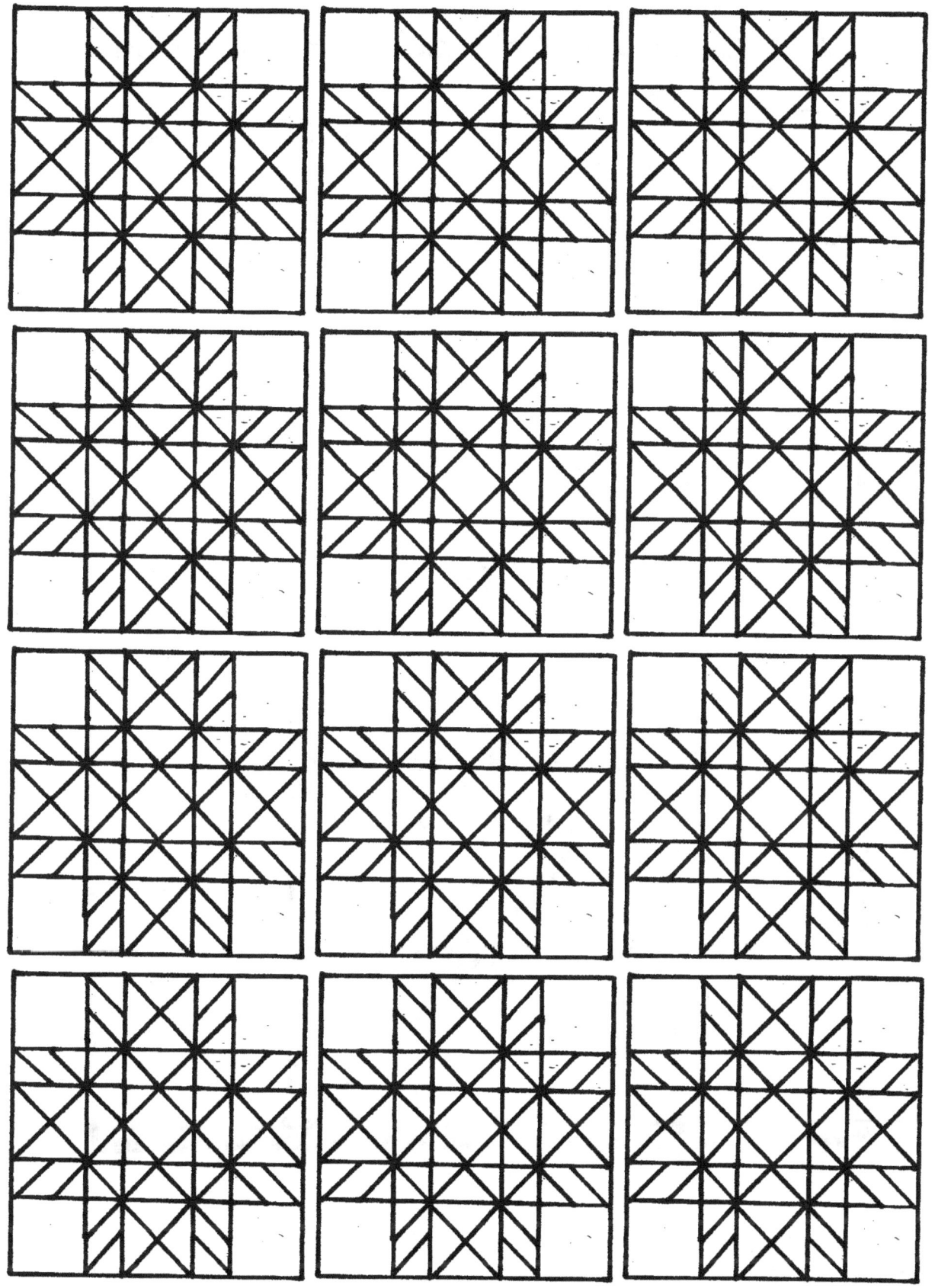

Patriotic Star
Dawson County Nebraska Barn Quilt Trail

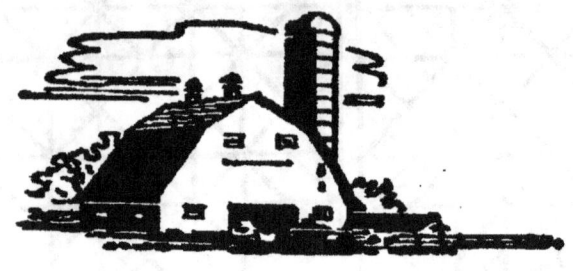

Quilt Block Location
Avenue C
Cozad, Nebraska

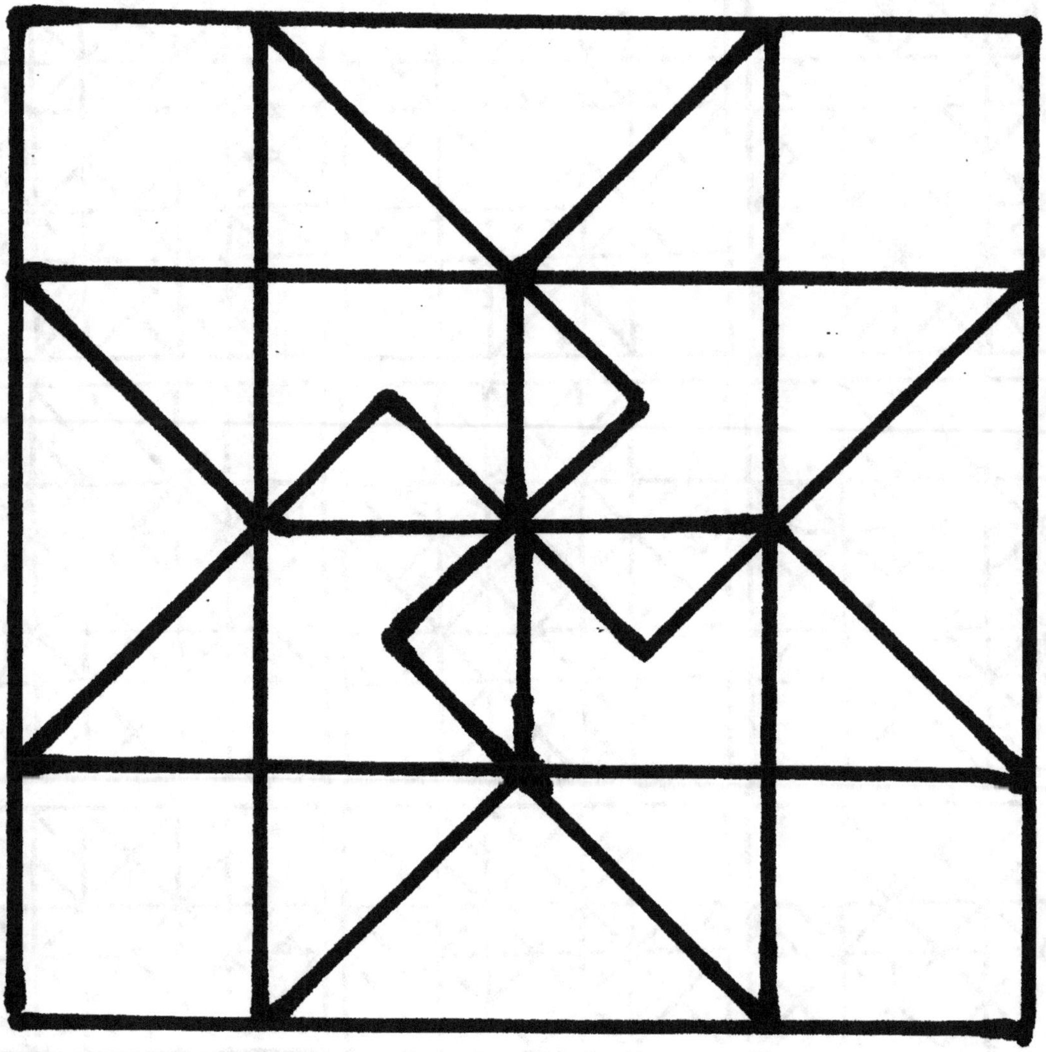

Dawson County Nebraska Barn Quilt Patriotic Star

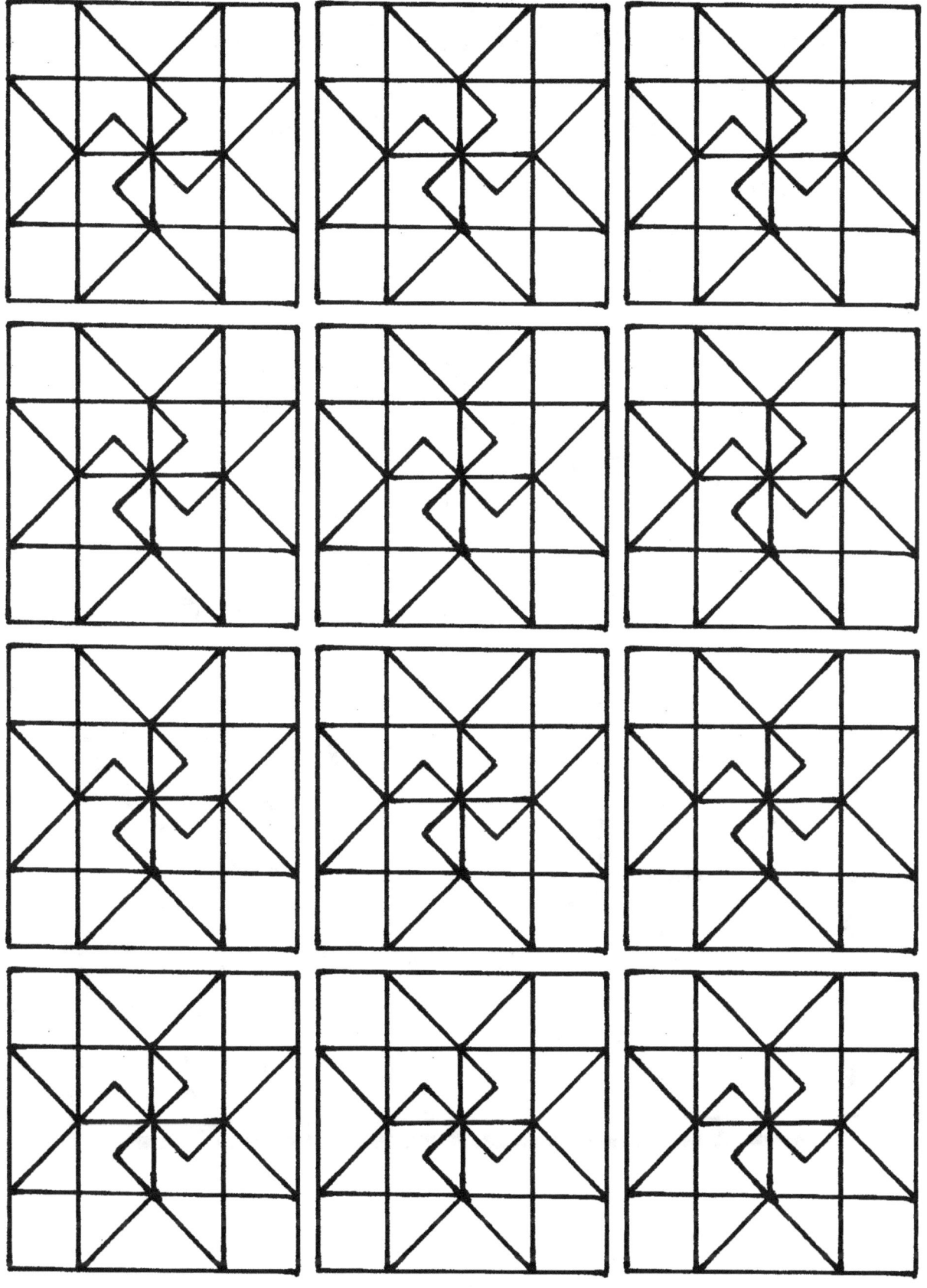

Piece by Piece
Dawson County Nebraska Barn Quilt Trail

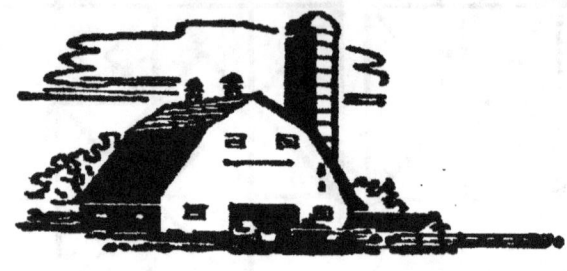

Quilt Block Location
East 12th Street
Cozad, Nebraska

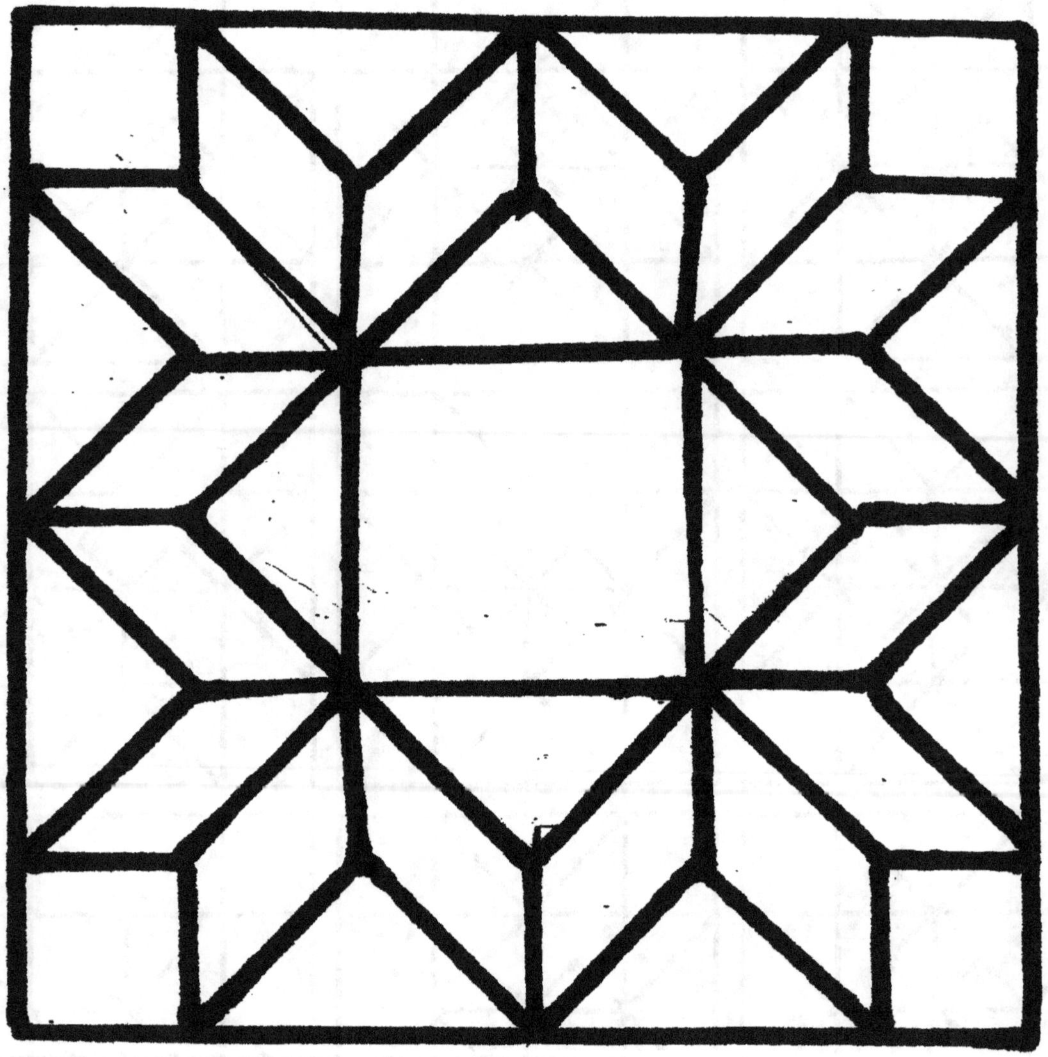

Dawson County Nebraska Barn Quilt Piece by Piece

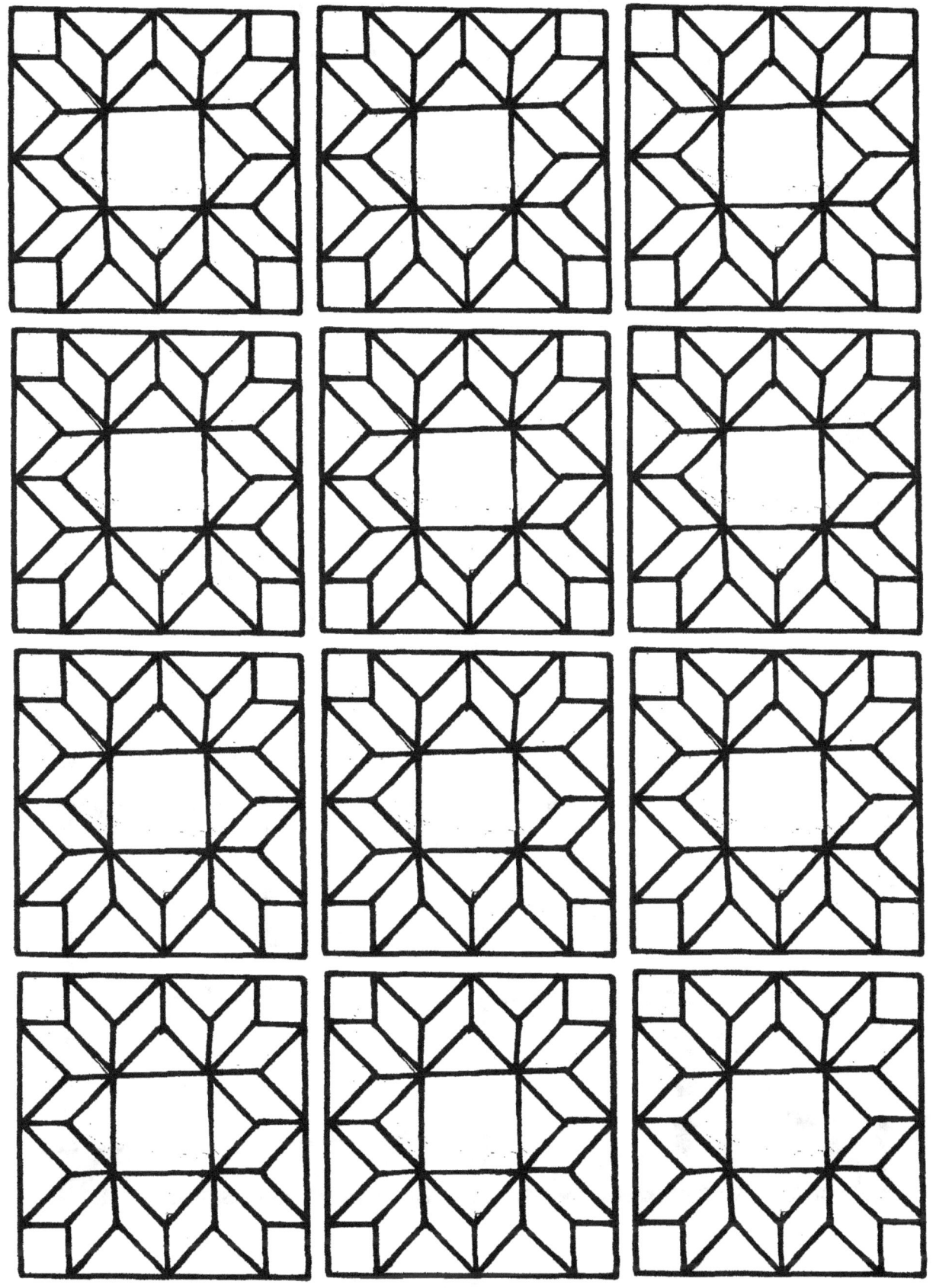

Pinwheel in a Pinwheel
Dawson County Nebraska Barn Quilt Trail

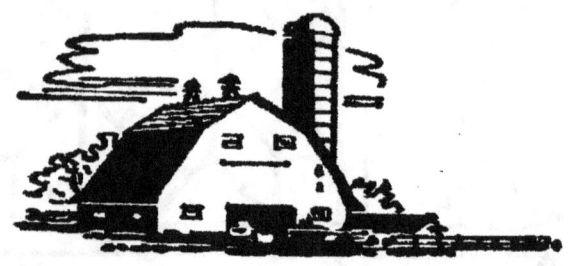

Quilt Block Location
Avenue J
Cozad, Nebraska

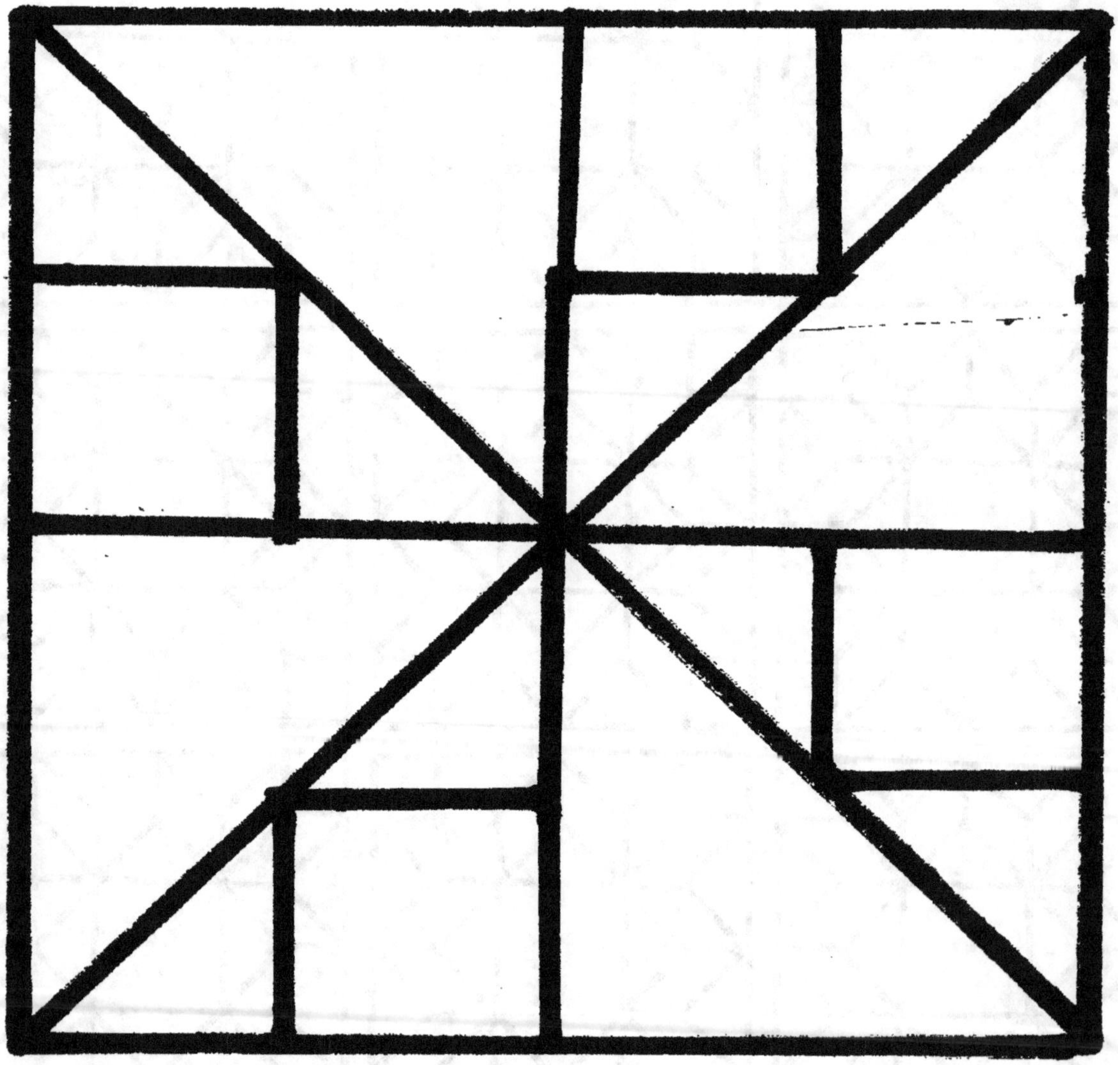

Dawson County Nebraska Barn Quit Pinwheel in a Pinwheel

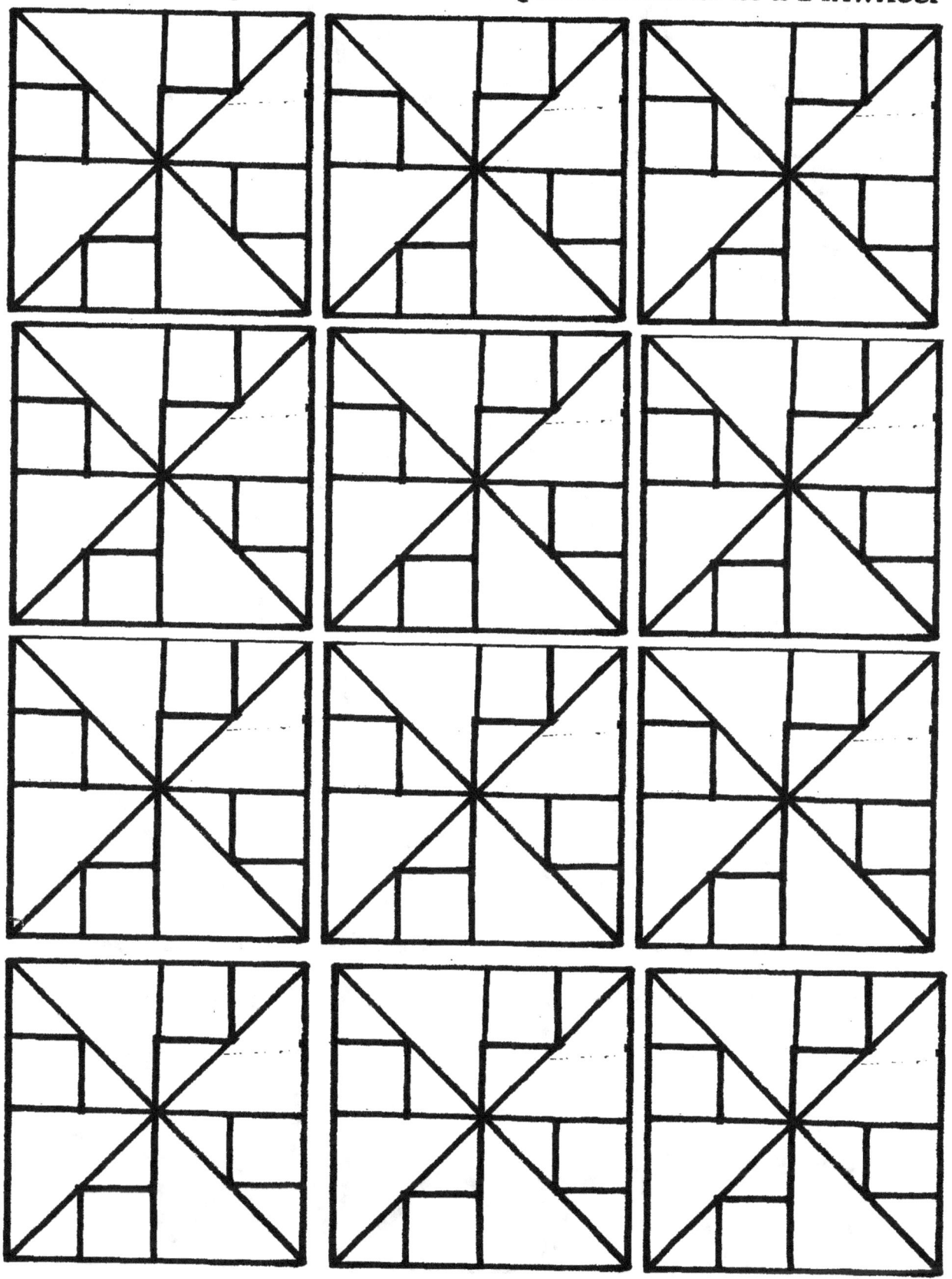

Prairie Wildfire
Dawson County Nebraska Barn Quilt Trail

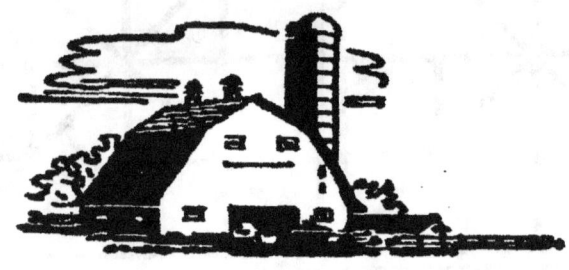

Quilt Block Location
Road 419
Eusits, Nebraska

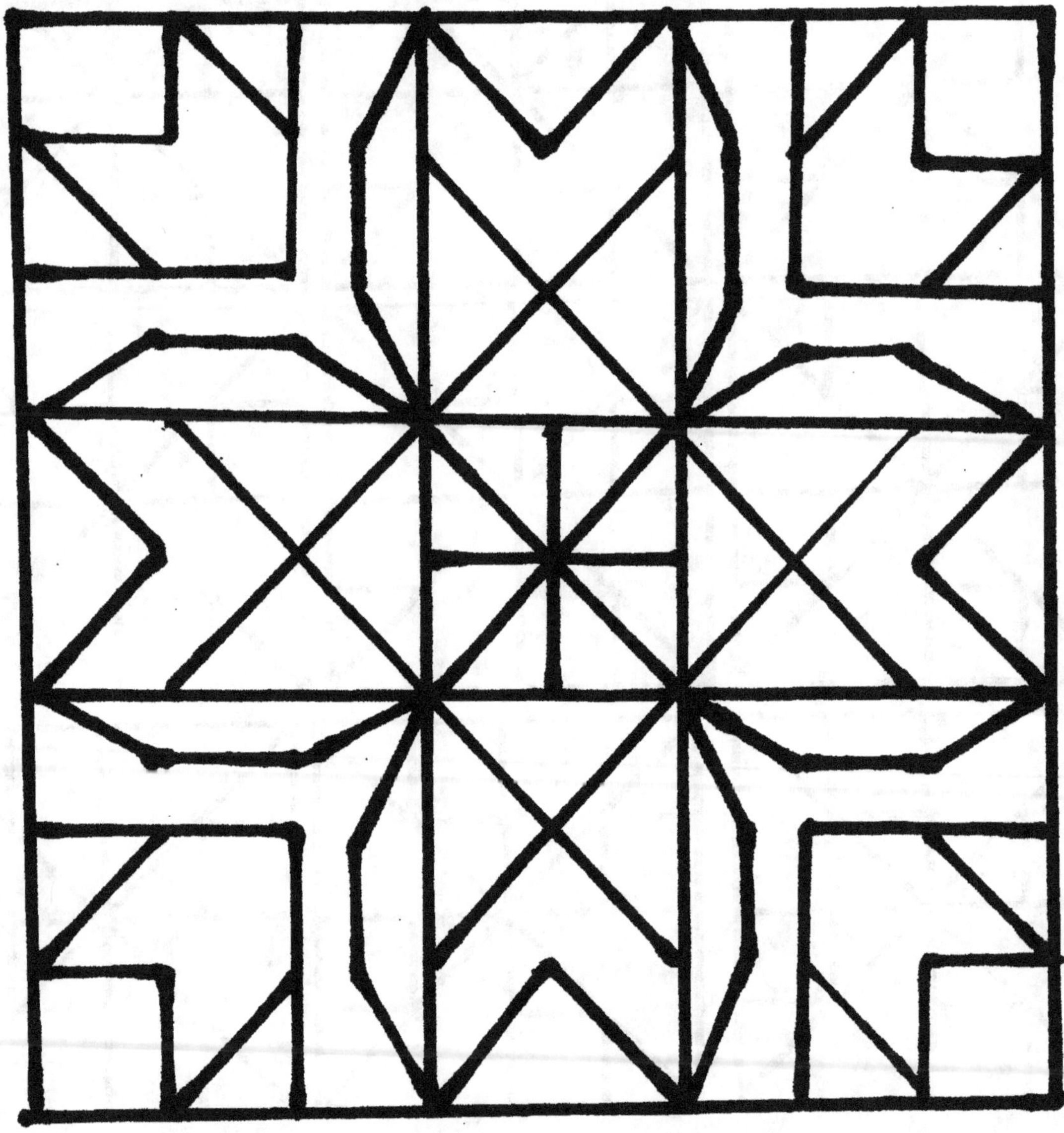

Dawson County Nebraska Barn Quilt Wildfire

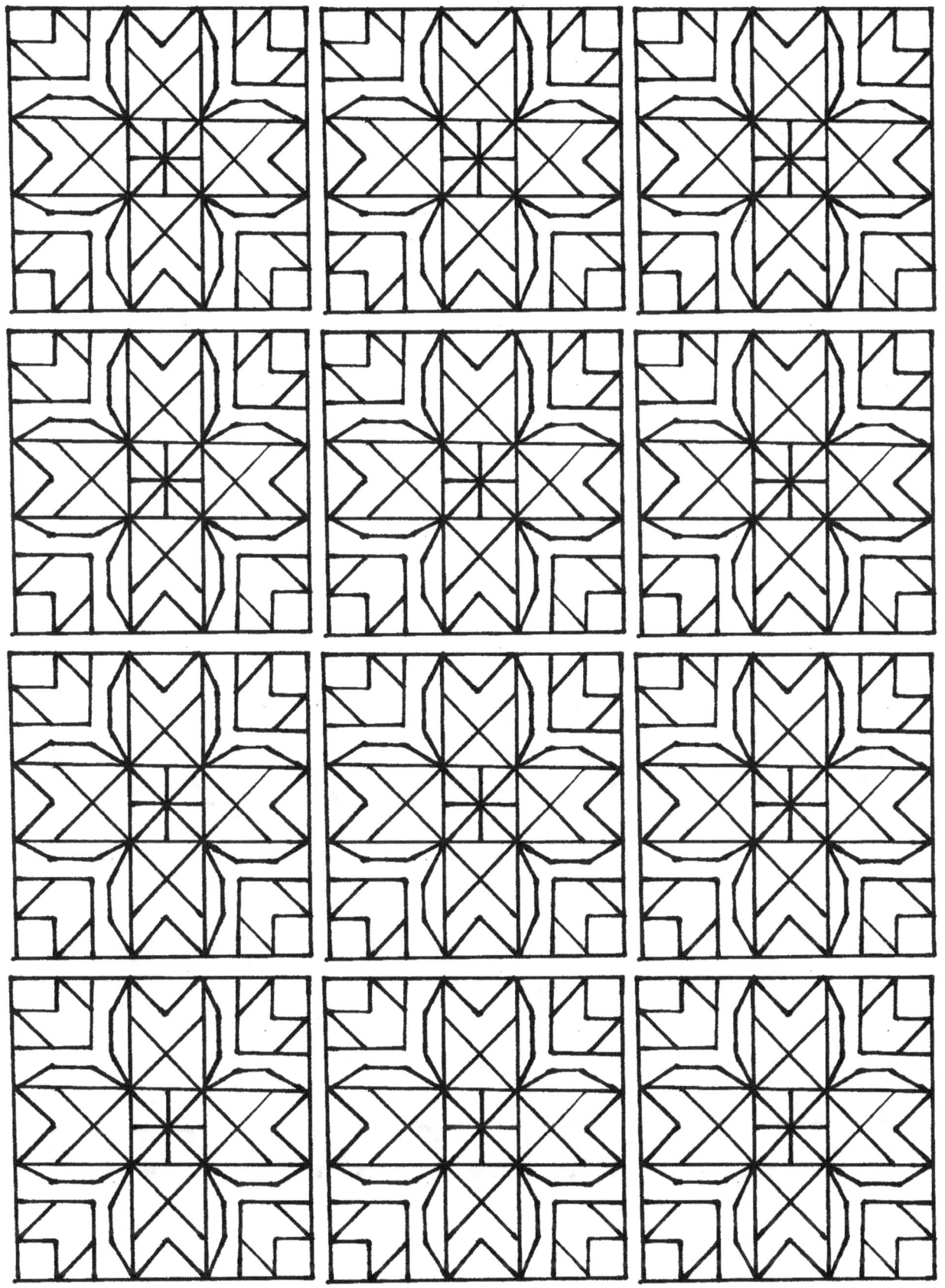

Red, White and Blue Runs True
Dawson County Nebraska Barn Quilt Trail

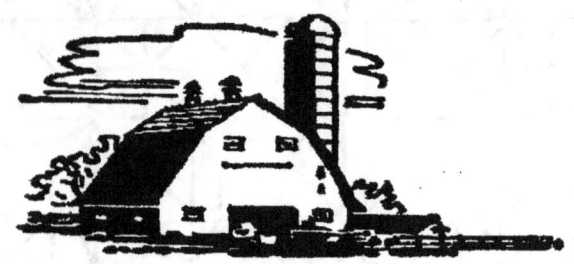

Quilt Block Location
East 12th Street
Cozad, Nebraska

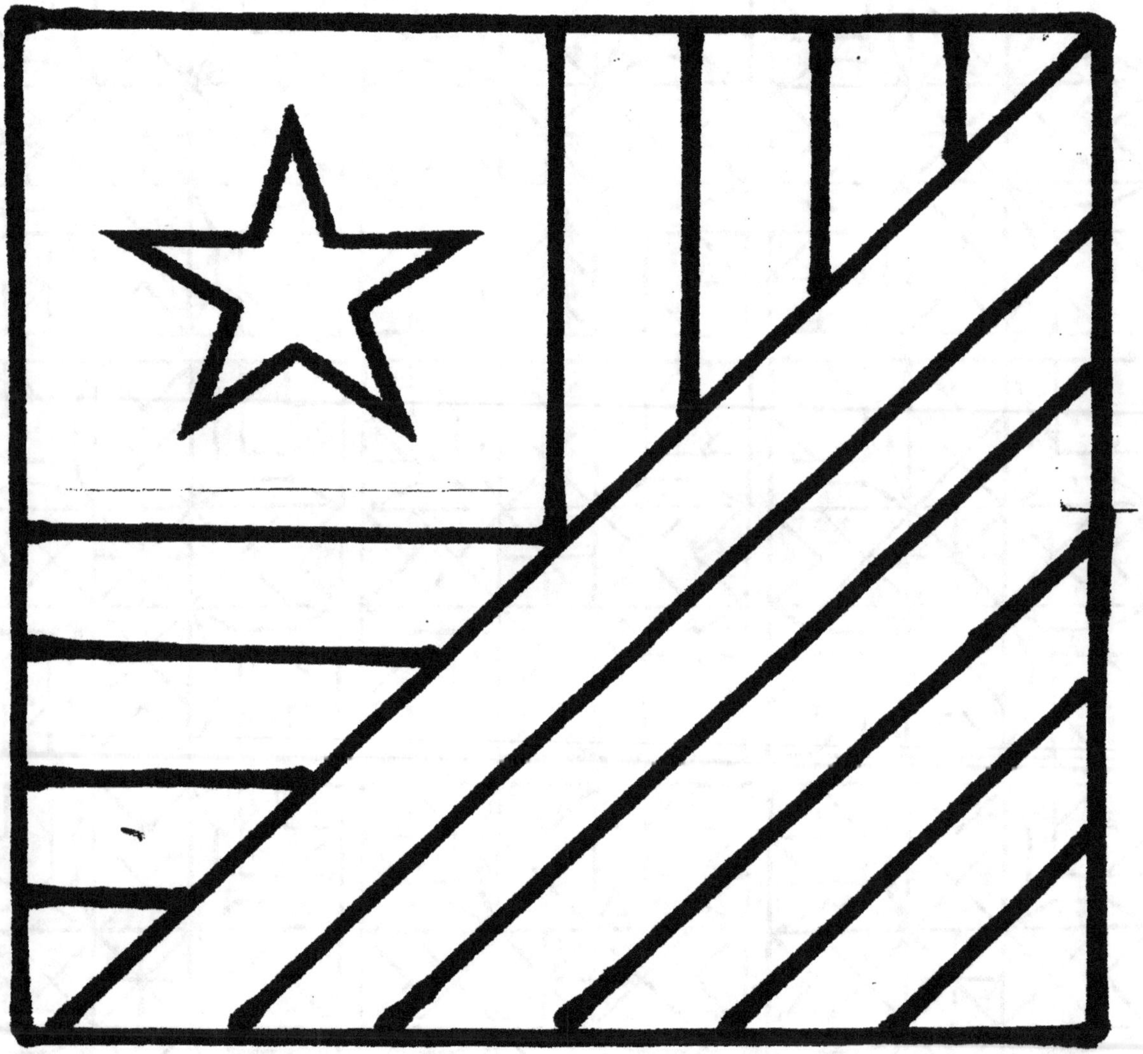

Dawson County Nebraska Barn Quilt Red, White & Blue Runs True

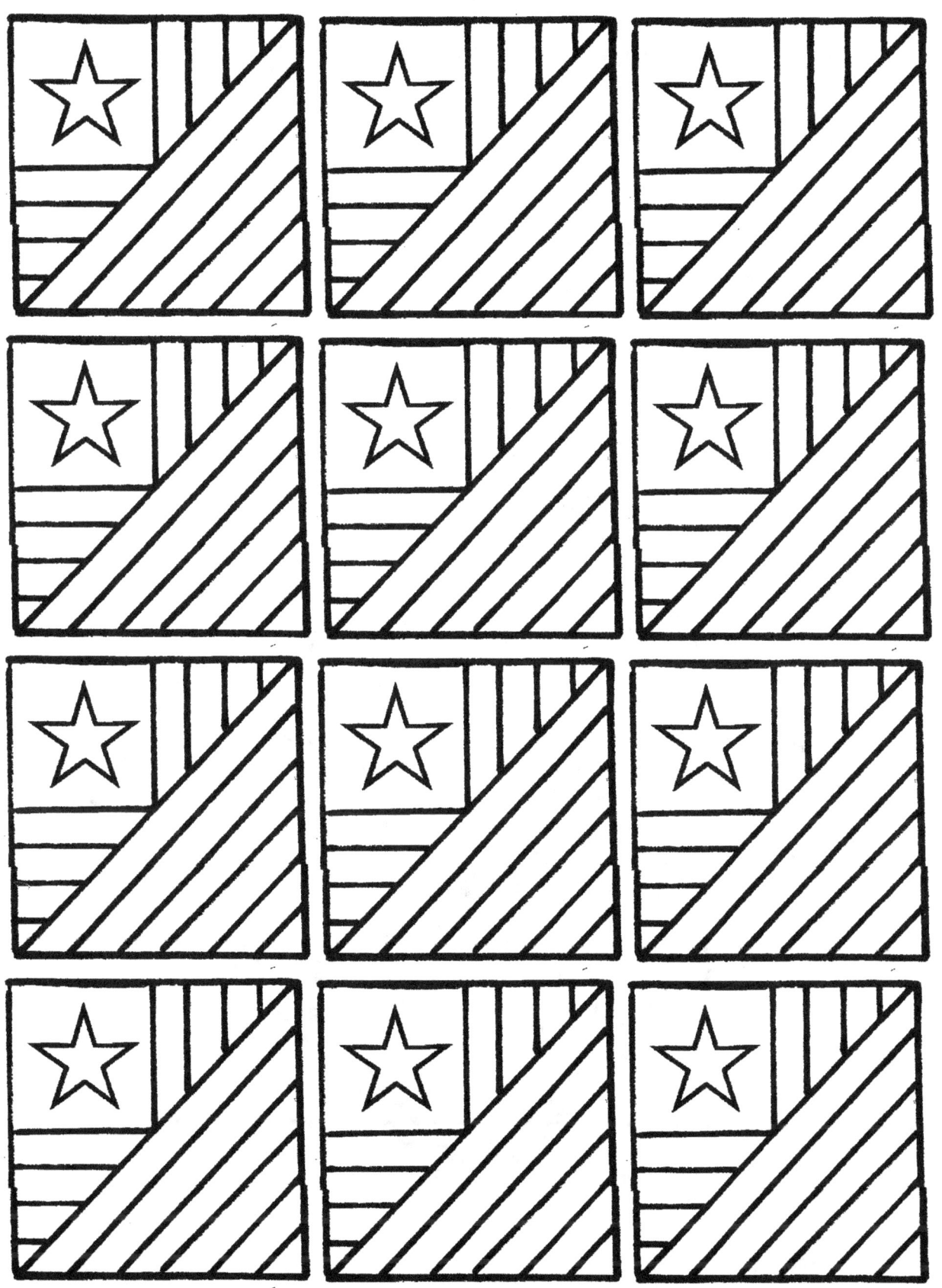

Scatter Joy
Dawson County Nebraska Barn Quilt Trail

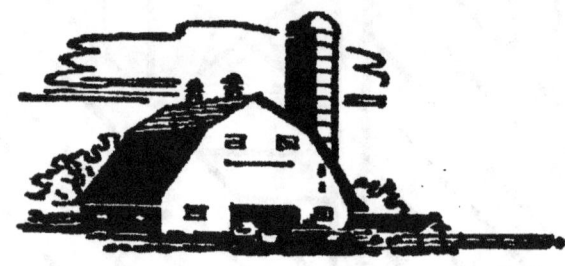

Quilt Block Location
West 13th Street
Cozad, Nebraska

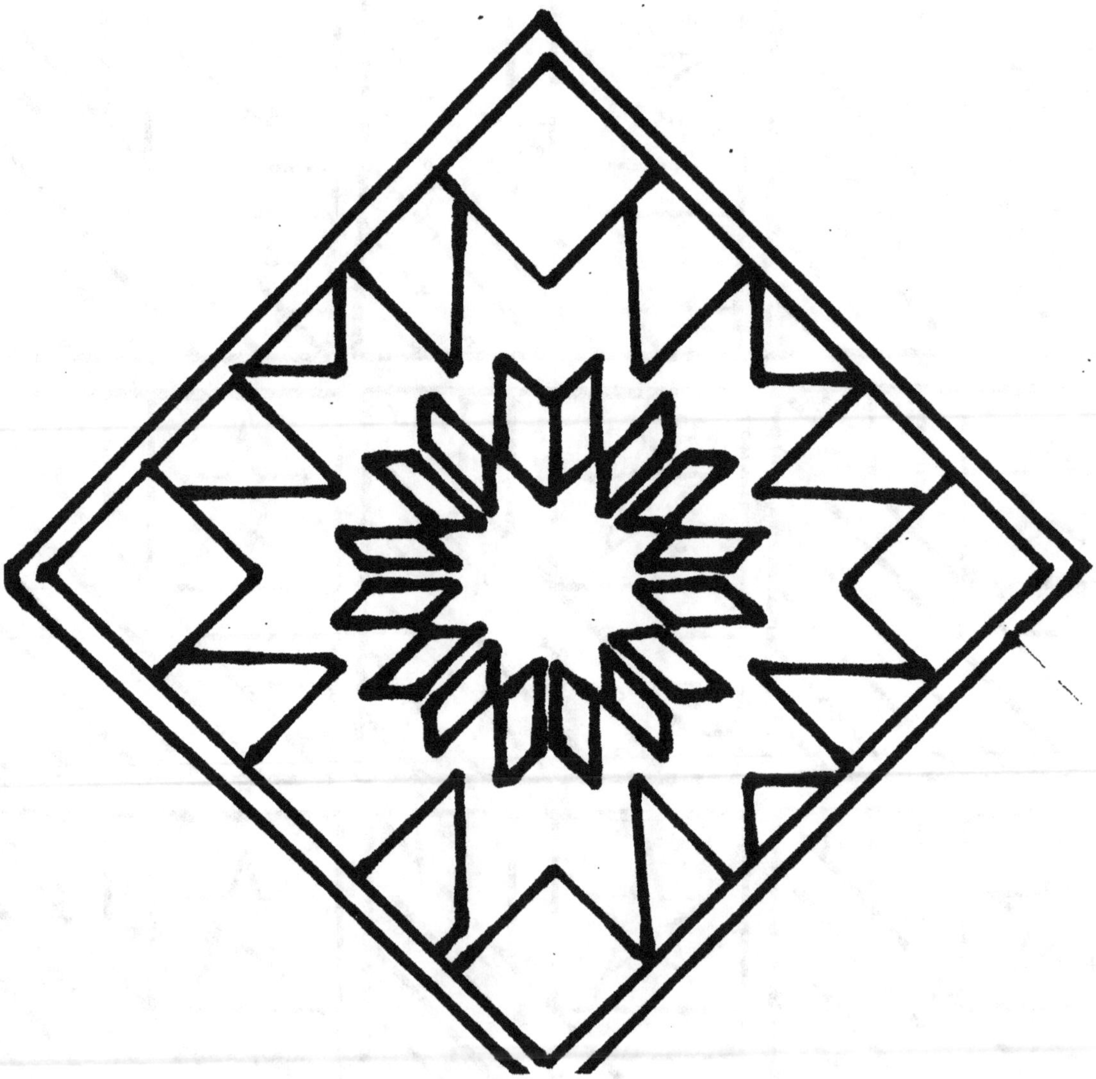

Dawson County Nebraska Barn Quilt Scatter Joy

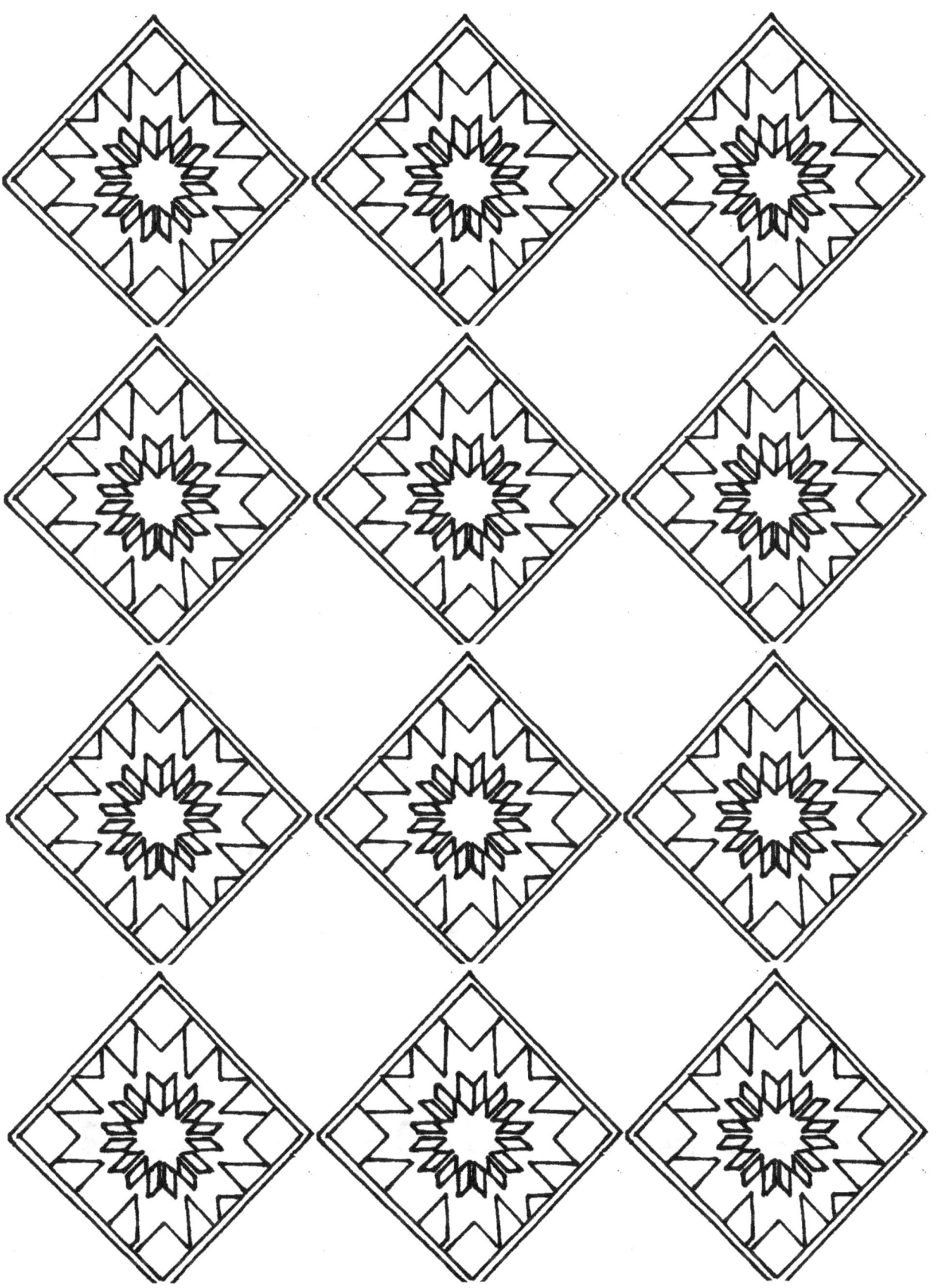

Security First Bank
Dawson County Nebraska Barn Quilt Trail

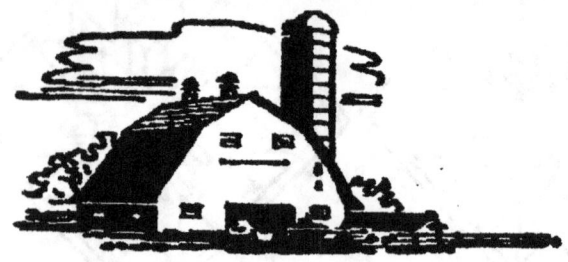

Quilt Block Location
Avenue F
Cozad, Nebraska

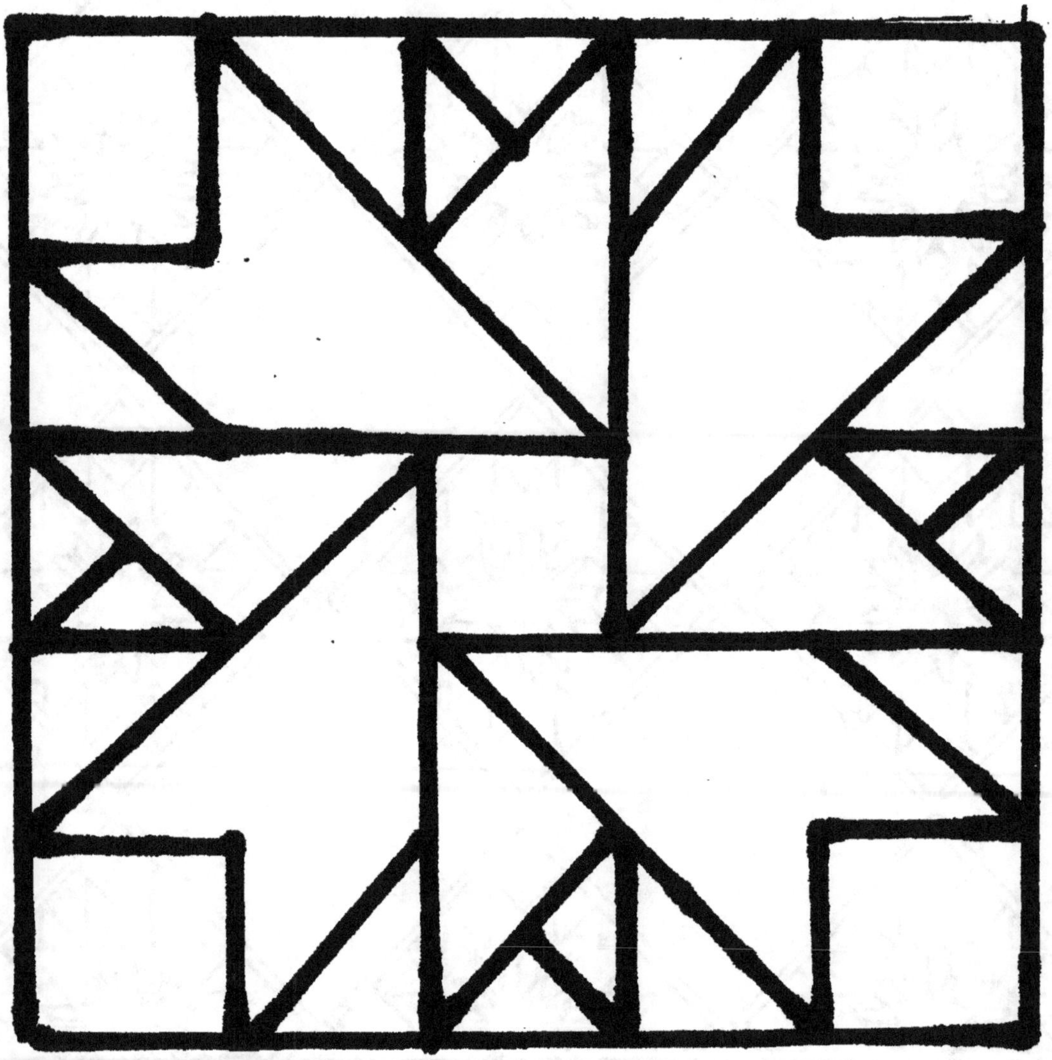

Dawson County Nebraska Barn Quilt Security First Bank

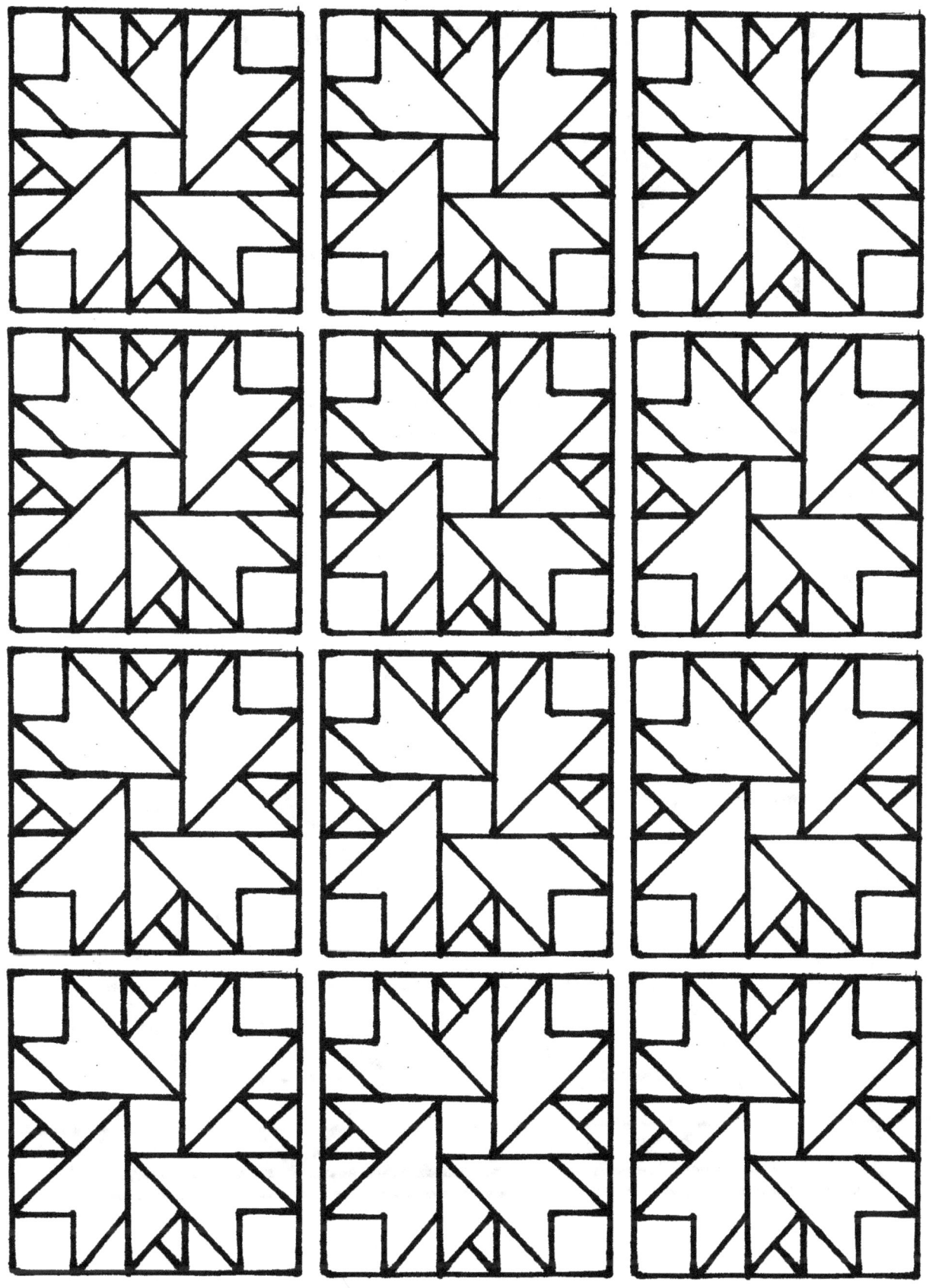

Sesqui Ear
Dawson County Nebraska Barn Quilt Trail

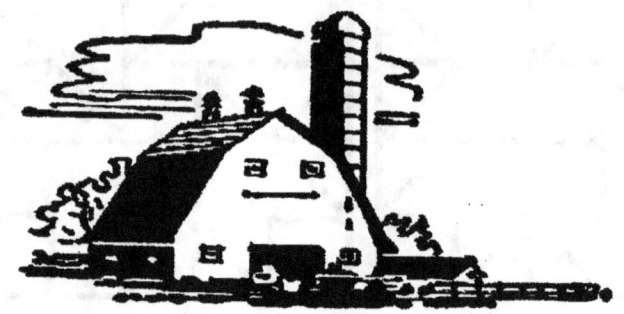

Barn Quilt Location
North Taft
Lexington, Nebraska

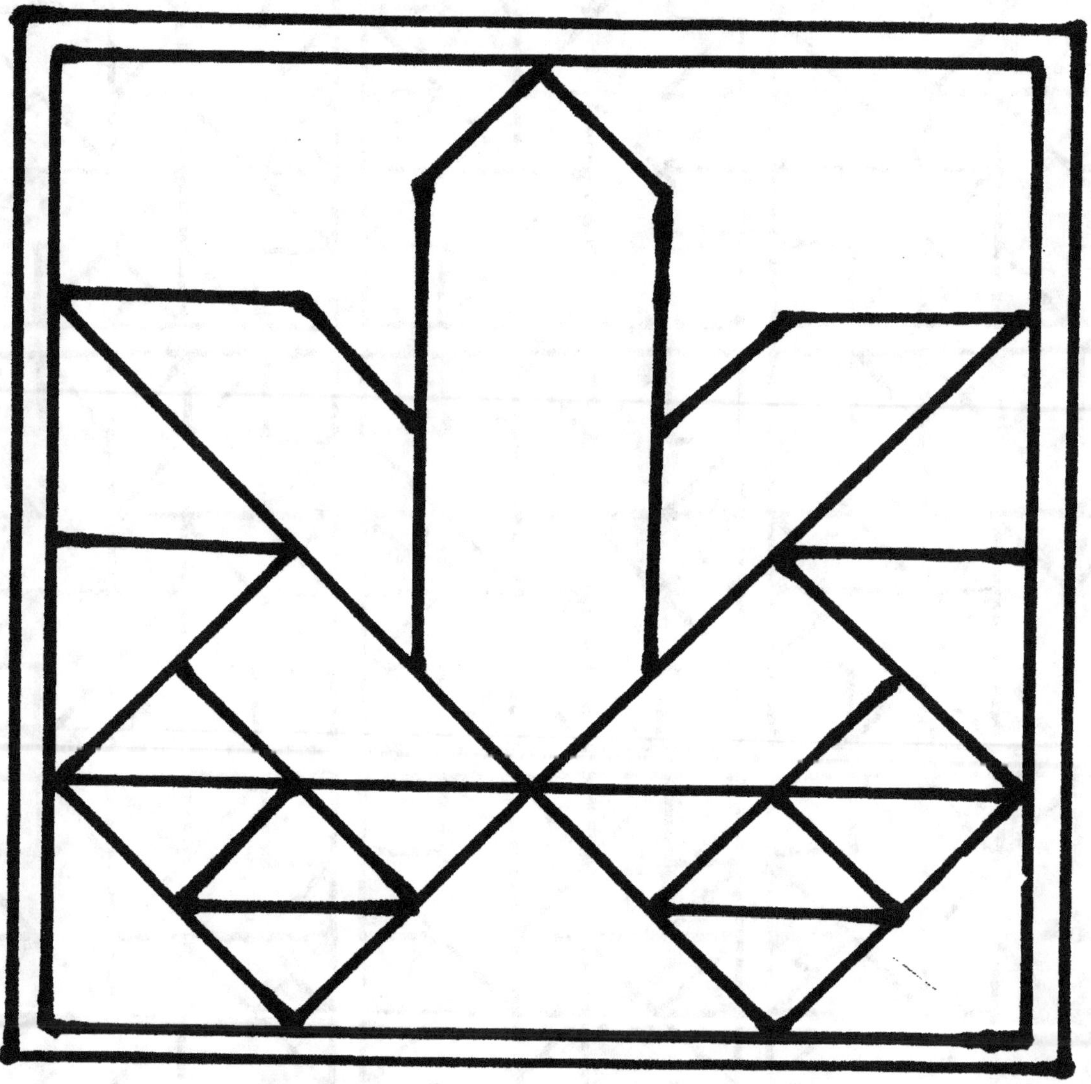

Dawson County Nebraska Barn Quilt Sesqui Ear

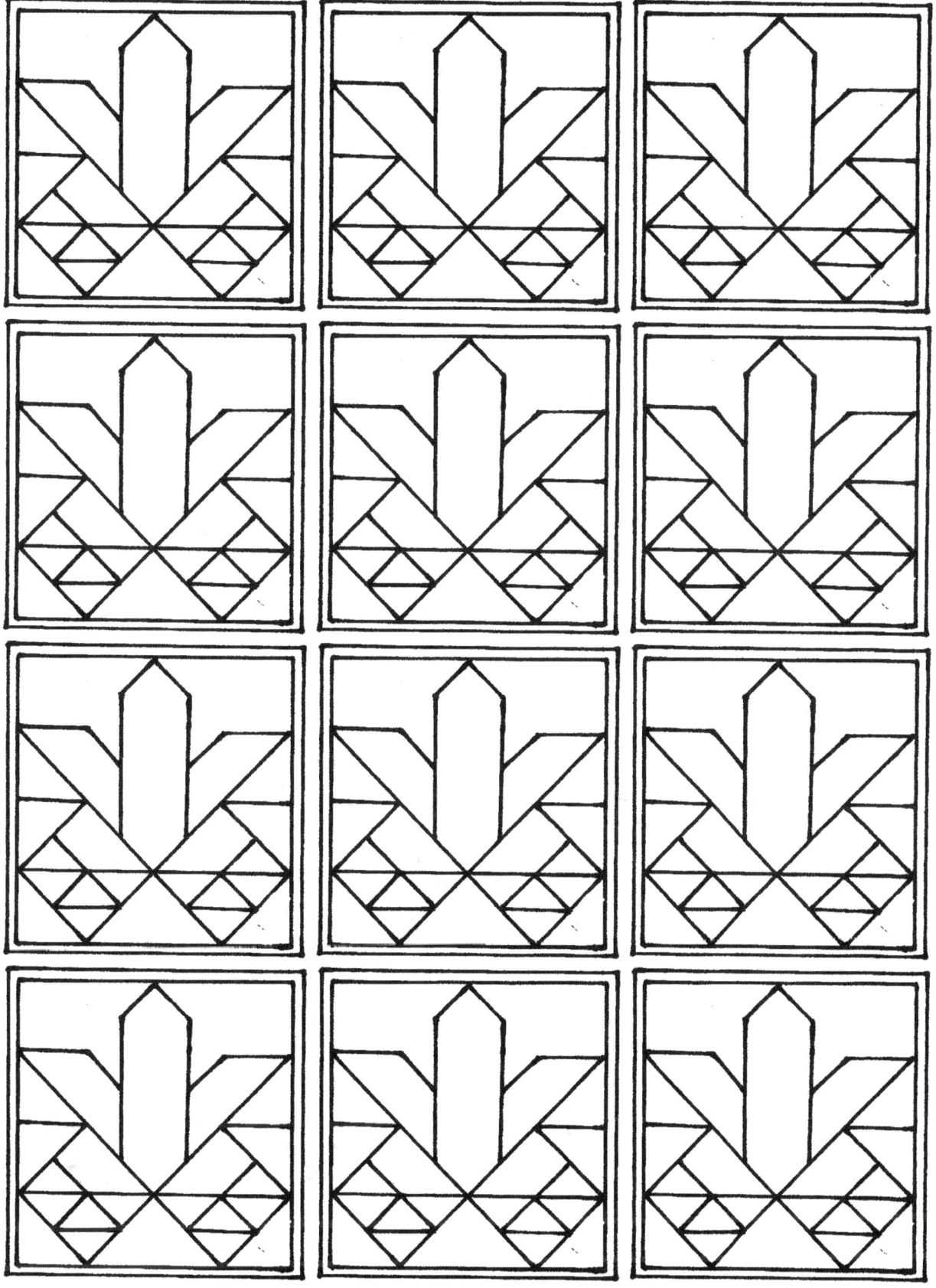

Staton Shop
Dawson County Nebraska Barn Quilt Trail

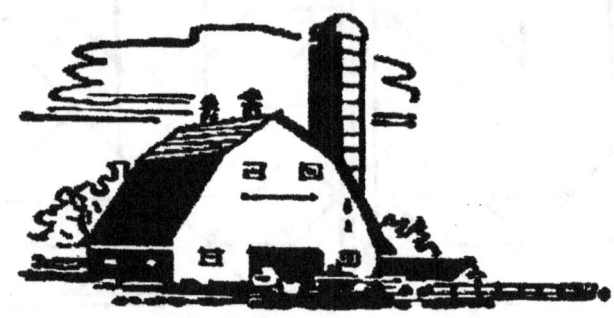

Barn Quilt Location
Adams Street
Cozad, Nebraska

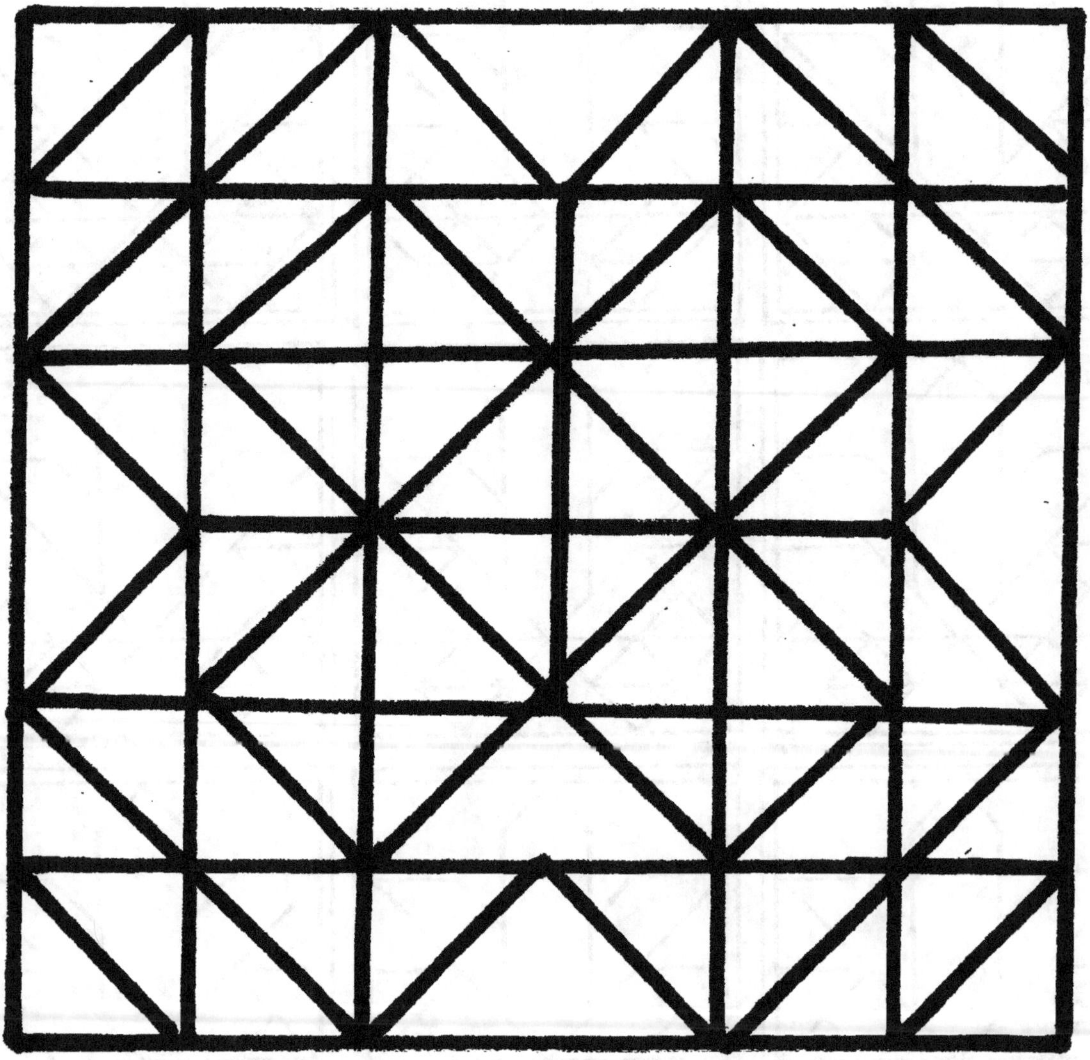

Dawson County Nebraska Barn Quilt Staton Shop

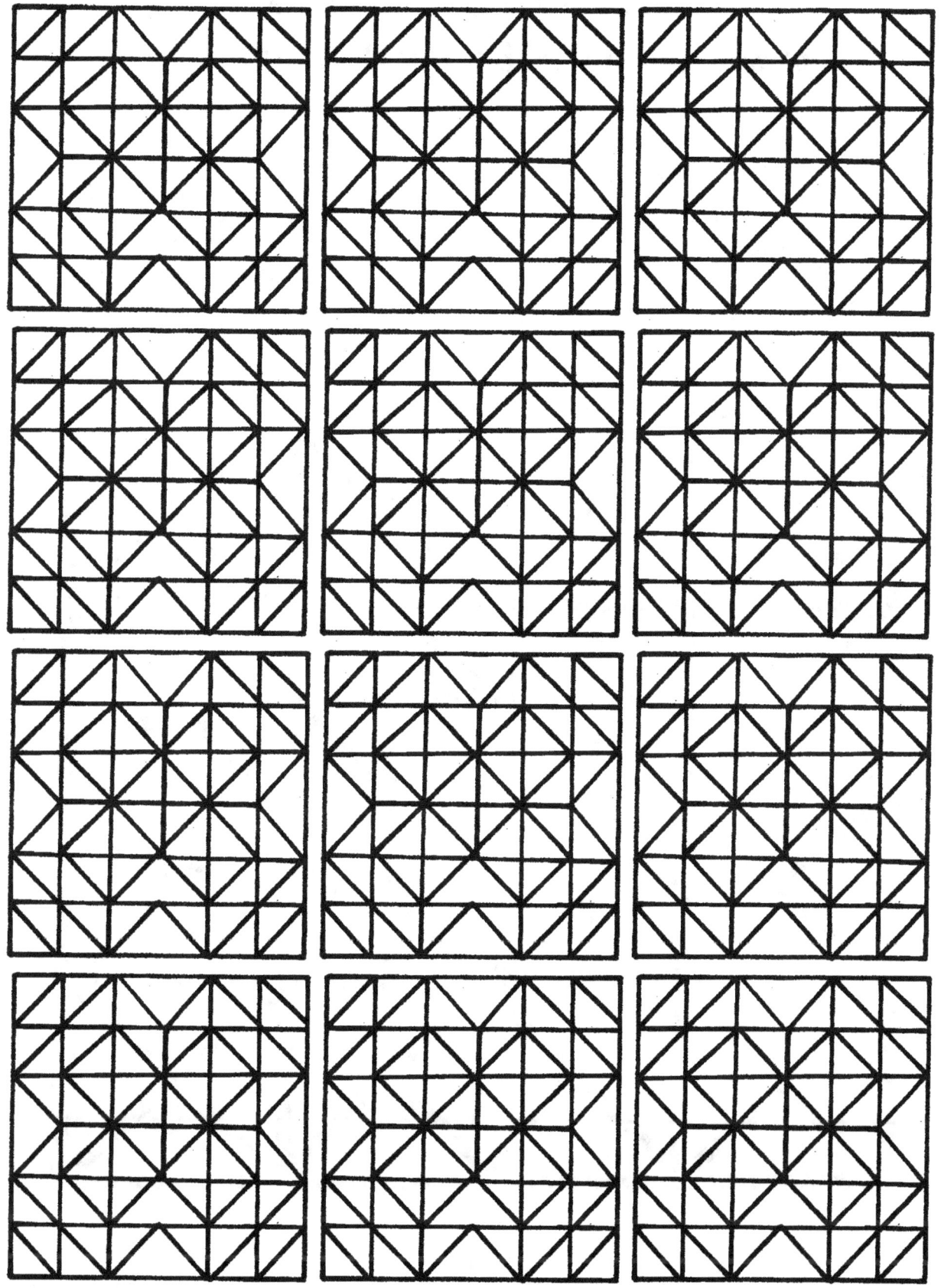

Summer Bliss
Dawson County Nebraska Barn Quilt Trail

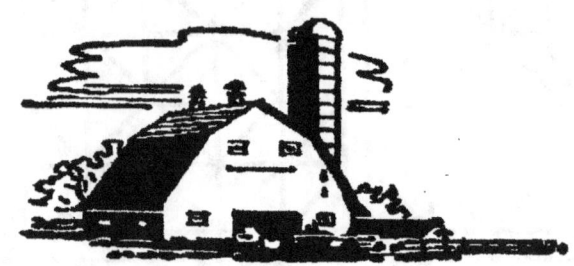

Quilt Block Location
21th Street
Gothenburg, Nebraska

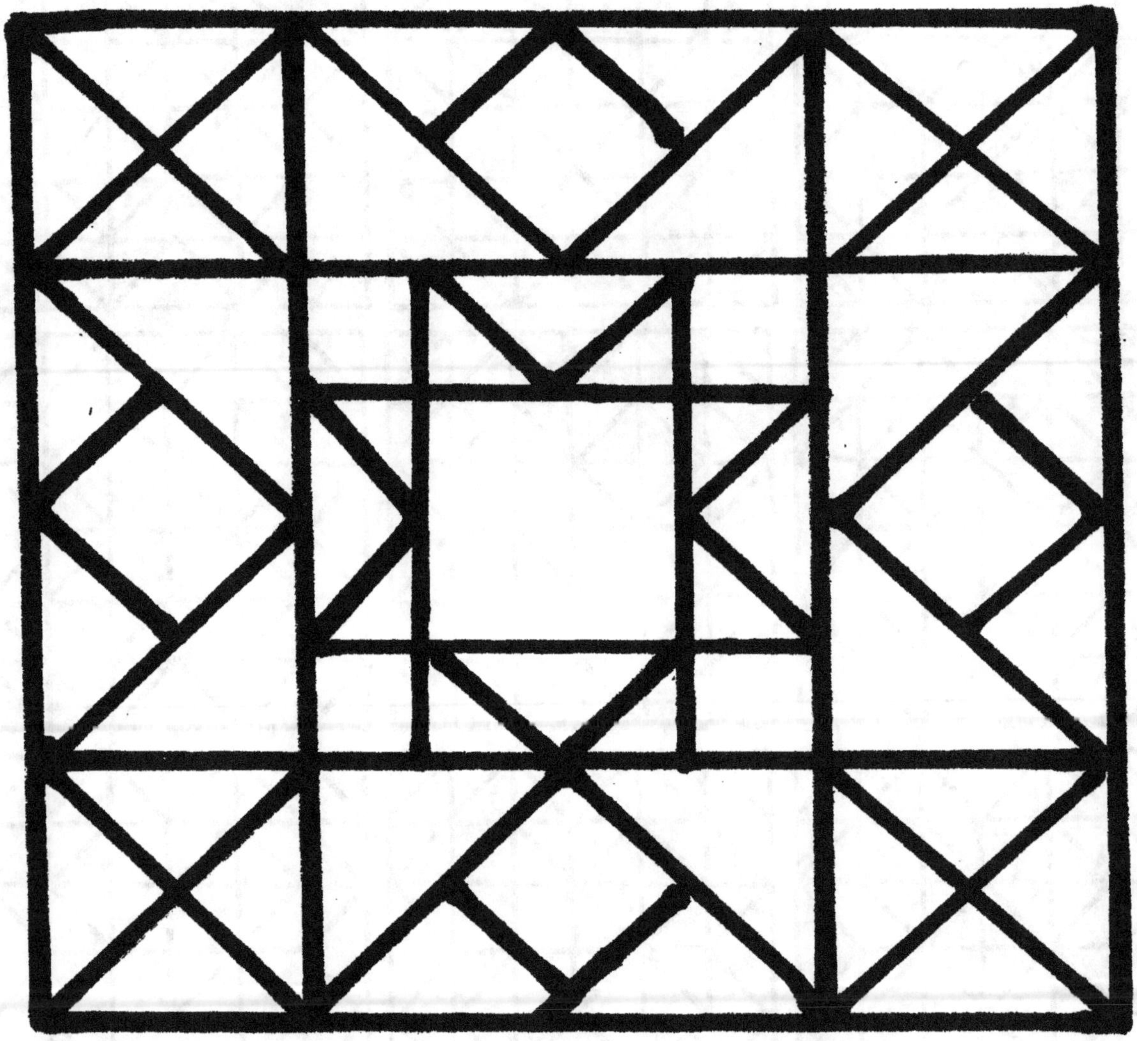

Dawson County Nebraska Barn Quilt Summer Bliss

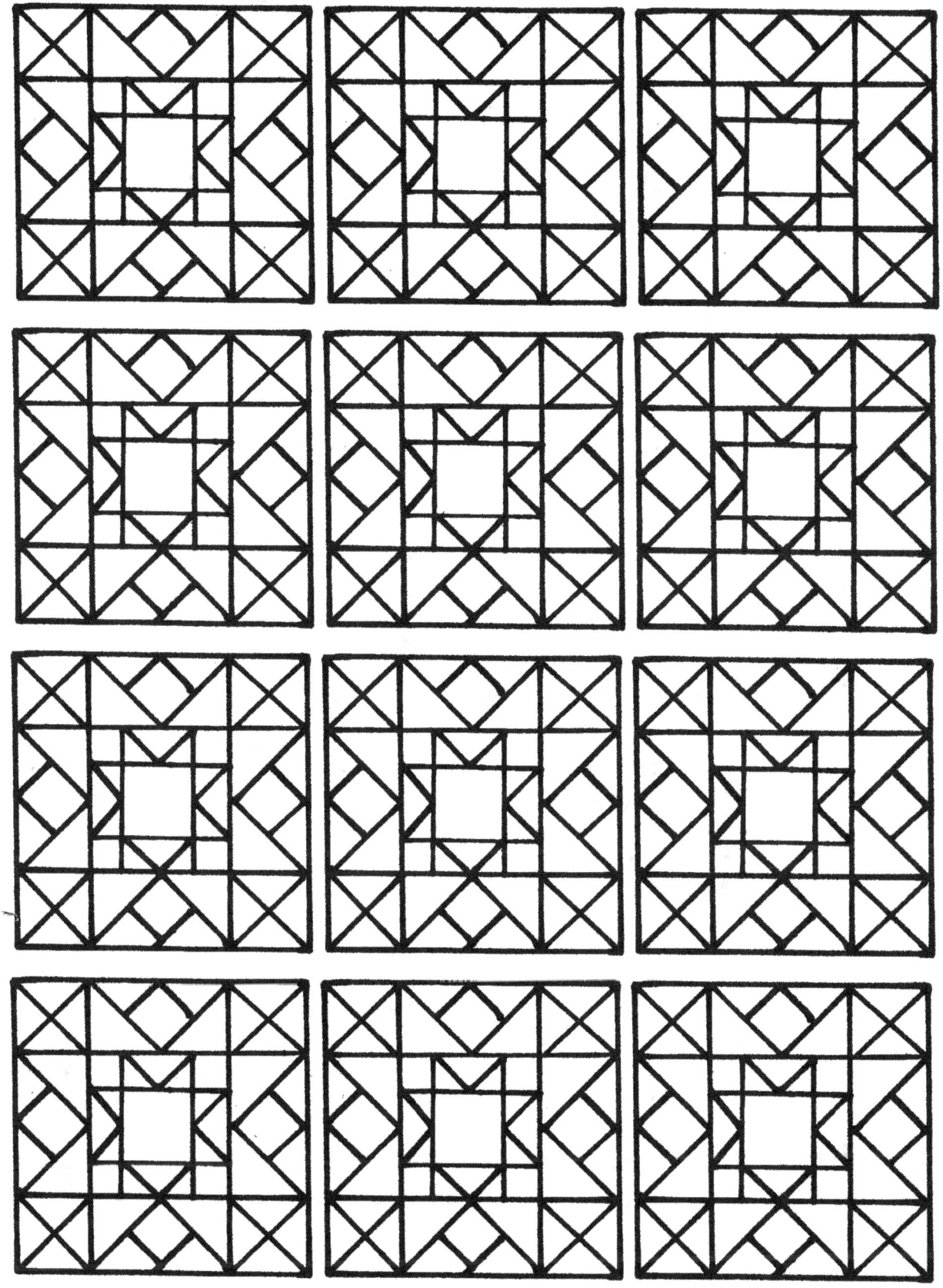

Swedish Weathervane
Dawson County Nebraska Barn Quilt Trail

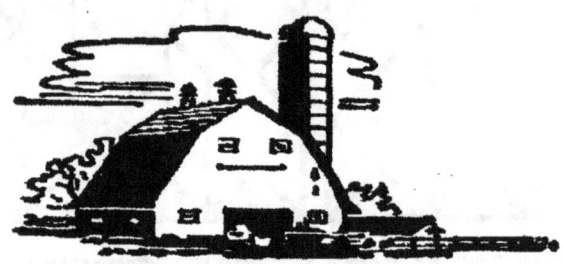

Quilt Block Location
Lake Avenue
Gothenburg, Nebraska

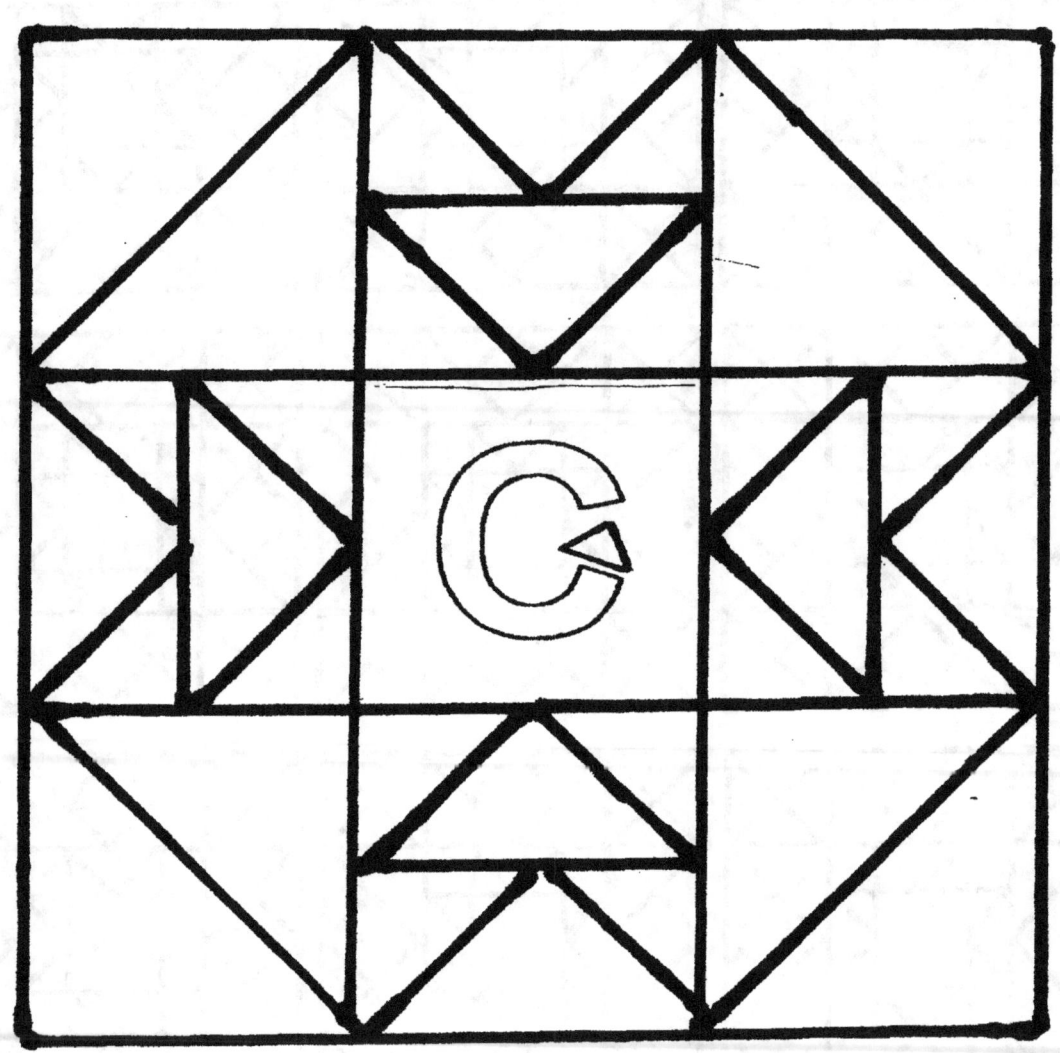

Dawson County Nebraska Barn Quilt Swedish Weathervane

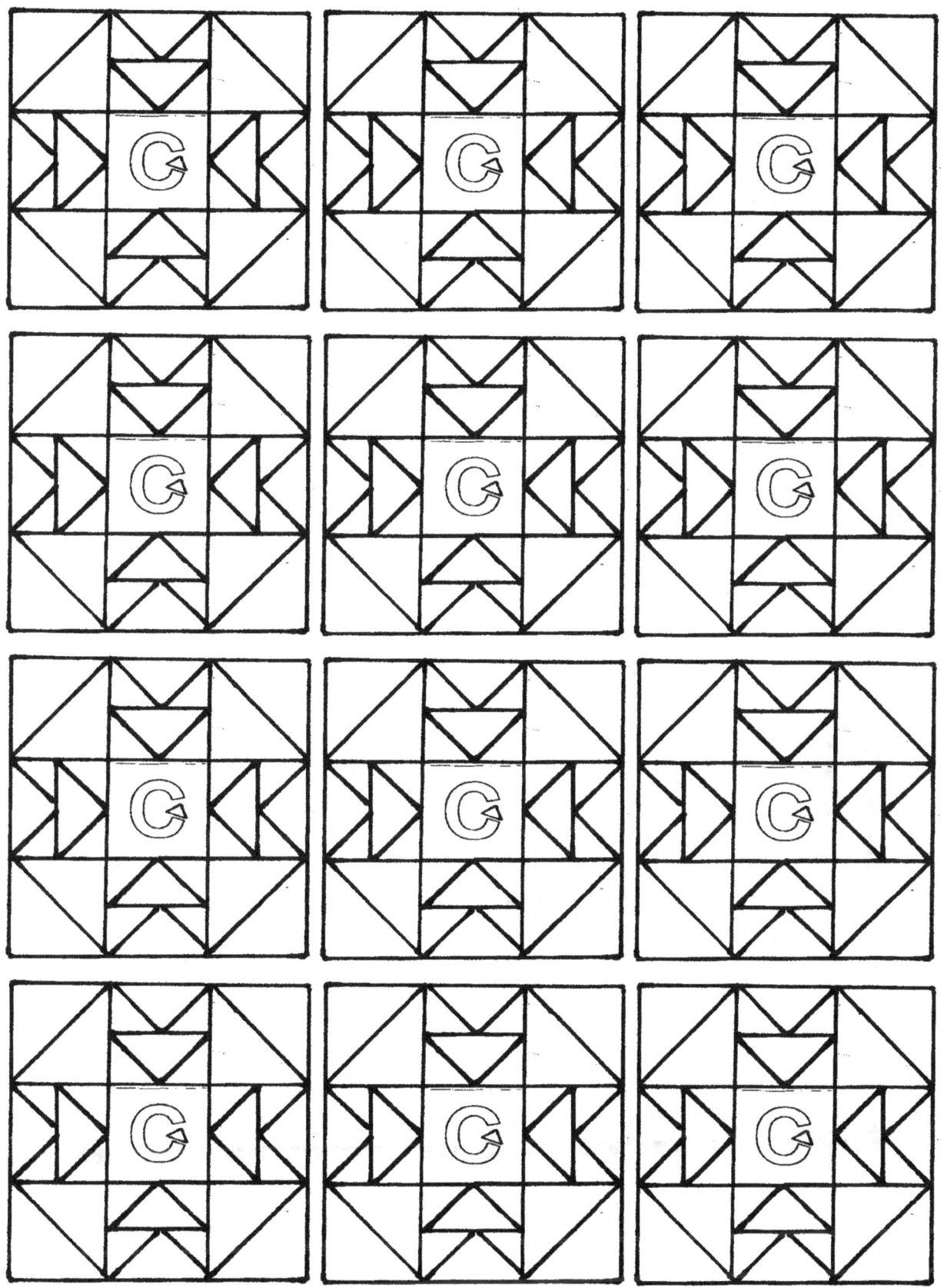

Thank You
Dawson County Nebraska Barn Quilt Trail

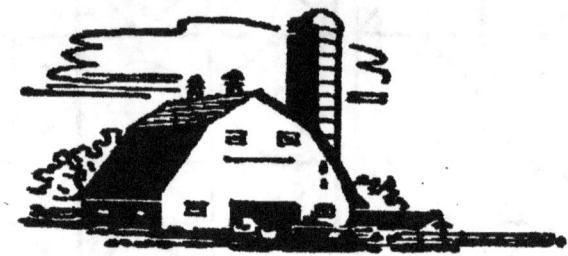

Quilt Block Location
North Shore Drive
Johnson Lake, Nebraska

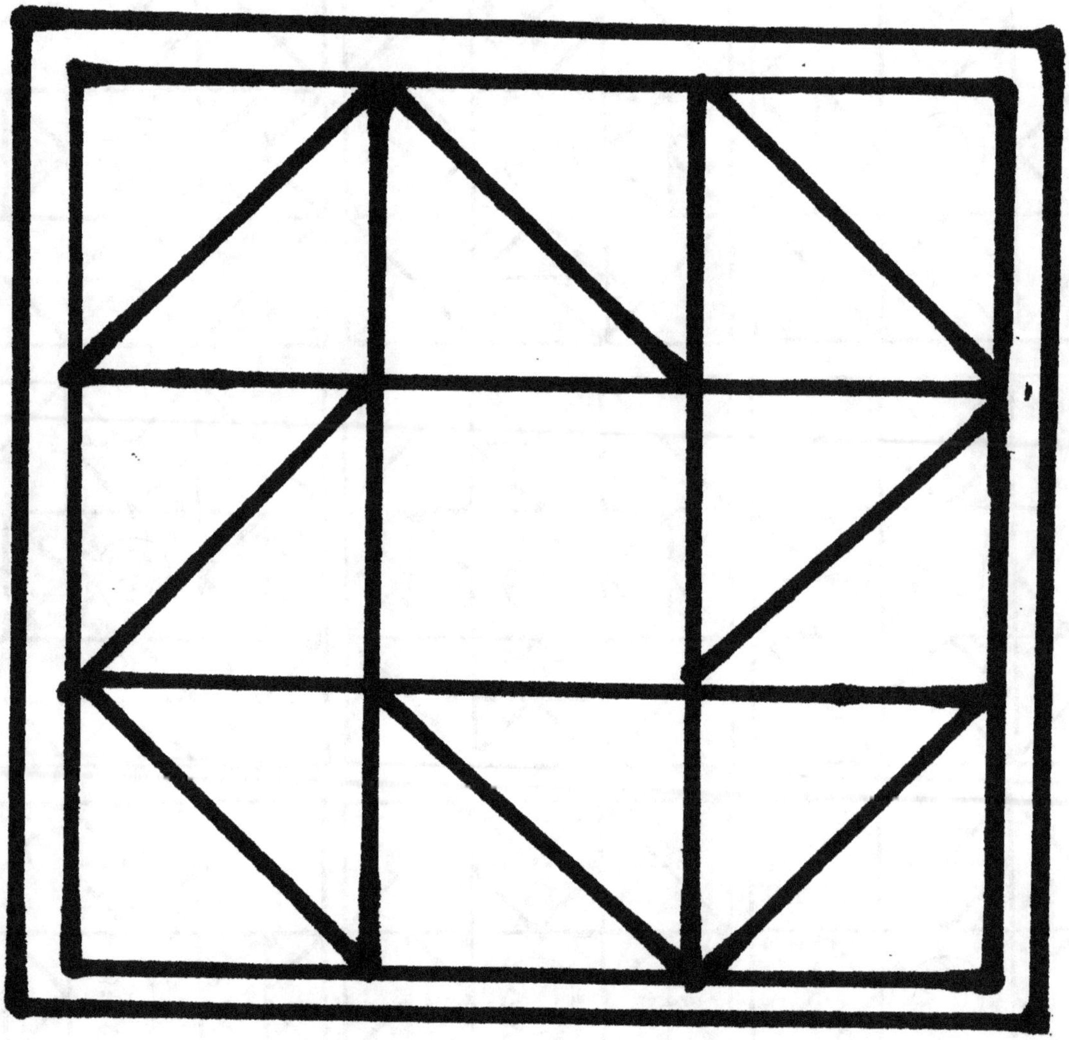

Dawson County Nebraska Barn Quilt Thank You

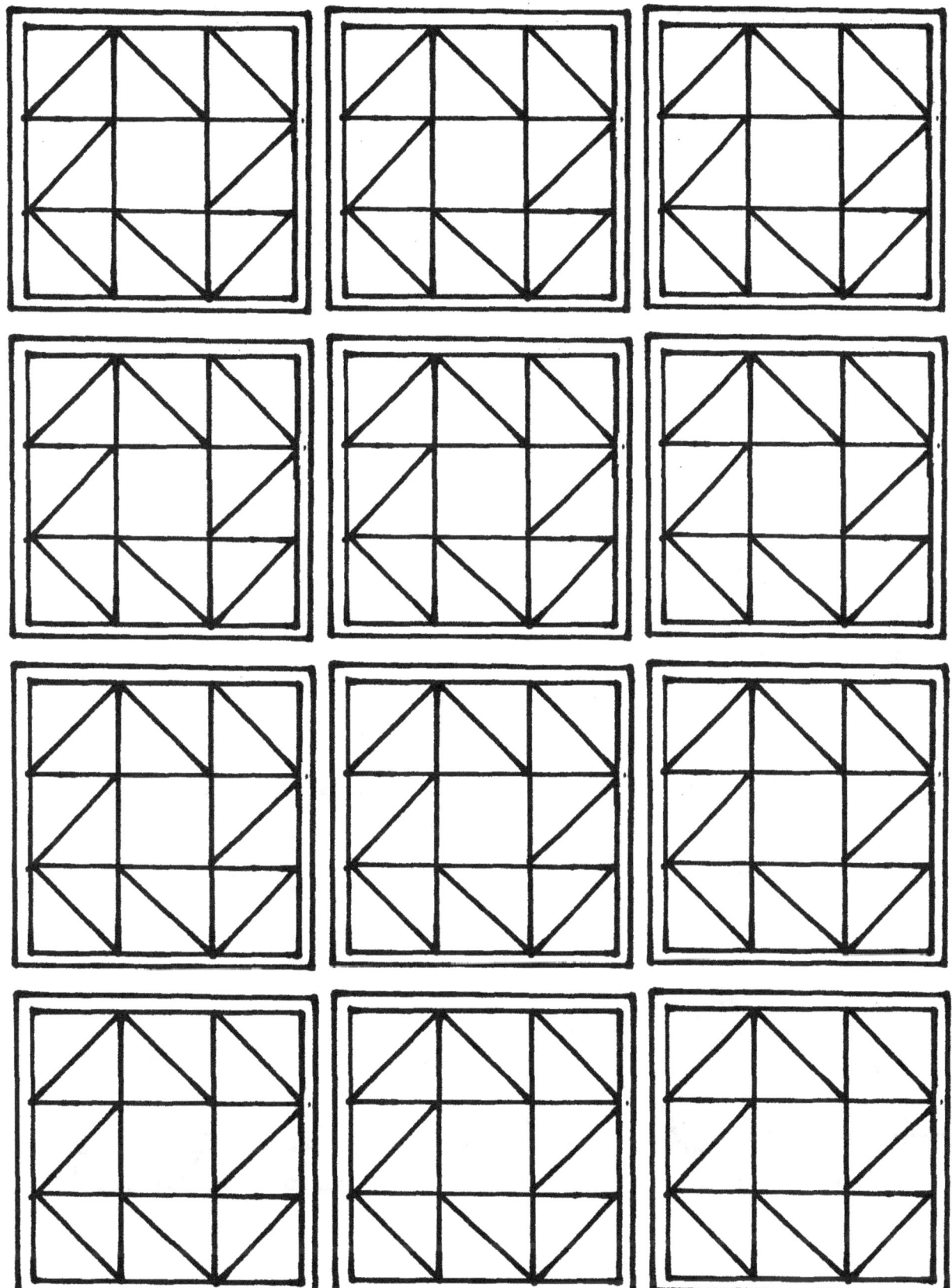

The Compass: Finding Our Way
Dawson County Nebraska Barn Quilt Trail

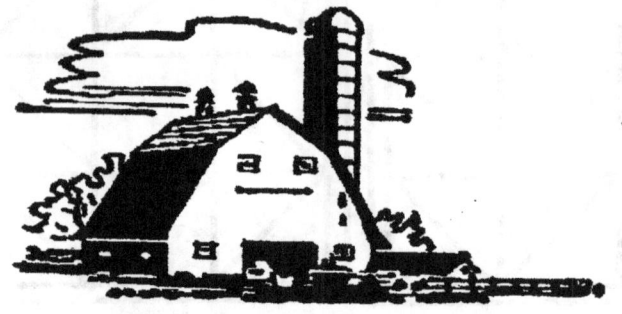

Barn Quilt Location
Meridian Avenue
Cozad, Nebraska

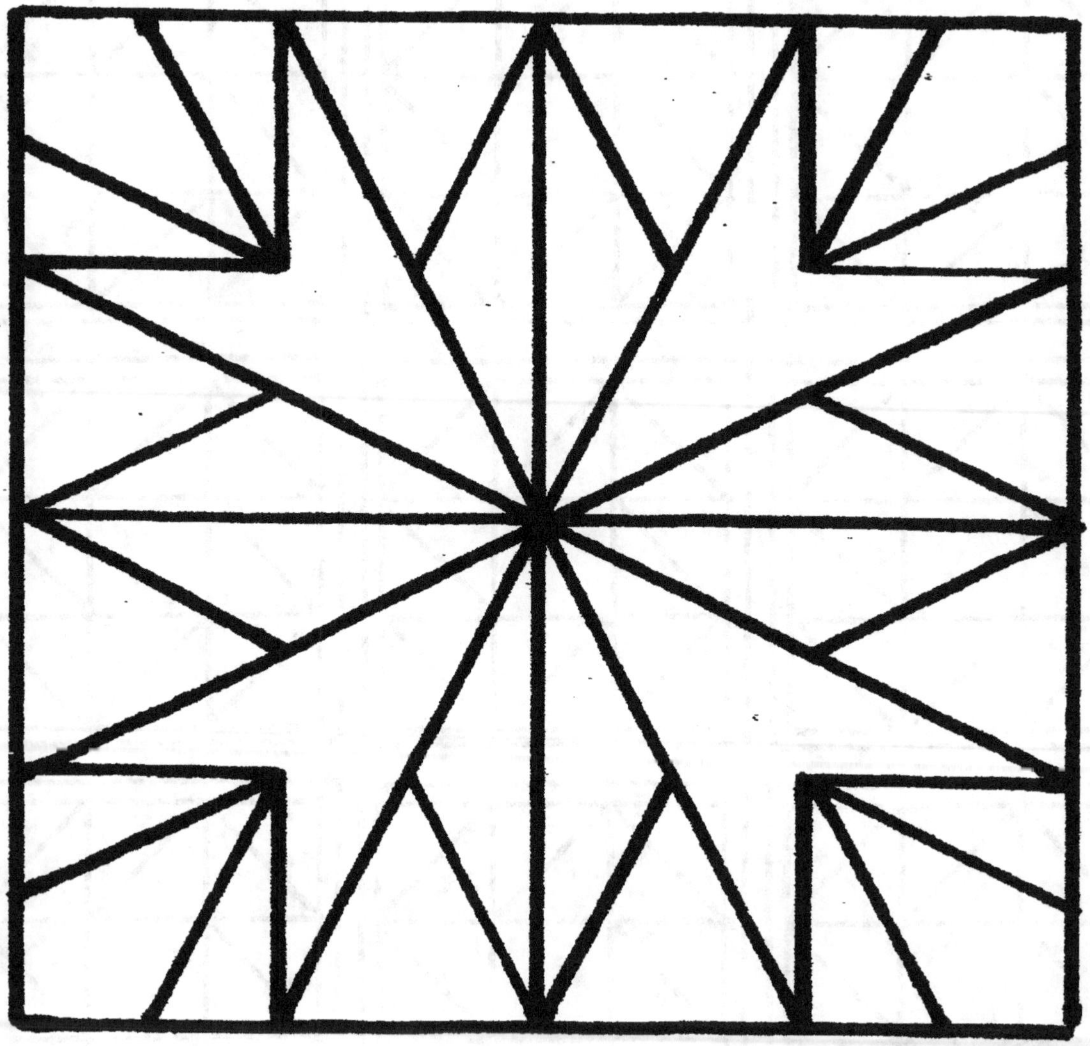

Dawson County Nebraska Barn Quilt Compass Finding Our Way

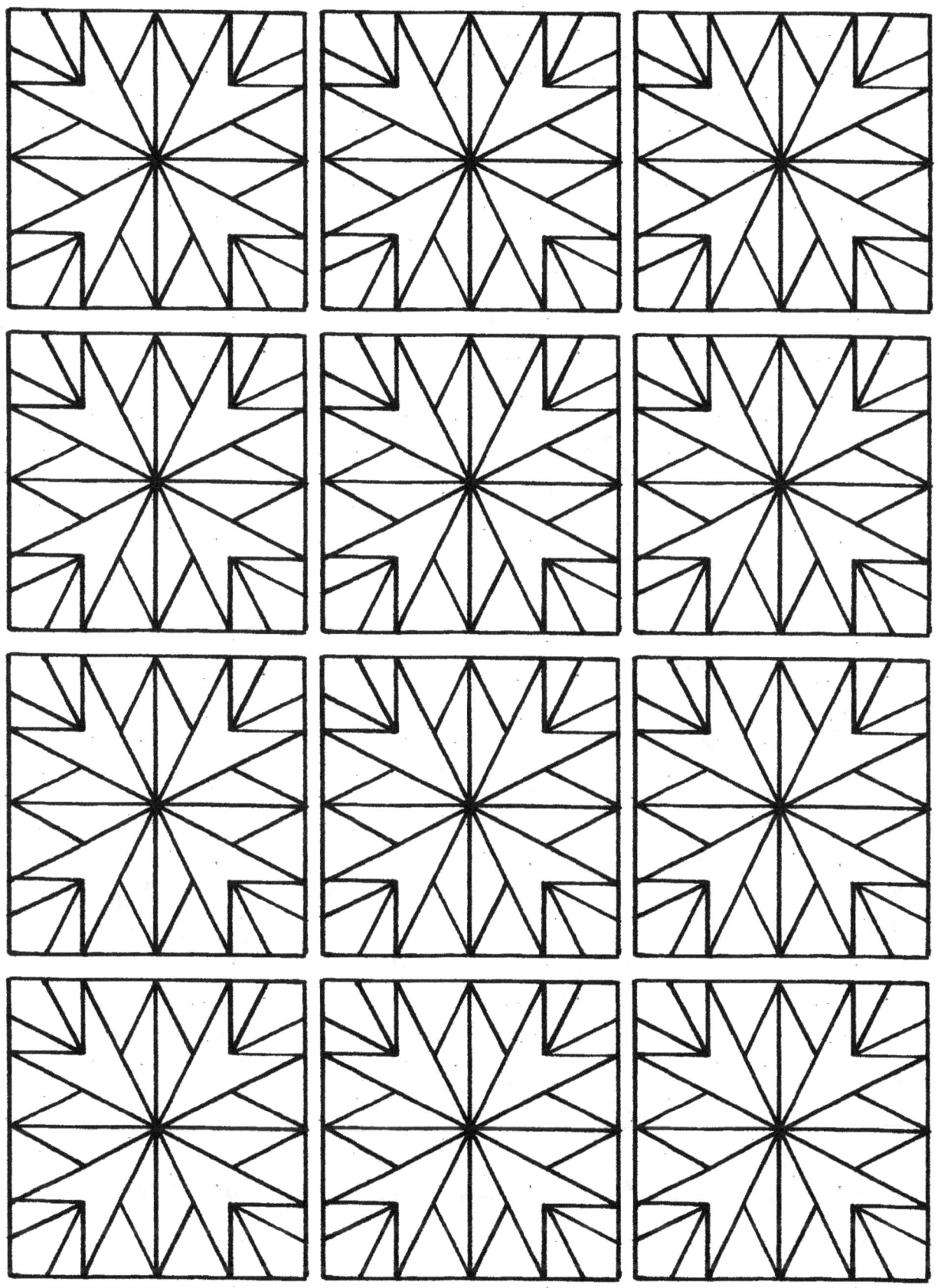

Variable Star
Dawson County Nebraska Barn Quilt Trail

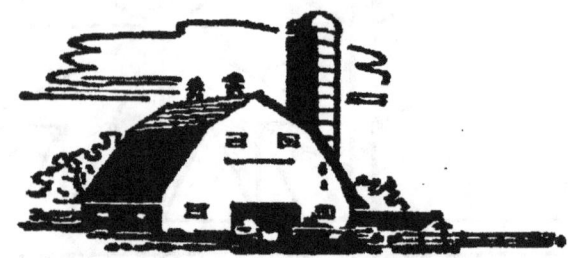

Quilt Block Location
West 14th Street
Cozad, Nebraska

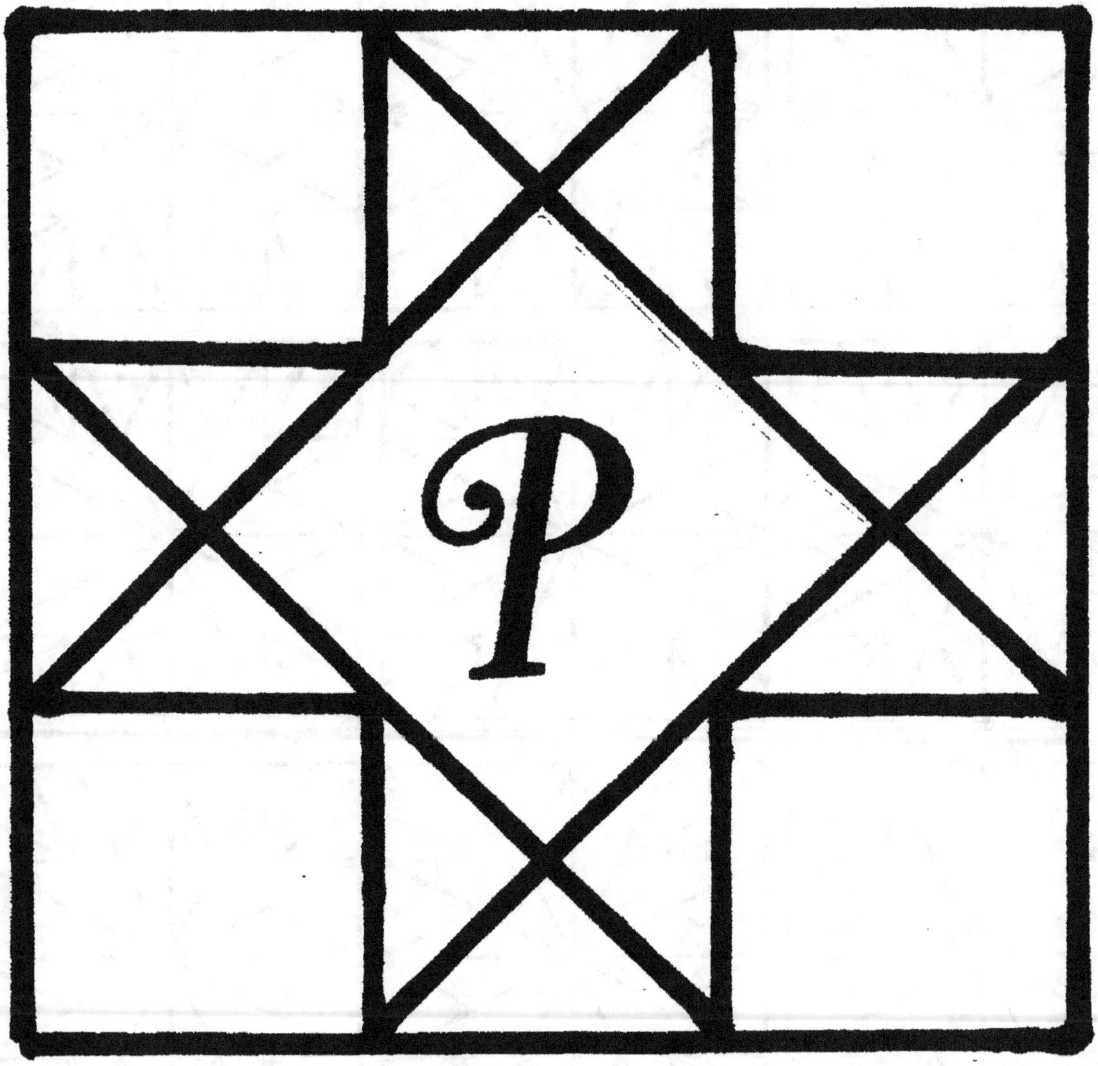

Dawson County Nebraska Barn Quilt Variable Star

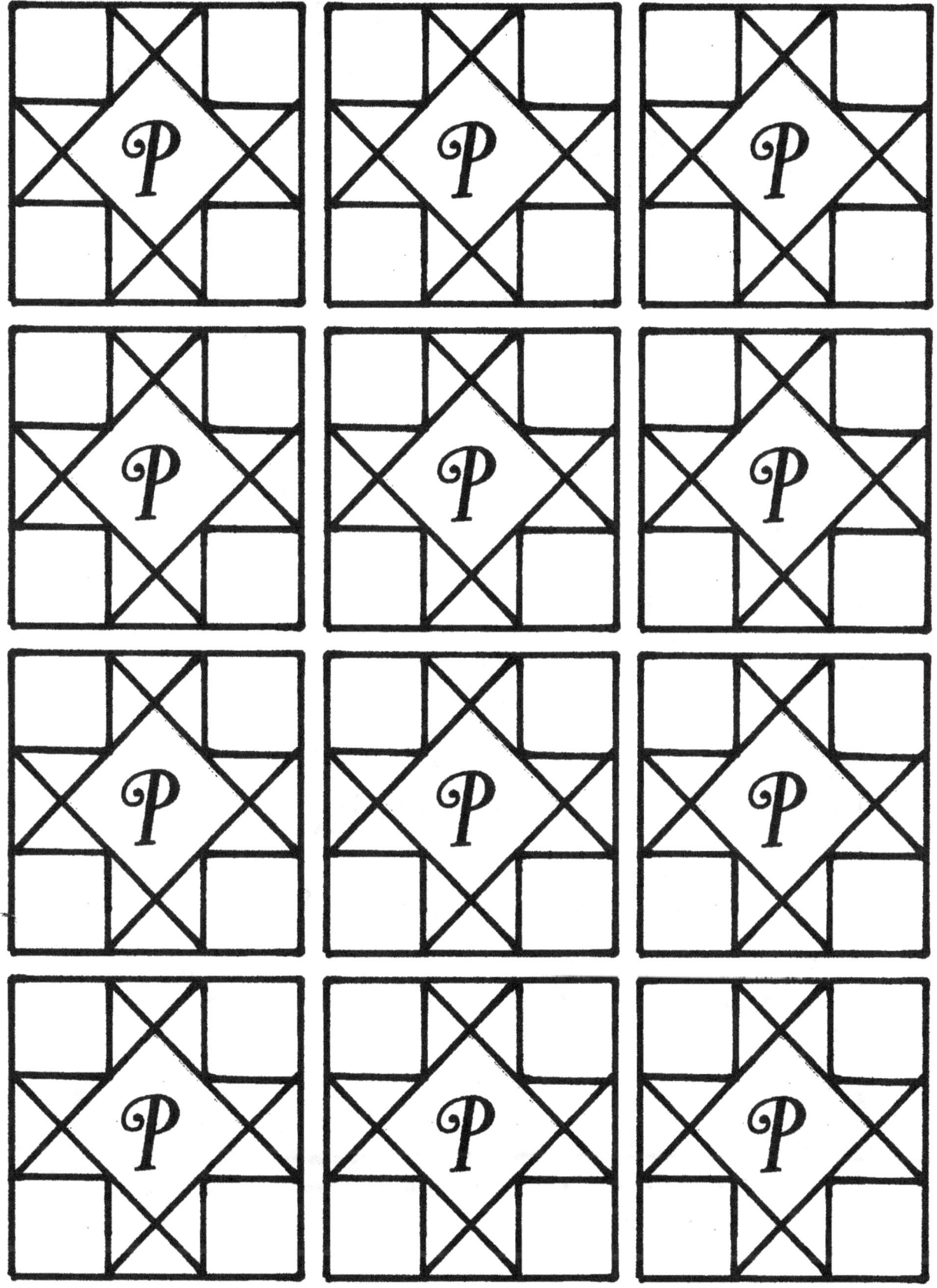

Vetters Corn

Dawson County Nebraska Barn Quilt Trail

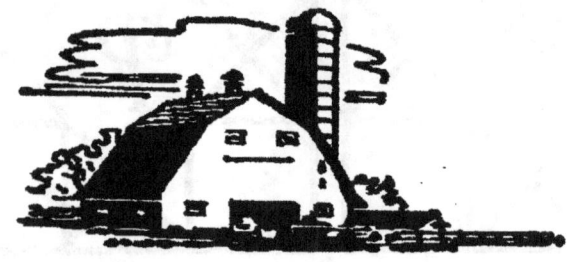

Quilt Block Location
Road 761
Cozad, Nebraska

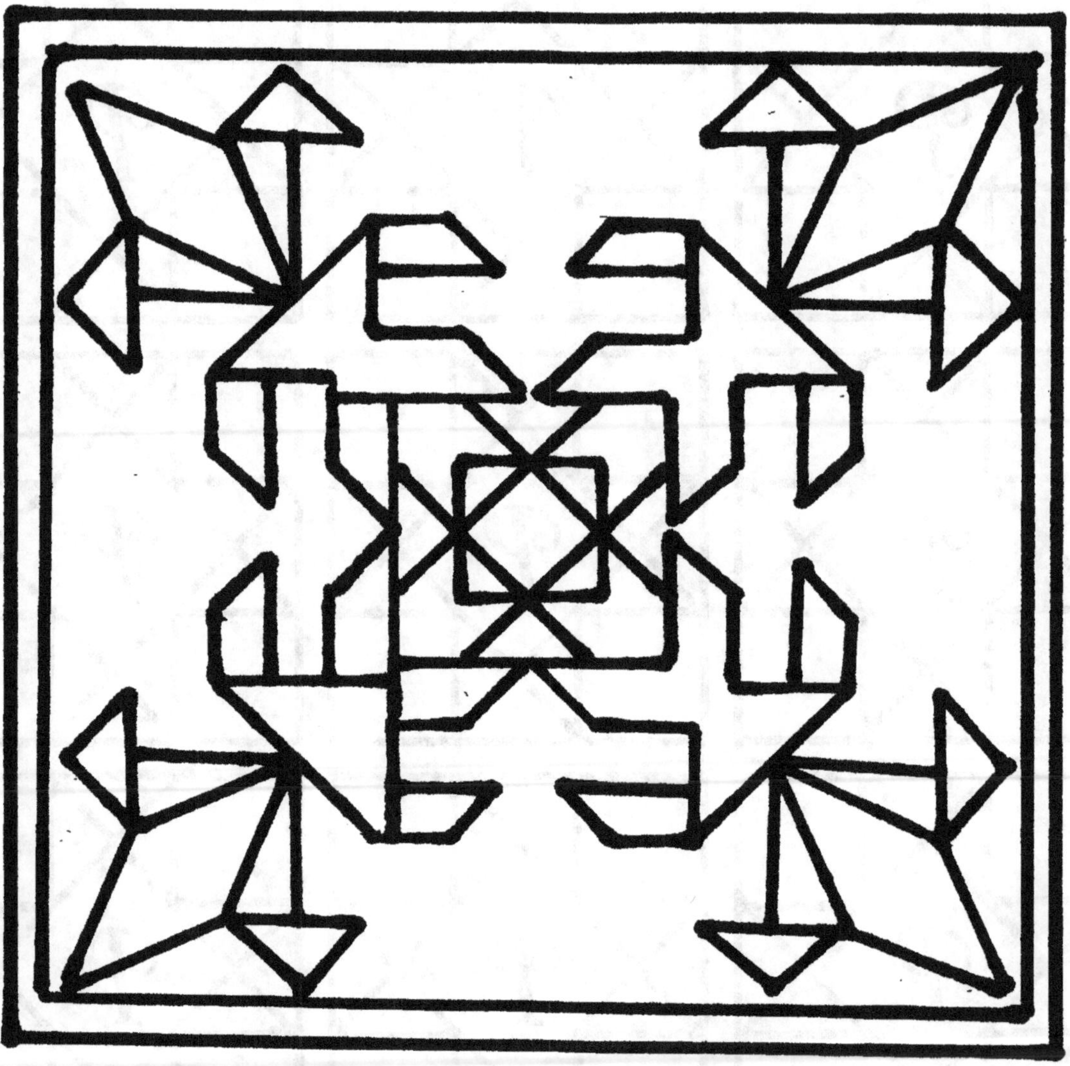

Dawson County Nebraska Barn Quilt Vetters Corn

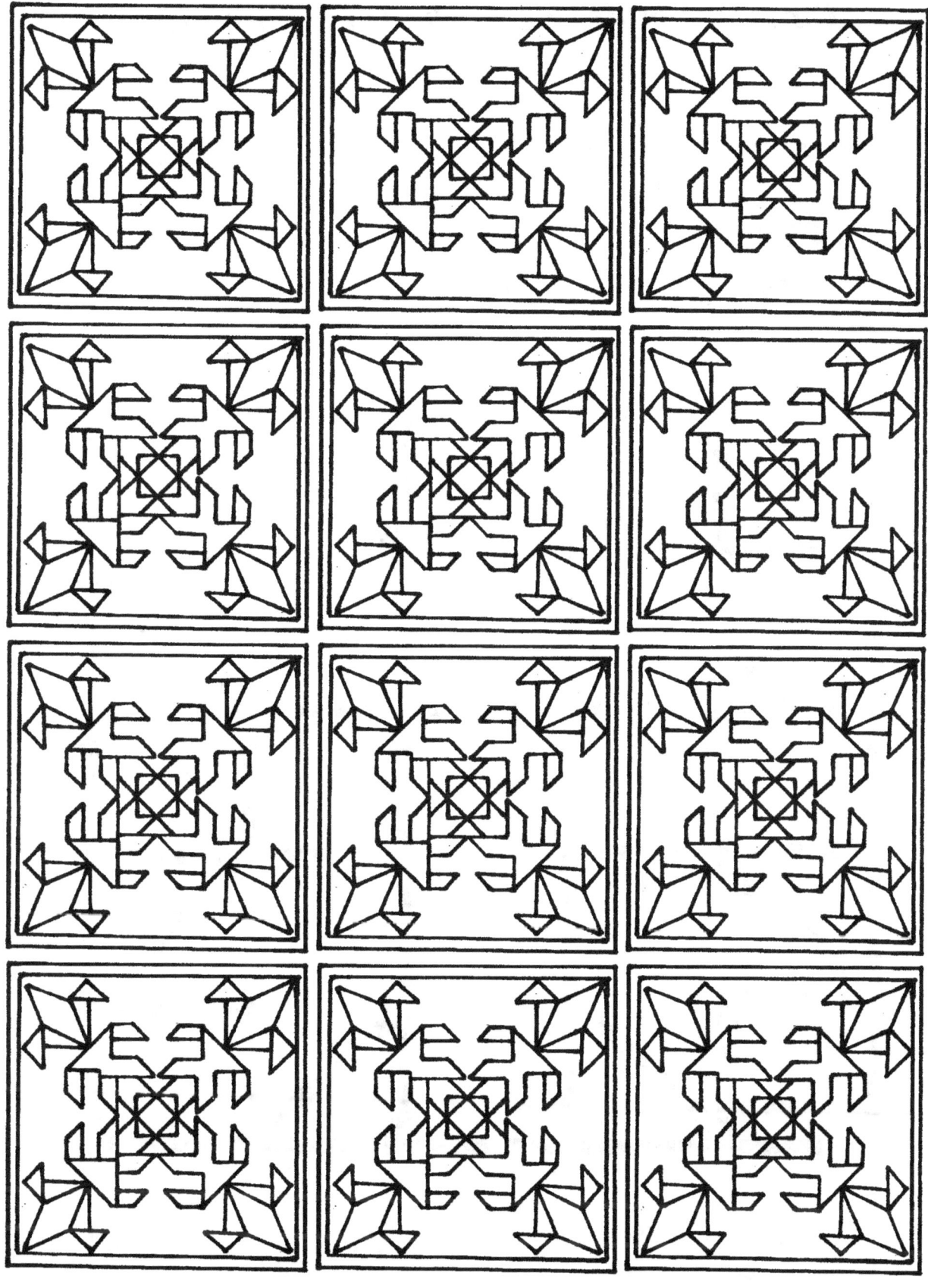

Wabi Sabi
Dawson County Nebraska Barn Quilt Trail

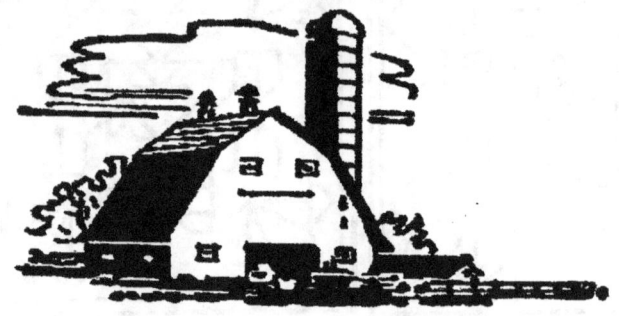

Barn Quilt Location
East 6th Street
Cozad, Nebraska

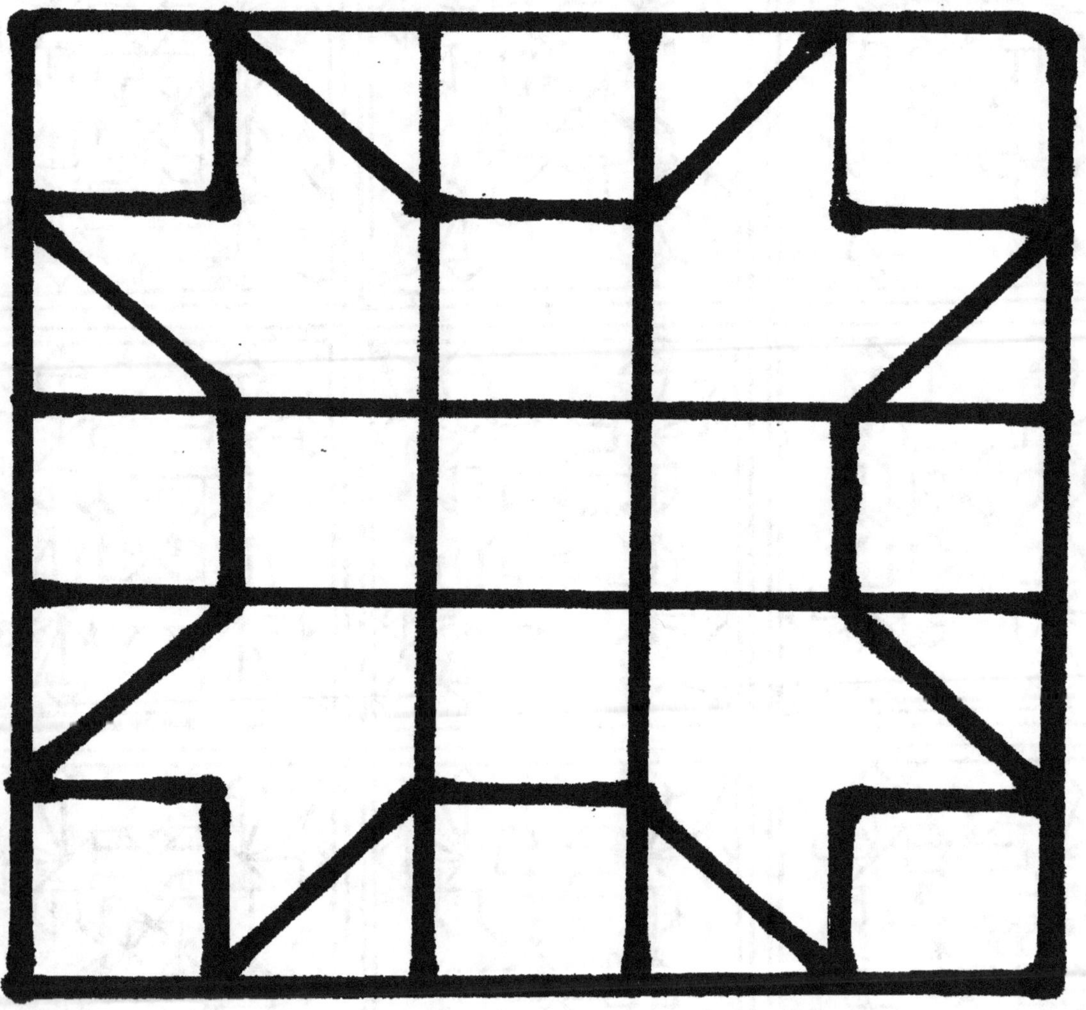

Dawson County Nebraska Barn Quilt Wabi Sabi

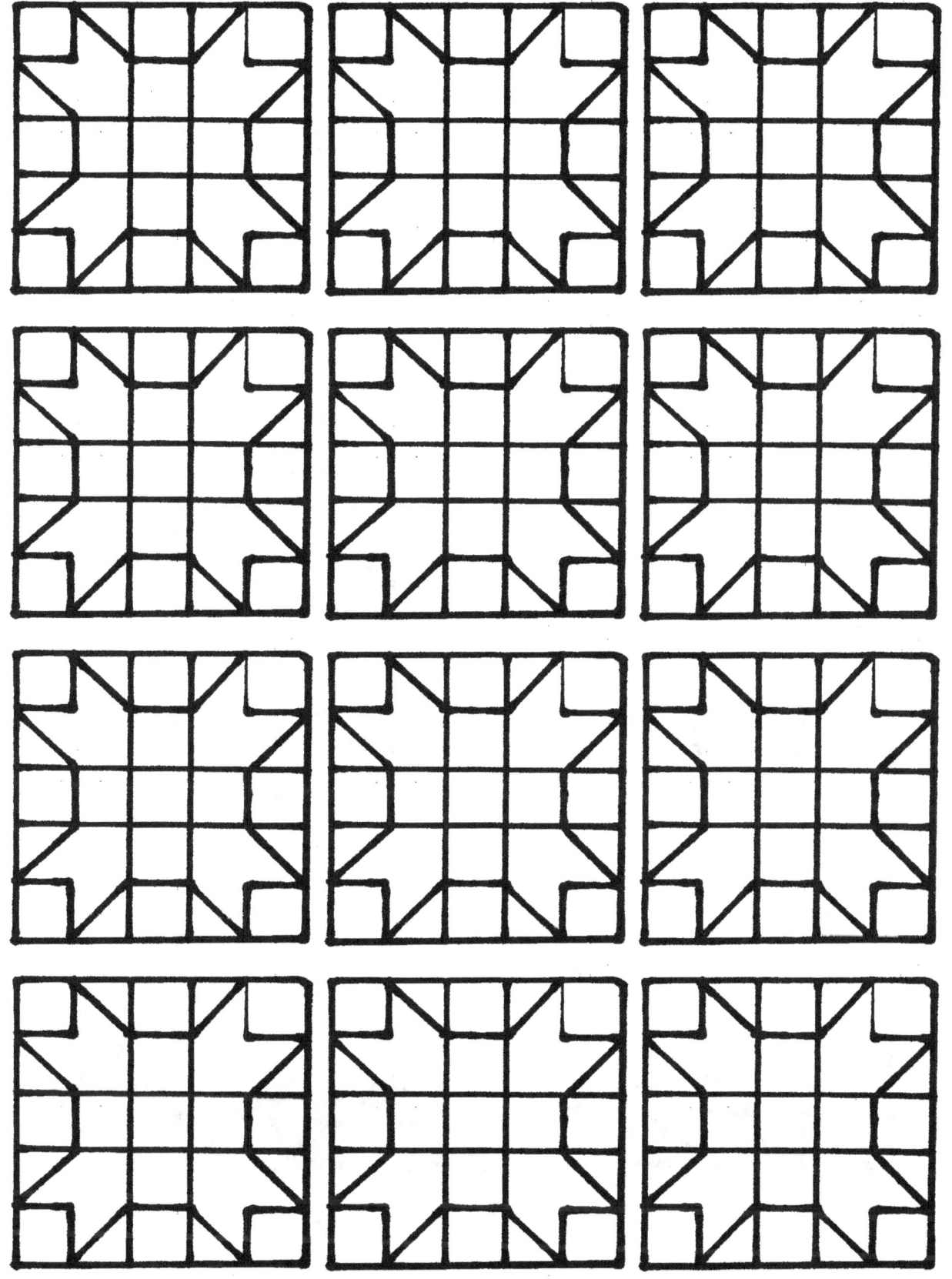

Weller
Dawson County Nebraska Barn Quilt Trail

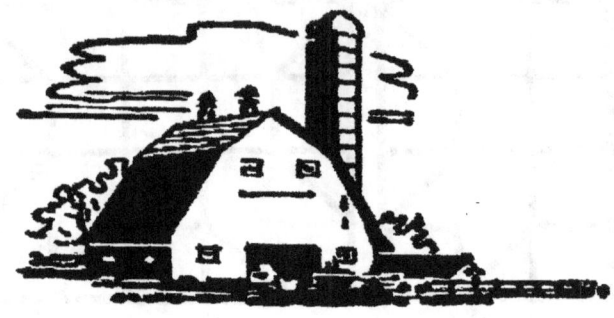

Barn Quilt Location
C Street
Cozad, Nebraska

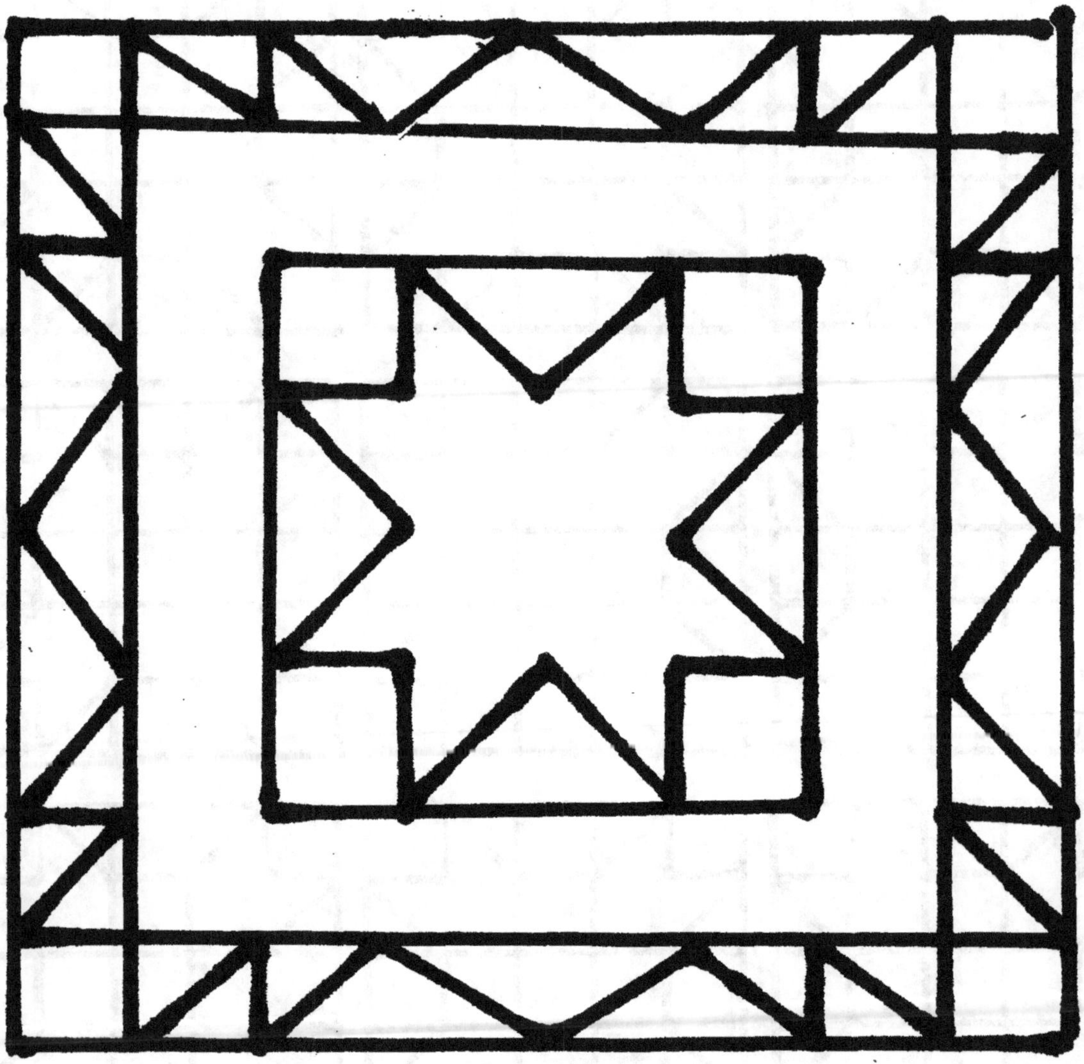

Dawson County Nebraska Barn Quilt Wabi Sabi

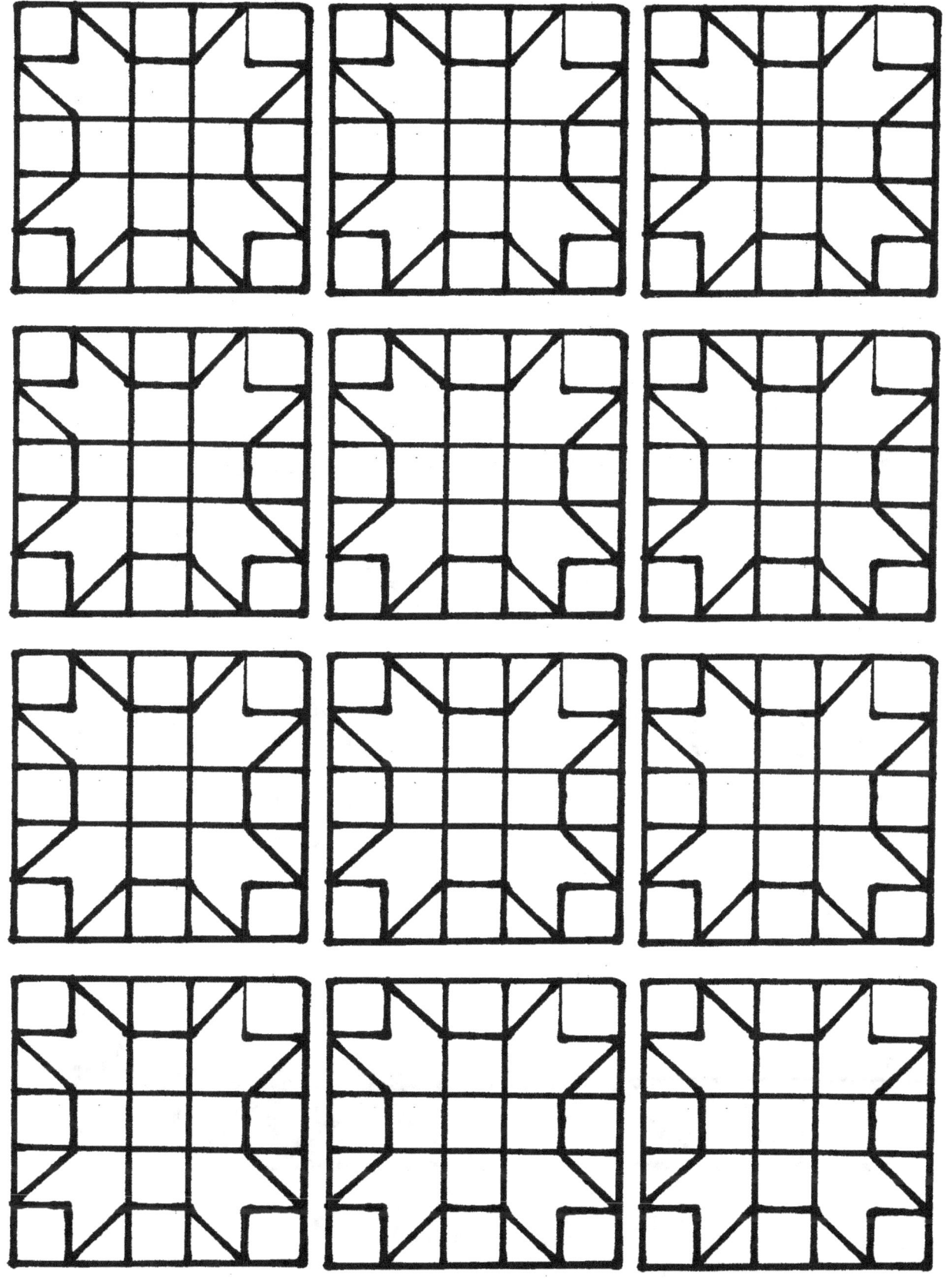

Weller
Dawson County Nebraska Barn Quilt Trail

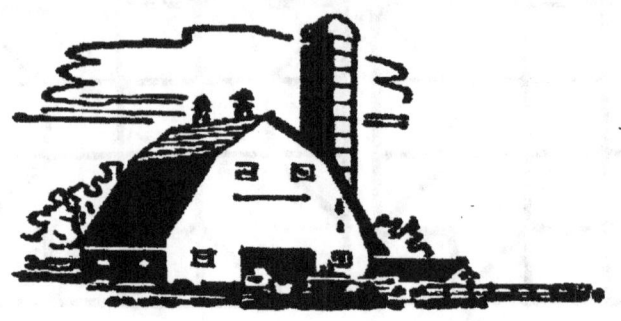

Barn Quilt Location
C Street
Cozad, Nebraska

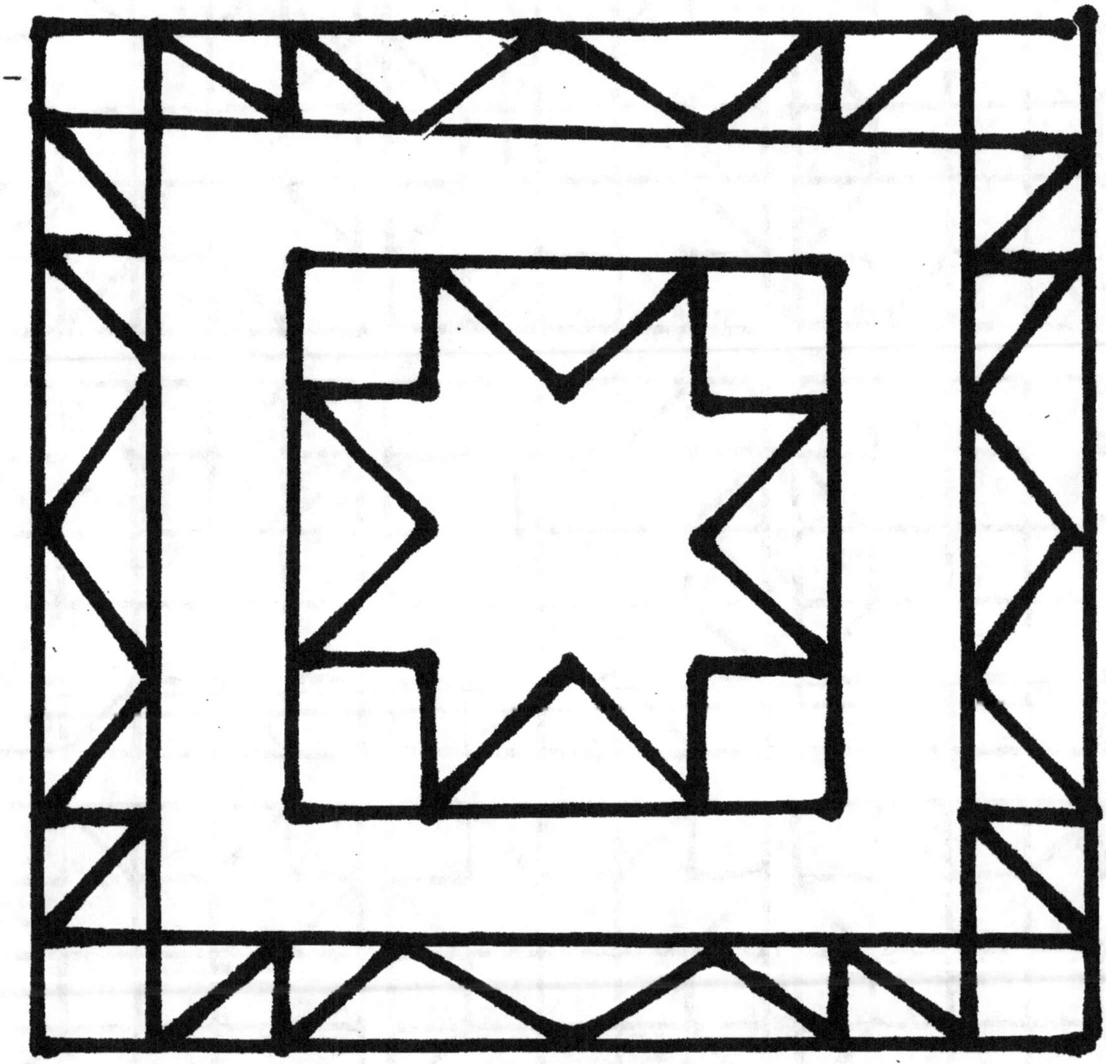

Dawson County Nebraska Barn Quilt Weller

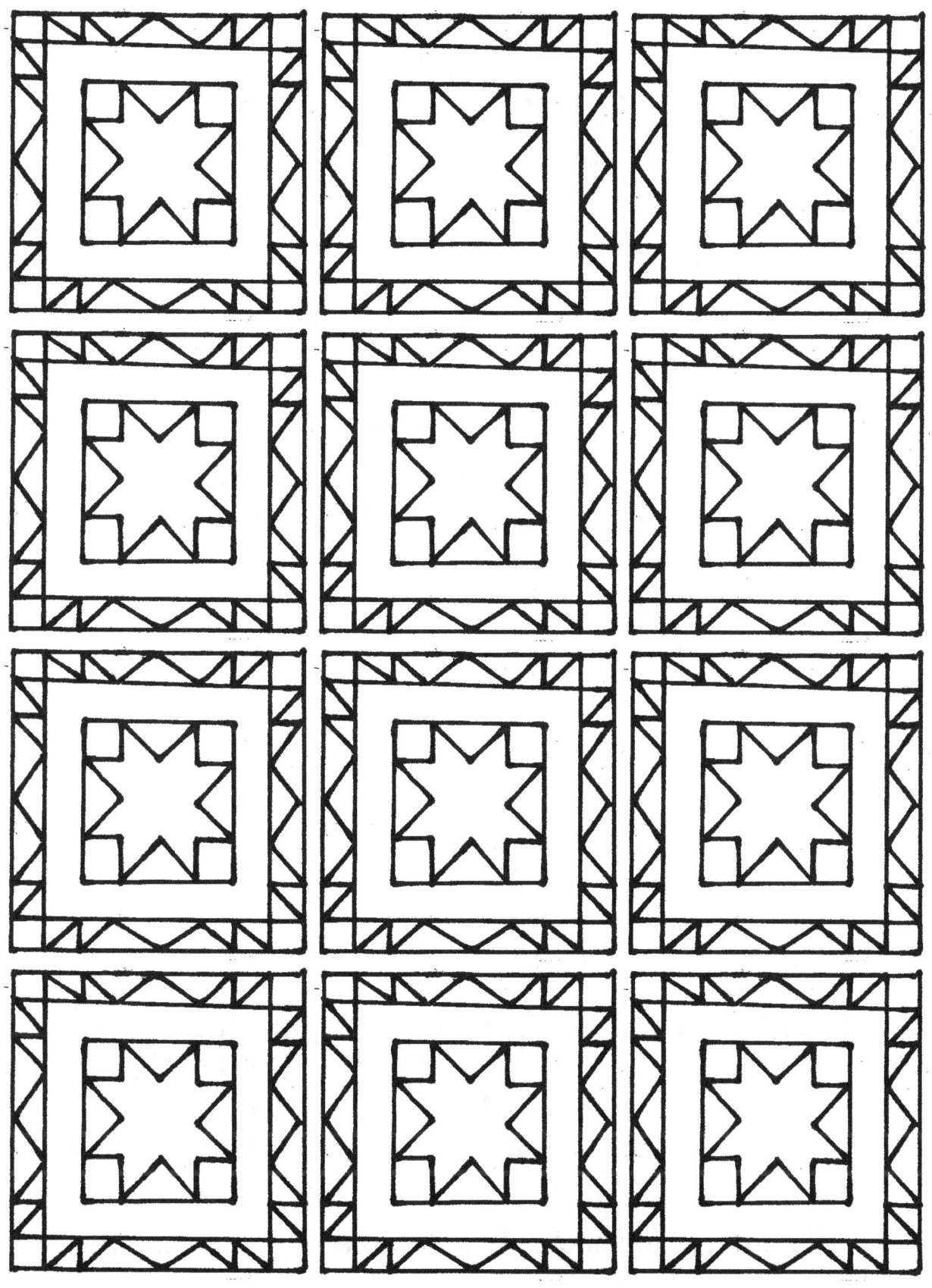

John Lettau Barn Coloring Book

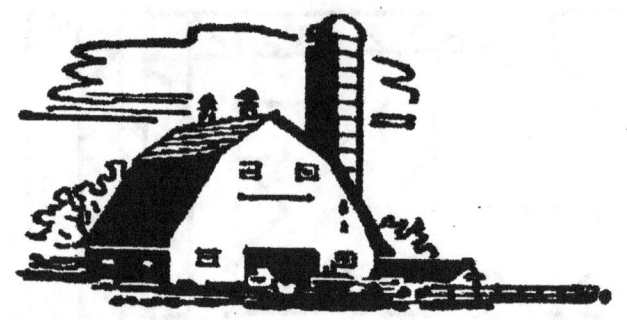

Barn Quilt Coloring Books

Shawano County Wisconsin Barn Quilt Coloring Books 1,2,3,and 4
Greene County Wisconsin Barn Quilt Coloring Books 1 and 2
Delaware County Iowa Barn Quilt Coloring Book
Franklin County Vermont Barn Quilt Coloring Book
Swanton Art Council Vermont Barn Quilt Coloring Book
Indiana Barn Quilt Coloring Books 1 and 2
Central & Northwestern Kansas Barn Quilt Coloring Book
Flint Hills Kansas Barn Quilt Coloring Books 1,2 and 3
Tennessee Appalachian Trail Barn Quilt Trail Coloring Books 1 and 2
Lake County California Barn Quilt Trail Coloring Book
Barn Quilts Around America

Geometric Pattern Coloring Books 1,2,3,4 and 5

Graph Paper Designs
Useful in the creation of your own Barn Quilt Patterns

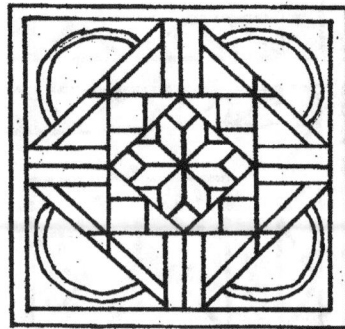 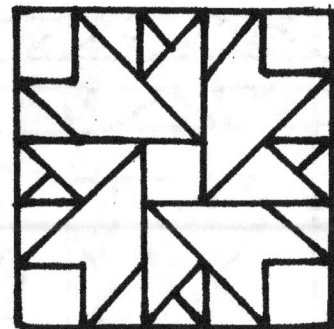 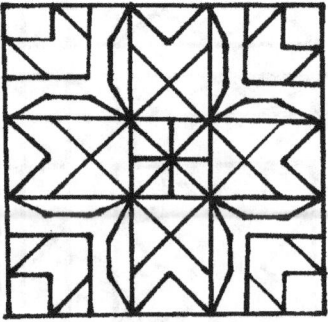

All Lettau coloring books available at Amazon.com

www.ingramcontent.com/pod-product-compliance
Lightning Source LLC
Chambersburg PA
CBHW080842220526
45467CB00008B/2359